Modern English Grammar

Author: Mr. Zissis Pispirikos
E-mail: zpispirikos@yahoo.com
Larisa September 2017
Greece

3

Contents

Modern English Grammar

1 MODAL VERBS		PRESENT / FUTURE	PAST
Can (Be able)	Ability	He **can** run fast.	She **could** / **was able to** run fast.
	Strong Possibility	He **can** still be at home. (**90% certain**)	-
	Prohibition	You **can't** leave the kids alone.	-
	Request	**Can** I use your car?	-
	Logical Assumption	He **can't** marry Ann. (**100% certain**)	He **can't have** married Ann.
	Permission	He **can** / **can't** have a party.	He **was(n't) allowed to** have a party.
	Offers	**Can** I do anything to help you?	-
	Suggestions	We **can** always leave early.	-
Could	Permission	**Could** I **be** excused?	-
	Weak Possibility or Speculation	She **could be** angry. (**50% certain**)	She **could have been** angry. (**Luckily she didn't.**)
	Request	**Could** I use your pen?	
	Logical Assumption	She **couldn't be** at work. (I don't think she... (negative))	They **couldn't have been** friends. (I don't think they were...(negative))
	Criticism	She **could** at least wait until 5 o'clock.	She **could** at least **have** waited...
	Suggestions	He **could** ask for advice.	He **could have** asked for advice.
May	Weak Possibility	She **may** be teaching. (**50% certain**)	She **may have** broken the vase. (**Perhaps she did it.**)
	Request	**May** I make a phone call? (**formal**)	-
	Permission	You **may** be excused.	-
	Prohibition	You **may** not talk during the test.	-
Might	Far more uncertainty	You **might** need to come tomorrow. (**30% certain**)	She **might have lost** her friends.
	Request	**Might** I borrow your pen? (**very formal**)	-
	Permission	**Might** I bring a friend to the wedding? (**More formal**)	-
Must	Duty	The children **must** follow their parents	The children **had to** follow their parents.
	Logical Assumption	He **must** be angry.	He **must have won** the game.
	Necessity	I **must** return to my work.	I **had to** return...(**I was obliged to**)
	Strong obligation	I **must** get more foods for the children.	I **had to** get more foods for the children.
	Prohibition	You **mustn't** cross the bridge	-
Ought to	Advice	You **ought to** follow the rules. (**Most people believe this**)	You **ought to have** followed the rules. (**But you didn't.**)
	Criticism	You **ought to** be more careful with this.	You **ought to have been** more careful... (**But you didn't do it.**)
	Necessity	We **ought to** reply to their proposal.	We **ought to have** replied to their proposal.
	Obligation	We **ought to** pay attention to kids.	We **ought to have paid** attention to kids.
	Duty	People **ought to** live in peace.	People **ought to have** lived in peace.
Have (got) to	Strong obligation	I **have (got) to** get more exercise.	I **had to** get more exercise.
	Necessity	She **has (got) to** buy a new car.	She **had to** buy a new car.
	Logical Assumption	The theft **have to have** happened this morning.	The theft **had to have** happened to weeks ago.
Had better	Advice	You **had better** tell her everything.	
Will	Probability	They **will** be in Canada tomorrow. (**100% certain**)	-
	Request	**Will** you give me a hand?(**very friendly**)	-

MODAL VERBS		PRESENT / FUTURE	PAST
Would	Permission	**Would** you mind **if** I open**ed** the door?	-
	Request	**Would** you mind help**ing** me?	-
	Offers	**Would** you like me to do it for you?	-
Shall	**Advice**	**Shall** I apply for this job ? (**Asking for advice**.)	-
	Suggestions	**Shall** we have a drink?	-
Should	Advice or **Weak obligation**	You **should** pay more attention.	You **should have paid** more attenti-on. (**But you didn't**.)
Need	Is necessary	**The tree needs** watering. **The tree needs to be** water**ed**.	**The tree** need**ed** watering. **The tree** need**ed** to be water**ed**.
Need not	It isn't necessary	**She needn't to** worry... **She need never to** worry...	**She** need**ed not to** worry... (**It wasn't necessary and she didn't worry**.)
Don't need to	It is<u>n't</u> necessary	**Penny** you **don't need to / don't have to** worry about it.	**Penny** you **didn't need to / didn't ha-ve to** worry about it.
Don't have to	It is<u>n't</u> necessary		(**It wasn't necessary and she didn't worry**.)
Needn't have	It was<u>n't</u> necessary, **but it happened.**		**You needn't have bought this book**. (**It wasn't necessary <u>but you did it</u>**.)
Mustn't	It is forbidden	You **mustn't** cross the street when the light is red.	-
Haven't got to	Future obligation	**Haven't** you **got to** be there tomorrow?	-
Ought not	Is used to **advise so-meone against doing** something.	Remember that "**Ought to**" loses "**To**" in **the negative**.	Margaret **ought to exercise more**. Margaret **ought not <u>exercise too mu-ch</u>**. It might cause injury.
Likely to/that	**Possibility**	Tom **is likely to** find a new job. It **is likely that** Tom **will** find a new job.	Tom **was likely to have** found a... It **was likely that** Tom **had** found..
Dare		Modals "**Dare**" and "**Need**" are mostly used in **negative contexts**. If "**Not**" <u>doesn't follow the verb</u>,"Dare" can be used **either with / without** "To"	<u>**No one**</u> would have **dared** (**to**) fight with him.

◊   **NOTE: Most modal verbs take <u>No</u> "-S" in the third person singular.**

◊   **NOTE: Needn't / Need never to , Don't have to / Don't need to**
         Needed not / Needed never to , Didn't have to / Didn't need to

Needn't to **Need never to** **Don't have** **Don't need to**	(+) **present infinitive**	Something is **not** necessary in the **<u>pres-ent or future</u>** and we **don't** know <u>**if the action will happen or not**</u>.

Needed not to Needed never to Didn't have to Didn't need to	(+) **present infinitive**	Something was **not** necessary in the **past** and we **don't** know **if the action happened or not**.
Needn't	(+) **Bare perfect infinitive**	We **know** that something **happened** in the **past** although it was **not** necessary.

◊ **Modal verbs + infinitive without "to"** can express **possibility** or **assumption** according to tenses.

■ **Present infinitive**   "**try**"

Simple present	I'm **sure** he tries hard.	He **must try** hard. (**Affirmative logical assumption**)
Future simple	**Perhaps** he **will** try hard.	He **may / might try** hard. (**Possibility**)

■ **Present continuous infinitive**   "**be trying**"

Present cont.	I'm **sure** he **is trying**.	He **must be trying**. (**Affirmative logical assumption**)
Future cont.	**Perhaps** he **will be trying**.	He **may / might be trying**. (**Possibility**)

■ **Perfect infinitive**   "**have tried**"

Simple past	I'm **sure** he **didn't** try.	He **can't have tried**. (**Negative logical assumption**)
Present perfect	I'm **sure** he **hasn't** tried.	
Past perfect	I'm **sure** he **hadn't** tried.	

■ **Perfect continuous infinitive**   "**have been trying**"

Past continuous	**Perhaps** he **was** trying.	He **may / might have been trying**. (**Possibility**)
Present perfect continuous	**Perhaps** he **has been** trying.	

◊ **OTHER VERBS with modal meanings**

Be supposed to...	(+) infinitive means "**Should**" When **someone else expects** something to be done.	You **are supposed to** be there at 5 o'clock. (**The boss expects from you to be there** at 5 o'clock.)
Be to...	(+) infinitive means "**Must**" When **someone else demands** sth.	I **am to** join in army. (**It is the law , I must obey**.)
Be bound to...	To express **likelihood , strong possibility**.	John **is bound to** pass the final exams.

Be likely to… **It is likely that**…	Means "**May**" (**Possibility**)	**He is likely to** go to Greece. **It is likely that** he will go to Japan.
Be allowed to…	To express **permission** , to say **what the rule is**.	**He was allowed to** tell the secret.
It is a foregone conclusion	To express **strong possibility**.	His victory is a **foregone conclusion**.
Would you like to.. **Would you like me to**…	Means "**Shall I ?**" Are used when we are **offer** ourselves to do sth.	**Would you like me** to help you?
How about… **What about**…	(+) **ing**? Are used to make **suggestions**.	**How / what about** going out for a walk?
Would you mind…	(+) **ing**? To express polite. (Formal request)	**Would you mind** waiting for ten minutes?
Why don't we…? **Let us / Let's**…	Are used to make **suggestions**.	**Why don't we** go out for a drink? **Let's** go out for a drink.
Was required…	To express **obligation**.	Everyone **was required** to try hard.
Managed to…	(+) <u>infinitive</u> To express **ability**.	How did they **manage to** <u>buy</u> this car?
Have succeeded in…	(+) **ing** To express **ability**.	They **have succeeded in** passing the final exams.
Might be prepared	(+) <u>infinitive</u> To express **willingness**.	She **might be prepared** <u>to help</u> us more.
Have refused…	(+) <u>infinitive</u> To express **unwillingness**.	The students **have refused** <u>to give</u> us more information.
The chances are… **In all likelihood**… **It is highly likely that**…	(+) <u>clause</u> To express **strong possibility**	**The chances are** <u>it will snow tonight</u>. **In all likelihood** <u>John will win the contest</u>. **it is highly likely that** <u>we'll continue to work on this project</u>.
…**it follows**…	(+) <u>clause</u> To express **conclusion** (**formal**)	From the fossils we have found, **it follows** <u>that there was an ancient city</u>.
…**conclude**…	(+) <u>clause</u> To express **conclusion**	We can **conclude** <u>that the project will be another blockbuster</u>.

- **Modal verb "HAVE TO" forms all tenses.**

Present simple	I **have to** visit Jane
Present cont.	I **am having to** visit Jane
Present perfect	I **have had to** visit Jane
Present perf. cont.	I **have been having to** visit Jane
Past simple	I **had to** visit Jane
Past continuous	I **was having to** visit Jane
Past perfect	I **had had to** visit Jane
Past perfect cont.	I **had been having to** visit Jane
Future simple	I **will have to** visit Jane
Future continuous	I **will be having to** visit Jane.
Future perfect	I **will have had to** visit Jane.
Future perfect continuous	I **will have been having to** visit Jane.

◊ **APPLICATIONS OF MODAL VERBS**

◊ **"CAN" / "BE ABLE" - "MAY" / "MIGHT"**

■ When we talk about **future ability** we use **"Will be able to"**	They **will be able** to sell this land. (**Future ability**)
■ We use **"Can"** or **"Be able to"** for **possible future arrangements**.	The manager **can / is able to** travel on abroad **next week**.
■ We use **"Be able to"** with <u>Perfect tenses</u>, <u>ing form</u>, <u>Modal verbs</u>, <u>Infinities</u>.	I **have**n't **been able to** buy a new car. Kate feels not be**ing able to** do anything. John <u>might</u> **have been able to** beat them. (**Modal verb**) They don't <u>seem to</u> be able to go climbing. (**Infinitive**)
■ **To draw a conclusion** about **past event**, saying that it was <u>not</u> **possible**. We use **"Couldn't + have + past participle"**.	Two young boys **couldn't have removed** this huge bookcase.
■ We usually prefer **"Can"** or **"Could"** with **verbs of** <u>senses</u>: (**"Feel"**, **"Hear"**, **"See"**, **"Smell"**, **"Taste"**, etc) and **verbs of** <u>Thinking</u> (**"Believe"**, **"Remember"**, **"Understand"**, etc)	I **can't remember** why George didn't come to our party. (**Present situation**) I **couldn't / wasn't able to remember** why George didn't come to our party. (**Past situation**)
■ To talk about a more <u>general possibility</u> of **something happening** we can use **"Can"** or **"May"**. We use **"Could"** to say that something **was possible** in **the past**.	This match **can / may** end in a tie. It **could** be a terrible mistake.
■ **To say that** that **things are not possible** or it is **possible that things are not on the case**. We can use **"May"** / **"Might"**, **"Can"** / **"Could"** in sentences with **negative meaning**, including those with words **like "Only"** or **"Hardly"**	The victory **can hardly** be attributed to them.
■ We <u>do not</u> use **"May"** to ask questions about <u>possibility</u> of something that is happening <u>in the present</u>. Instead we use **"Could"** or the phrase **"Be likely to"**.	**Could** this campaign last over a month? (**Question about possibility in the present**). How long **is** this conference **likely to** last?

■ **To say** that it is **possible** that **something will happen in the future**. We can use "**May**" / "**Might**" or "**Could**" + be + present participle.	The old building **may / might / could be** renovati**ng** in the next year.
■ **To say** that **situations** or **activities** that **were possibly happening** at a **particular past time** we can use "**May**" / "**Might**" / "**Could**" + have been + Present participle.	Do you believe he **might have been** stealing them? (**Activity** which possibly **was happening in the past**.)
■ **To say** that something <u>was likely</u> to happen in the **future**. We can use "**May**" / "**Might**" / "**Could**" + have + past participle.	John **may / might / could have sold** his house **by the time he decided to leave the city**. (The house **was likely** to be sold in the **future**.)
■ To express <u>uncertainty</u> about **something <u>in the past</u>**. We can also use "**May**" / "**Might**" / "**Could**" + have + past participle.	He **might have sold** his car **in 2011**. (**Uncertainty in the past**)
■ **To criticize someone** because <u>they didn't do something</u> that **we think they should have** we use "**Might** / "**Could**" (not "**May**") + have + past participle.	You <u>**might have kept**</u> it <u>in its case</u>. Why did you throw it before asking me?
■ We use "**May**" to express a **fervent wish**.	**May** God be with you!

◊   "**WOULD**" / "**WILL**"

■ We use "**Would**" to talk about <u>willingness</u> in the future.	I **would** take the initiative to call all the members of the team tomorrow. (<u>**Willingness**</u> in the <u>Future</u>)
■ We <u>**do not**</u> use "**Would**" to talk about <u>willingness</u> in the past.	Last year he **took** the initiative to call all members of the team. (<u>**Willingness**</u> in the <u>Past</u>)
■ We use "**Would**" to say that we are **willing** <u>but unable</u> to do something.	He **would** be pleased to win the competition. (**But he is unable to win**.)
■ We also use "**Would**" in conditionals.	If I were you , I **wouldn't** speak to him again. (**Conditional**)
■ To **talk** about <u>imaginary</u> past situation we can use: "**Would have + past participle**".	John told me that he **would have studied** all night long. (**He didn't study**.)
■ To show that <u>we think</u> a <u>past</u> situation actually happened. We use "**Will have + past participle**".	He **threw** her picture outside the window. I <u>**believe**</u> (**think**) that his brother **will have seen** something.
■ To talk about **characteristic behavior**. We can use "**Will**" or "**Would**".	Many people **will protest** against the new reforms.(Characteristic behavior)
■ To talk about <u>things</u> or <u>habits</u> that **are true now** or **were true in the past** we can also use "**Will**" and "**Would**".	Every year two kids **will / would** represend our school in local festival. (**True habit in the present / past**.)

■ We **mainly** use "Would" to talk **about things** that <u>happened repeatedly</u> in the past.	**Every year** the annual conference **would** last for about an hour. (**Repeated every year**)
■ We **don't** use "Would" to talk about <u>past states</u>.	We **used to** live in a small house betause we were poor. (**Past state**) <u>NOT</u> We **would** live in a small house beause we were poor.

◊ **"MUST"**

■ When we **decide for ourselves** that something is **necessary** or **important** we use "Must".	I **must** see the doctor. (**It's important**)
■ When we want to express <u>certainty</u> or <u>near-certainty</u> for **something** happened **in the past** we use "**Must have + past participle**" rather than "**Have to**".	She **must have** visit**ed** Tom at <u>least three times</u>. (**Certainty**)
■ **To draw a conclusion** about **something** that is **happening around the time of speaking** we can use "**Must be + present participle**".	Look! Tom has passed the final exams. His friends **must be going** to congratulate him <u>now</u>. (**Conclusion**)
■ **To draw a conclusion** about **something** that is **happening at a particular** <u>past time</u>, saying that it was **likely** or **certain** we use: "**Must have been + present participle**".	In the previous summer they **must have been** sharing the same flat for a month. (**Conclusion**)
■ **To draw a conclusion** based on <u>what we know</u> about a **present action** we use "**Must have to**".	He **must have to** visit his sister , <u>he has left me a notice about his absence</u>. (**He knows about his absence.**)
■ **To draw a conclusion** based on <u>what we know</u> about a **past action** we use "**Must have had to**".	<u>As far as I know</u> he **must have had to** visit her sister **last week**. (**He knows about his absence last week.**)

◊ **"SHOULD" / "OUGHT TO"**

■ The use of "**Should**" and "**Ought to**" is for **actions** or **events** the speaker **sees as desirable**.	I **should** buy this car, I don't want to miss the chance. (**Desirable action**)
■ To talk about something that <u>didn't happen in the past</u> , particulary when we want to imply **some regret** or **criticism** we use: "**Should have + past participle**" as well as the form: "**Ought to have + past participle**"	You **should have studied** history again. (**Criticism**) I **ought to have kept** this watch in my safe. (**Regret**)

◊ **"HAVE TO" / "HAVE GOT TO"**

■ "**Have to**" suggests that **someone else** or **an** <u>outside circumstance</u> or <u>authority</u> makes something necessary. It is also prefered **in questions**.	<u>The committee</u> **had to** postpone two games because of bad weather.
■ We use "**Have to**" with <u>Adverbs of Frequency</u> or with other **Modal Verbs**.	We <u>always</u> **have to** pay more taxes every year. All members **should have to** pay a sum of money for the annual subscription.

- "**Have got to**" is more **informal** than "**Have to**". If "**Have**" is <u>contracted</u>, we must add "**Got**".

  They'**ve** got to postpone the meeting.

◊ **NOTE**:

- We generally use "**Modal verb + be + ing form**" when we talk about **possible plans**.

  I **may be** going to **Swiss** <u>in April</u>.
  (**Possible plan**)

- "**Should**" + **be** + **ing form** relates to an event <u>**already happening**</u>.

  John **should be** sleeping <u>now</u>.
  (**Already happening**)

- "**Would**" + **be** + **ing form** relates to a <u>**past situation**</u> which refers to a **present** or **future event**.

  His house **would** not **be** selling up <u>**as it was protected by the law**</u>.
  (<u>**Past situation**</u> which refers to a **future event**.)

2 TENSE FORMS - ACTIVE & PASSIVE VOICE

◊ TENSE FORMS	ACTIVE VOICE	PASSIVE VOICE
		Passive voice is formed with the appropriate tense of verb **to be+past participle** , and the object becomes subject. <u>There is **no object** in **Passive** form.</u> Only **transitive** verbs (which take **an object**) can be put in to passive.

Present

Present simple All / Every day Sometimes Always Never Often	They **repair** the road. Present simple expresses unchanging , repeated or permanent states.It can also represent a widespread truth or laws of nature.	The road **is** repair**ed** by them. **(In the passive voice)**
Present cont. Now At the moment At present Today Always	They **are** repair**ing** the road. Present continuous (or progressive) tense describes an ongoing action that is happening at the the moment of speaking.	The road **is being** repair**ed** by them. **(In the passive voice)**
Present perfect Just Always Ever , Never Yet How long So far Recently This week	They **have** repair**ed** the road. Present perfect tense describes recently completed actions. Actions that begun in the past and completed in the present at an unspecified time. Evidence in the present. We use present perfect to talk about **repeated actions** that <u>might happen again</u>. We use present perfect to talk about **completed actions** or **series of actions** when we are <u>interested in result</u>. When we give **news** or **information** we often **introduce a topic** with the **present perfect**. When referring to **something** that **will happen** at <u>some time</u> in the **future**.	The road **has been** repair**ed** by them. **(In the passive voice)** I've finish**ed** three pages of work this week <u>so far</u>. I **have bought** new batteries <u>hoping that they will last even more</u>. The **construction of the new stadium has** finish**ed**. <u>As soon as</u> I **have** finish**ed**, you can come in.
Present perfect continuous Just Always Ever , Never Yet	They **have been** repair**ing** the road. Present perfect continuous (or progressive) tense describes an action in progress in the past , which is still in progress until now.	The road **has been** being repair**ed** by them. **(In the passive voice)**
How long So far Recently This week	We often prefer **present perfect continuous** to say <u>how long</u> the action **has been in progress** or to refer to **something** that has **recently stopped**.	I **have been** stand**ing** on the top of the building <u>for the last 30 minutes</u>. **Have** you **been** sleep**ing**? **(Now you are not sleeping**.)

Past

Past simple	They repair**ed** the road.	The road **was** repair**ed** by them.
Yesterday		**(In the passive voice)**
Last week	Past tense expresses an action that was started and finished in the past.	
How long ago		
Just now		
Then / When	When we talk about **two or more past completed actions** that **followed** one another we, use the **past simple** for **both**.	I **got up** and help**ed** her to lift the box. **(Two completed actions**.)
In 1992 etc		

Past continuous	The company **was** repair**ing** the road **during the period** of the local festival.	**During the period** of the local festival the road **was being** repair**ed** by the company.
While		**(In the passive voice)**
When		
As	Past continuous (or progressive) tense describes a past ongoing action which was happening when another action occurred.	
The moment that		

Past perfect	They **had** repair**ed** the road when I went back home.	When I **went back** home the road **had been** repair**ed** by them. **(In the passive voice)**
For		
Since		
Already	Past perfect tense describes an action that took place in the past before another past action.	
After		
Just		
Never / Yet		
Before	We use the past perfect when we say **how many times** something happened **in a period** up to a particular **past time**.	He **had read** the text **only one time until** Friday.
By / By the time		

Past perfect cont.	They **had been** repair**ing** the road **for an hour** before Tony arrived.	The road **had been** being repaired by them **for an hour** before Tony arrived. **(In the passive voice)**
For		
Since	Past perfect continuous (or progressive) describes a past ,ongoing action that was completed before another past action.	
	When we use the **past perfect continuous** before another action in the past is a good way to show **cause** and **effect**.	Jason **was tired** because he **had been** jogging and he didn't manage to play tennis with us.

Future

Future simple	They **will repair** the road.	The road **will be** repair**ed** by them.
Be going to	They **are going to repair** the road.	The road **is going to be** repair**ed** by them.
Tomorrow		**(In the passive voice)**
Tonight	Future tense expresses an action or situation that will occur in the future.	
Next week, soon, etc		

Future cont. **Be going to** Part of one's routine	They **will be** repair**ing** the road. They **are going to be** repair**ing** the ro- ad when the president arrives tonight. I **will be** watch**ing** TV when she arrives tonight.	The road **will be** being repair**ed** by them. When the president arrives tonight the road **is going to be** being repair**ed** by them. (**In the passive voice**)
	Future continuous describes an ongoing ac- tion that will take place in the future or will be interrupted by a shorter action.	
Future perfect **Be going to** Before By By then By the time until (only in **nega- tive sentences**.)	They **will** have repair**ed** the road by the end of the next month. They **are going to** have repair**ed** the road by the **end of the next month**.	The road **will have been** repair**ed** by them , by the end of the next month. The road **is going to** have been repair**ed** by them , by the **end of the next month**. (**In the passive voice**)
	Future perfect tense describes an action tha- t will be completed at a specific time in the f- uture.	
Future perfect continuous	**By** the **end of the month** they **will have been** repair**ing** the road **for 60 days**.	**By** the **end of the month** the road **will have been** being repair**ed** by them **for 60 days**. (**In the passive voice**)
Be going to By...for	**By** the **end of the month** they **are going to** have been repair**ing** the road **for 60 days**.	**By** the **end of the month** the road **is go- ing to** have been being repair**ed** by th- em **for 60 days**. (**In the passive voice**)
	Future perfect continuous (or progressive) describes a duration of an event that occurs until some specific future time.	

Future in the past: Is formed with:

Was / Were going to	**Future** in the past is used when we talk about a **future activities** or **events** at a **certain moment in the past**, which may have happened or **not**.	I **was going to** travel on abroad , but I postponed the trip. (**It didn't happen**) I told you that John **was going to come** to the party. (**It really happened**)
Would + verb	"**Would**" is used for **promises** , **volunta- ry actions** or **predictions**.	I knew that he **would help** him. He had **promised** to him.
Was to / Were to + infinitive	We use "**Was to** " / "**Were to**" + infinitive when we **don't know** whether the event actually happened unless the context make this clear.	He went to the cinema, afterwards he **was to go** to Tom's party. (**Did he go**?)
	We use "**Was to** "/ "**Were to**"+infinitive when we refer to **future** events **which people either can control or not**, at a certain moment **in the past**.	He left his house last summer for a walk, but it **was to spend almost** six months , **maybe more**, until the day he returned to his family again. (**We can't control how many months he has spent**.)
Was to / Were to + Past participle	With "**Was to** " / "**Were to**" + past partici- ple used for **things** that **were expected** but they **didn't actually happen**.	I **was to have gone** to museum, **but the union were on strike**. (**He expected to go to the museum** but it **didn't** actually happen.)

◊ **NOTE**:

■ We usually use **continuous tenses** with **adverbs** such: "**Always**", "**Constantly**", "**Continually**" and "**Forever**" to **emphasize** that something which is done so often is **characteristic** of a **person**, **group** or **thing**.

He **is always** tell**ing** me lies.
(**Characteristic of him**.)

■ We often use the **Present continuous** or the **Past continuous** tense:

To make **a REQUEST** or **an OFFER more polite**.

John, **were** you mov**ing** this box over there? (**Request**)

When we want to express an **uncertainty** to an **INQUIRY** or to a **STATEMENT**.

Is he go**ing** to marry her?
(**Uncertain inquiry**)

◊ **NOTE**: We use **"Be to + infinitive"**

■ In "**News**" & "**Reports**".

Another two hybrid models **are to be made** by TOYOTA this year. (**News**)

■ To talk about "**Rules**", "**Plans**", or "**Instructions**".

The vice president **is to announce** the new business activities. (**Plans**)

■ We **do not** use "**Be to+infinitive**" to talk about **future events** that people **cannot** **control**.

The mist **will** still be dangerous even in summer.
NOT: The mist **is** still **to be** dangerous even in summer.
(People **cannot** control the mist.)

◊ **NOTE: Expressions with future meaning**

To be about to... , **To be on the verge / point of...** , **To be bound / certain / (un)likely to...** ,
To be on the brink of...

◊ **NOTE**: We can also use **the Future continuous**, **Future perfect** and **Future perfect continuous** to say **what** we **believe** or **what** we **imagine** is **true**.

I won't **be** sell**ing** my car, I **think** it is not the right time for selling it.
Mary **will have** forgot**ten** how I look like.
My track has been broken down. The clients **will have been** wait**ing** for me at the station for at least two hours.

◊ **NOTE**: What's the difference ? **"Will" vs "Be going to"**

■ **Will + infinitive**	A **decision** <u>at</u> the **moment of speaking**	Julie: There is no milk. John: Don't worry! I **will** go to the super market to buy some.
	A **prediction** based **on opinion**.	**I think** the Conservatives **will** win the next elections.
	A **future** fact	John **will** leave tomorrow.
	For **promises / requests / refusals / offers**.	I **will** help you tomorrow, if you like. (**Offer**)
	Willingness	I **will** give you further information.

■ **Be going to + inf.**	A **decision** <u>before</u> the **moment of speaking**. (**Scheduled decision**).	Julie: There is no milk. John: **I know**. **I'm going to** buy some, when I finish my job.
	A **prediction** based on something we can **see** (or **hear**) <u>now</u>.	The Conservatives **are going to** win the elections.They **already** have the most of the votes.
	A **prediction** based on <u>outside eviden-ce</u>.	Look **at this place**! I think they **are going to** remove that old statue.

◊ **NOTE**:

| ■ **Present simple with future meaning.** (**Timetables / Programmes**) | The match **begins** at **6 o'clock** this evening. |
| ■ **Present continuous with future meaning.** (**Fix arrangement in near future**) | He **is** meeting his son **this Sunday**. |

◊ We **can't** use the <u>present continuous</u> tense for <u>future events</u> which **people** <u>can not</u> **control**.

There are a lot of clouds in the sky, I think that it **is going to** rain this afternoon.
<u>NOT</u>: There are a lot of clouds in the sky, I think that it **is** rain**ing** this afternoon.

◊ **Stative verbs**

Stative verbs express a **state that lasts for some time** rather than an **action**.They are <u>not</u> used in **continuous** forms.

Verbs of senses	Feel , Hear , Look , Listen , See , Smell , Taste , Watch , etc
Verbs of emotions	Adore , Detest , Dislike , Enjoy , Forgive , Hate , Hurt , Like , etc
Verbs of opinion	Agree , Believe , Suppose , Understand , etc
Other verbs	Belong , Concern , Depend , Know , Mean , Own , Possess , Need , Prefer , Want

◊ **NOTE**:

■ "Feel" and "Hurt" | Can be used in **either** <u>continuous</u> or sim-ple form. | She **feels** / **is** feeling better.

■ "Look" , "Listen" , "Watch" | Express **deliberate action** and **can be used** in **continuous form**. | He **is** listen**ing** to some records.

◊ **Stative verbs in the continuous form**

■ **Some** stative verbs can be used in **continuous** form if they refer to a **temporary action**. | Now, I'm lik**ing** read**ing** detective stories more **than usual**. (Temporary action)

■ **Some** stative verbs can be used in **continuous form** suggesting that a **process is going on** at **the time of speaking** or empha-sizing that the **process continues to develop**. | I'm regrett**ing** buy**ing** this old house. (Emphasizes that I started to regret it and **this regret may grow**.)

◊ **Some** stative verbs have **continuous** forms but there is a **difference** in meaning.

STATE	ACTION
I **see** them coming towards us.	I have the ability.
She's **seeing** her doctor today.	She is visiting.
These flowers **smell** nice.	They have a nice smell.
Why are you **smelling** the food?	Why are you checking the smell of...
The soup **taste** delicious.	Its flavor is good.
She is **tasting** the soup.	She's testing the flavor.
It **feels** like velvet.	It has the texture of velvet.
He is **feeling** the cloth.	He is touching the cloth.
He **has** a house.	He possesses.
We are **having** a nice time.	We are enjoying ourselves.
Do you **like** this car?	Is it nice?
How are they **liking** the party?	Are they enjoying?
I **think** he has left.	I suppose , I believe
I'm **thinking** about his suggestion.	I'm considering...
It **looks** as if it's going to snow.	It appears.
They **are looking** at the statue.	They are viewing.

- **"Have gone to" / "Have been to" / "Have been in"**

He **has gone to** New York.
(He is on his way to New York or he is there now . He **hasn't** come back yet.)

He **has been to** New York.
(He has visited New York , but he **isn't** there now. He **has** come back.)

He **has been in** New York.
(He lives in New York now.)

- **"Since" / "For"**

Since It is used when we refer to a **previous point** of **time**. It is **normally** used with **perfect tenses**.	I've **been** here **since July**.
For Expresses **duration** of **an action**.	We've **been** here **for** three years.

◊ **"Used to + infinitive" / "Would + infinitive" / "Be used to + ing form" / "Was going to + infinitive"
/ "Get used to + ing"**

Used to + infinitive Expresses **past habitual actions**, or **past states**, that no longer happen now.	We **used to live** in a small house because we were poor. (**Past state**)
Would + infinitive Expresses **past <u>repeated</u> actions** and **routines not states**.	When I was a child , I **would go** to the football ground **every** Sunday.
Be used to + ing (In **all tenses** of "Be") Be **in a habit** of...	Tom **is used to** study**ing** history in the evenings.
Was going to **Usually** expresses **actions** one intended to do but he / she **didn't** do.	He **was going to** buy a car but **he lost all his money**.
Get used to + ing **Familiarize** with sth.	I **am** gett**ing used to** driving my new car.

- **We never use <u>future</u> forms after:**

After	**Once**
As long as	**Suppose / Supposing**
As soon as	**Till / Until**
Before	**Unless**
By the time	**When** (<u>Time conjunction</u>)
If (conditional)	**Whenever**
In case	**While**

- **"When"**

| Used as a **question word**. | It can be used with <u>future</u> forms. | When <u>will</u> the next bus leave? |

- **"If"**

After :

| I don't know
I doubt
I wonder | It can be used with <u>future forms</u> meaning **"Whether"**. | We **don't know if** he <u>will</u> stay at home or not. |

◊ **Time words**

Ago	**Back** in time from **now**. (Used with <u>**Past Simple**</u>)	Tom <u>left</u> an hour **ago**.
Before	**Back** in time from <u>then</u>. **"Before"** is also used with <u>present</u> or <u>past</u> forms to show that an action preceded another.	**Suzan** told me that Tom had left an hour **before <u>the end of the game</u>**. You should be here **before** they <u>leave</u>. He **had** cook**ed** the dinner **before** she <u>came</u> home.
Already	Is used with **perfect** tenses in **mid** or **end** positions in statements or questions.	He **had already** fix**ed** the car when they arrived. **Have** you got dress**ed already?**
Yet	Is used with **perfect tenses** in negative sentences after a **contracted auxiliary** verb or **at the end** of the sentence. It can also be used at the **end** of **questions**.	He has**n't yet** call. He has**n't** call **yet**. Have they arrived **yet**?
Still	Is used in statements or questions **after** the <u>auxiliary</u> verb or **before** the **main** v-erb. **"Still"** comes **before** the <u>auxiliary</u> verb in **negations**.	She <u>can</u> still dance well. He **still wants** to buy this house. She **still <u>hasn't</u>** reply to my letter.

◊ **USING THE PASSIVE VOICE**

◊ **Changing from Active into Passive.**

- <u>Active voice</u>

Subject	Verb	Object	Agent
Tom	fixed	the car	---

- <u>Passive voice</u>

Subject	Verb	Object	Agent
The car	was fixed	---	by Tom

- **We often use the passive voice**:

When the **agent** (the **person** or **thing that performs** the **action**) is **unknown**. When the **agent** is "<u>people in general</u>".	His car **was** dama**ged** last Sunday. (**By someone who is unknown**.) The toys can **be found** at the playroom. (<u>**Anyone can find this toys**</u>.)
When the **agent** does **not** want to reveal **his / her identity**.	Some children **were gone** to restricted area. (By an **agent** who **does not want to reveal** his / her **identity**.)
When the **agent** is **unimportant** , or is **obvious**:	Only four students **have been awarded**. (The **agent** is **clearly the school's authority**.)
To **describe procedures** or **processes**, focusing on **what was done** rather than **who did it**.	The old cars **were repaired** last year.
To **avoid repeating** the <u>agent</u> in a **description** or **narrative**.	Apple corp. has introduced the new **i-phone**. **It has been** introduc**ed** to Europe and USA. **Rather than**: Apple corp. has introduced the new i-phone. <u>**Apple corp**</u>. has introduced it to Europe and USA.

- In **informal contexts** we often use <u>**active**</u> **sentences** with a **subject** such as: "**People**" , "**Somebody**" , "**Someone**" , "**Something**" , "**We**" , "**They**" or "**You**".

  <u>People are</u> drinking alcohol at their homes. (Informal "**People**" = subject) Alcohol **is being drunk** by **people**. (**More formally** "People" = object)

- **Stative verbs** that <u>do not usually</u> form the **passive voice**: "**Be**" , "**Become**" , "**Belong**" , "**Exist**" "**Have**" , "**Lack**" , "**Resemble**" , "**Seem**".

- Some stative verbs <u>can form</u> their passive voice: "**Believe**" , "**Intend**" , "**Know**" , "**Like**" , "**Love**" "**Need**" , "**Own**" , "**Understand**" , "**Watch**" , etc

◊ **PASSIVE FORMS**

- **Verb + to-infinitive + object**
(Active voice)

  They **started to repair** the **house**.

  Verb + to be + past participle
(Passive voice)

  The **house started to be** repair**ed** by them.

- **Verb + <u>Object</u> + to-infinitive**
(Active voice)

  They **allowed** <u>him</u> **to sell** the house.

  <u>**Subject**</u> **+ be + past participle + to-infinitive**
(Passive voice)

  <u>He</u> **was allowed to sell** the house.

■ **Verb** + <u>Object</u> + **bare infinitive** with the verbs:	They **make** <u>him</u> **scream** with anger.
"**Make**" , "**Let**" , "**Hear**" , "**Help**" , "**See**" , "**Feel**" , "**Observe**". (Active voice)	
<u>Subject</u> + **be** + **past participle** + **to-infinitive** (Passive voice)	<u>He</u> **was made to scream** with anger.
■ **Verb** + **ing** + **object** (Active voice)	More and more people **avoid** buy**ing ex-pensive clothes**.
Verb + **being** + **past participle** (Passive voice)	The expensive clothes **avoid being bo-ught** by more and more people.
■ **Verb** + <u>Object</u> + **ing** with the verbs:	Mun **caught** <u>Jane</u> steal**ing** money.
"**Bring**" , "**Catch**" , "**Find**" , "**Hear**" , "**Keep**" , "**Notice**" , "**Obs-erve**" , "**See**" , "**Send**" , "**Show**". (Active voice)	
<u>Subject</u> + **be** + **past participle** + **ing** (Passive voice)	<u>Jane</u> **was caught** steal**ing** money by mum.
■ <u>Some</u> **verbs** & <u>Some</u> **stative verbs** + <u>Object + to-infinitive</u>.	We **want John to win** the competition. (Active voice)
"**(Can't) bear**" , "**Hate**" , "**Like**" , "**Love**" , "**Need**" , "**Prefer**" , "**Want**" , "**Wish**"	(**NOT**: **John <u>is</u> want<u>ed</u> to win** the...) (**No** passive voice) BUT: His colleagues **hate** him. (Active voice) He **was hated** by his colleagues. (Passive voice)

◊ **NOTE:**

■ After **some verbs** the **direct object** can be followed by an **ob-ject complement** , **a noun** or **an adjective** , which **describes** or **classifies** the object.("**Appoint**" , "**Declare**" , "**Make**" , "**No-minate**" , "**Vote**" , "**Call**" , "**Name**" , etc)	The Queen **made Sir George** a <u>knight</u>.
■ When these clauses are put in the **passive**, these **objects com-plements** become <u>subject complements</u>, and they are placed after the verb.	**Sir George was made** a <u>knight</u> by the Queen.

◊ **NOTE:**

■ **Get + Past participle**: is used to talk about **events** we **see as unwelcome** or with **events** the **speaker** sees as **positive**.	Get **drunk**! (**Unwelcome**)
	When <u>I</u> **get succeeded** in the exams... (A **positive** event)
■ We **<u>don't</u>** use **Get + Past participle** with verbs describing **sta-tes**.	He **lived** in a small house. (**NOT**: He **got lived** in a small house.)

◊ **MODAL VERBS in the Passive Voice**

**Modal verb + be + past participle
(Present)**

Can / Could be **made**
May / Might be **hidden**
Must be **warned**
Have to be **done**
Should be **done**
Will be **grown**

Modal verb + have been + past participle (Past)

Could have been **made**
Might have been **hidden**
Must have been **warned**
Had to have been **done**
Should have been **done**
Would have been **grown**

◊ **NOTE**: In the passive voice:

■ **By + agent is omitted** when **the agent** is: **unknown** , **unimportand** , **obvious from the context** or words such: **Someone** , **People** , **I** , etc.

They will give more information soon.

More information **will be given** soon.
("**By them**" is omitted.)

■ **By** + **agent** is used to say **Who** or **What** did the action.

She was knocked down **by a lorry**.

■ **With** + **instrument** or **material** is used to say what the **agent** used.

The **policeman was** stabb**ed with** a **knife**.

■ **Verbs** following by a **preposition** (**Looked after** , **Accused of** , **etc**) , take the preposition **immediately after** them when turn into passive.

She looks **after** her father well.

Her father **is** look**ed after** well.

■ **In passive questions with** : "**Who**" , "**Whom**" or "**Which**" we do **not** omit "**By**".

Who offered **her** the job?

Who was she offered the job **by**?

■ "**Hear**" , "**See**" , "**Watch**" can be followed by **present** participle in **active** and **passive** voice.

We **heard** him play**ing** the guitar.

He **was heard** play**ing** the guitar.

■ The Stative Verbs: "**Believe**" , "**Expect**" , "**Feel**" , "**Hope**" , "**Know**" , "**Report**" , "**Say**" , "**Think** , **etc** are used in the following **passive patterns** in **personal** and **impersonal** constructions.

Teachers **expect** that he will improve soon. (Active voice)

Subject (**person**) + passive verb+ **to-inf**.
He is expected **to improve** soon.
(Passive **personal** construction)

It + passive verb + **that clause**.
It is expected **that he will improve** soon.
(Passive **impersonal** construction)

■ **Transitive & Intransitive Verbs**

◊ **A transitive verb** , used with a **direct object** , **transmits action** to an **object** and **may** also have an **indirect object** , which indicates **to whom** or **for whom** the **action is done**.

She **sent** the **letter**. ("**Send**" is the **transitive verb**.)
She **gave** the **lecture**. ("**Gave**" is the **transitive verb**.)

"**Letter**" = the **direct object** of **sent**.
"**Lecture**" = the **direct object** of **gave**.

- In these sentences , something is **being done** to an <u>object</u>.

  A **transitive** verb can also have an **indirect object** that <u>precedes</u> the **direct object**.
  The **indirect object** tells **to whom** or **for whom** the <u>action is done</u> , although the words "**to**" and "**for**" **are not used**.

- He **sent Robert** the **letter**.	The <u>direct object</u> **letter receives** the action. (**sent**) **Robert** is the <u>indirect</u> object **for whom the action is done**.
- She **gave** her **class** the **lecture**.	The <u>direct object</u> **lecture** receives the action. (**gave**). The <u>indirect object</u> **class** is the group **to whom** the lecture was given.

- **NOTE**:

  Usually the "**Indirect object**" is a **group of people** and the "**Direct object**" is a **thing**.

- After many verbs <u>with two objects</u>, we can **reverse the order of the objects** if we put "**For**" or "**To**".	I granted my **brother** an **old bike**. ("**Brother**" = the Indirect object) ("**Old bike**" = the direct object) I granted an **old bike** for **my brother**.
- We use "**Verb** + <u>Direct object</u> + FOR + <u>Indirect object</u>" with verbs as: "**Build**" , "**Find**" & "**Get**".	Father **built this house** for **me**. (Father **built me this house**.) Go out and **find a ticket** for **me**. (Go out and **find me a ticket**.)
- We use "**Verb** + <u>Direct object</u> + TO + <u>Indirect object</u>" with verbs as: "**Give**" , "**Offer**" & "**Show**"	He **gave a pencil** to **me**. (He **gave me a pencil**.)
- We use "**For**" or "**To**" + <u>Indirect object</u> with verbs as: "**Play**" , "**Read**" and "**Write**" sometimes with a **difference** in **meaning**.	I wasn't able to explain this message, so I had to **write** a letter **to him**. He wasn't able to write himself, so I **wr**ote the letter **for him**. (**Instead of him**)
- Sometimes the **meaning** is **very** similar.	Reading reports for / to <u>young students</u> is a necessary process.
- **Some verbs** with **two objects** <u>cannot</u> have their **objects reversed** with "<u>For</u>" or "<u>To</u>", including: "<u>Ask</u>" , "<u>Guarantee</u>" and "<u>Refuse</u>".	I **asked** my brother a sum of money. <u>NOT</u> I **asked** a sum of money **to** my brother.
- If the **direct object** is a <u>pronoun</u>, we **usually** use: "**Direct object (pronoun)** + FOR / TO + Indirect object"	I left <u>it</u> here for **my wife**. Give <u>it</u> to me.

■ **Verb + Object + Adjective**

Some verbs: "Assume" , "Believe" , "Consider" , "Declare" "Find" , "Hold" , "Judge" , "Pronounce" , "Prove" , "Report" , "Think" can **be followed by** an "Object + **Adjective**".	He **believes** driving car **fast** , is the absolute freedom. (**Formal** English)
	He **believes** that car driving **to be fast** is the absolute freedom. (**Less formal** alternatives)

◊ **An intransitive verb** does **not** take an object and **can't** have a **passive form**.

She **sleeps** too much. She **complains** frequently.	In these sentences **nothing** receives the action of verbs "**sleeps**" and "**complain**".

■ **NOTE: Other verbs** usually **intransitive (Verb + No object)**

"Appear" , "Arrive" , "Come" , "Cough" , "Faint" , "Fall" , "Go" , "Happen" , "Hesitate" , "Interact" , "Matter" , "Occur" , "Remain" , "Sleep" , "Sneeze" , "Swim" , "Wait".

■ **NOTE:**

Many verbs can be either **transitive** or **intransitive** depending **on how** they are used in the sentence.

She usually **leaves (transitive)** the **books** on the table.	The **verb (leaves)** is followed by an **direct** object (**books**).
The train sometimes **leaves (intransitive)** early **on Sunday**.	Is **not** followed by an **direct** object. It is followed by a prepositional phrase (**on Sunday**).

◊ **"There is"** , **"There being"**

"There being" is simply the **passive form** of **"There is"**. **"There is"** relates the next clause to a **subject** where **"There being"** puts the **"blame"** on the **object**.	"I think / feel **there is** too much salt in the **food**."
	"Emma said **there is** too much salt in the **food**."
	In these examples, there is a **subject** (I, **Emma**) and "**food**" is the **direct object** of the sentence.
	"I'm tired of **there being** too much salt in the **food**.
	In this example, "**food**" is the **object** of the sentence. It's the food's fault that there is so much salt, the **speaker** is **not involved**. (The food may contain a salty ingredient.)
This pattern often **introduces a** REASON and it is used mainly in **formal** writing.	The stadium is still closed, **there being** many angry people who are protesting outside of the gates. (The reason why the stadium is closed is people who are protesting outside of it.)

◊ **NOTE**:

"Being" as "**verb-ing**", is required in **all such instances**.

Would you mind being quite for a moment.
I look forward to being interviewed on the current affairs programme.
She was afraid of being accused of a crime which she did not commit.
I am tired of being taken for granted and expected to do all the house work.

◊ **NOTE**: "**Have had**" / "**Has had**" (**Present perfect form of** "**Have**")

Consider the **present** tense.

He **has** a lot of homework this week. (This means that he has a lot of homework **now that we are talking**.)

On the other hand we use the **present perfect** tense of "Have" as a **main verb**, to describe **an event** <u>from the past</u> that has some **connection** to the **present**.

He **has had** a lot of homework this week. (**It is possible that** he might have a lot of homework to do **all the week**, and he could say something like this on Thursday, for example.)

Compare with:
He **had** a lot of homework this week. (A **completed** event. Either because there is no expectation of more homework, or the week is over.)

◊ **NOTE**: "**Had had**" (**Past perfect form of** "**Have**")

We use "**Had had**", as a **main verb**, to describe our **experiences** and **actions**. We use it when we are talking about **past** and we **want to refer** <u>back to</u> an **earlier past time**.
We can use: "<u>Before</u>" , "<u>Already</u>" , "<u>By the time</u>" as time expressscions.

After she **had had** a cup of coffee she **felt** much better. (**Action**)
By the time he **was** thirty he **had** <u>already</u> had four different jobs. (**Experience**)

◊ **NOTE**: "**Have been having**" / "**Had been having**"

We use "**Have been having**" for **events** (especially a **series** of **events**) or other **duration**-based things.

How long **have** you **been having** these symptoms?
(The symptoms are **still existed** and **may continue to exist** for unknown time in the future.)

We use "**Had been having**" for **events** (especially a **series** of **events**) or other **duration**-based things which have **already stopped**.

How long **had** you **been having** these symptoms?
(The symptoms **were still existed** for a period of time in the past but **now they have stopped**.)

◊ **NOTE: Spelling rules - Doubling consonants**

- We **double** the **final letter** when **one-syllable verb** that **ends** in "Consonant + **Vowel** + Consonant".

  St**o**p --> St**o**pping --> St**o**pped
  R**o**b --> R**o**bbing --> R**o**bbed
  S**i**t --> S**i**tting

- We **double** the **final letter** when **one-syllable adjective** that **ends in** "Consonant + **Vowel** + Consonant" , in **comparative** and **superlative degree**.

  Wet --> Wetter --> The wettest
  Big --> Bigger --> The biggest
  Sad --> Sadder --> The saddest

- We **double** the **final letter** when a word has **more than one syllable**, and when the **final syllable** is **stressed in speech**.

  Begin --> Beginning
  Prefer --> Preferring --> Preferred

- If the **final syllable** is **not stressed in speech** we **do not double the final letter**.

  Listen --> Listening --> Listened
  Happen --> Happening --> Happened

- In **British English** the **verbs** "Travel" and "Cancel" are **excepttins** to this rule, as well as the **verbs** "Write" & "Bite".

  Travel --> Travelling --> Travelled
  Cancel --> Cancelling --> Cancelled

  Write --> Writing --> Written
  Bite --> Biting --> Bitten

◊ NOTE: **We do not double the final letter when**:

A word ends in **two consonants** (-**rt** , -**rn** , etc).

Start --> Starting --> Started
Burn --> Burning --> Burned

Two vowels come **directly before** the <u>final letter</u>.

Remain --> Remaining --> Remained

We do **not double** "**W**" or "**Y**" at the **end** of the words "**Play**" & "**Snow**".

Play --> Playing --> Played
Snow --> Snowing --> Snowed

◊ **NOTE**:

Verbs ending in "-**c**" change to "-**ck**" before "-**ing**"

It is important not to panic if you loose your way. Panicking will only make matters worse.

3   GERUND - INFINITIVE

■   Gerund

◊   **What is a gerund** , and how does it differ from a **present participle?**

The **present participle** is the **ing** form of a **verb** used as an **adjective**.	(Running shoes , breaking story , **etc**)
The **gerund** is the **ing** form of a **verb** used as a **noun**.	(Running , fishing , etc)

◊   The **gerund form** of a verb looks exactly like the **present participle** , but they **function differently** in a sentence.
The **gerund** will **fill** a noun slot (**subject , direct object , etc**) but the **present participle** will be **either** an **adjective** or **part verb**.

Running is good exercise.
(Gerund as a noun (subject))

Are those the new running shoes?
(Participle as an adjective).
He **is** running his last race now.
(Participle as a part of a verb).

◊   **Forms of the -ing**

Forms of the -ing	Active voice	Passive voice
Present	Trying	Being tried
Present cont.	---	---
Perfect	Having tried	Having been tried
Perfect cont.	---	---

◊   **Verbs followed by gerund**

Acknowledge	Dread	Prohibit
Admit	Encourage	Propose
Advise	Enjoy	Put off
Advocate	Escape	Quit
Allow	Excuse	Recall
Anticipate	Face	Recollect
Appreciate	Fancy	Recommend
Avoid	Finish	Regret
Begin	Forget	Relish
Begrudge	Go (Physical activities)	Remember
Can't bear	Grudge	Report
Can't help	Hate	Require
Can't resist	Imagine	Resent
Can't see	Involve	Resist
Can't stand	Keep	Resume
Catch	Leave off	Risk
Cease	Like	Spend
Complete	Love	Start
Consider	Mention	Stop
Continue	Mind	Suggest
Defend	Miss	Tolerate
Delay	Necessitate	Try
Deny	Observe	Understand
Despise	Overhear	Urge
Discover	Permit	Waste (Time / Money)
Discuss	Postpone	Worth
Dislike	Practice	
Don't mind	Prefer	

Like + to-inf = I think that something is right.	I like **to** help people.
Like + gerund = Enjoy something	I like gett**ing** up early in the morning.

◊ **Prepositions followed by gerund**

Example: **Instead of** study**ing** for the exams , she goes out every night.

About (how / what)	Besides	Instead of
After	By	On
Apart from	In	Since
Because of	In spite of / despite	Without

◊ **Verbs with prepositions followed by gerund**

Example: He **accused** her **of** steal**ing** his money.

Accuse of	Consist of	Pay for
Adjust with	Cope with	Prevent sb from
Admit to	Decide against	Protect from
Apologize for	Decide for	Put off
Approve of	Depend on	Rely on
Ask about	Die of	Spend money on
Ask for	Dream about / off	Spend time on
Begin by	Escape from	Succeed in
Believe in	Feel like	Suspect of
Be used to	Forgive for	Take part in
Blame for	Get used to	Talk about / of
Care for	Give up	Thank for
Carry on	Insist on	Think of
Complain about	Keep on	Use for
Concentrate on	Look forward to	Warn against
Congratulate on	Object to	Worry about

◊ **Adjectives** with / **without** prepositions followed by **gerund**

Example: I am **interested in** visit**ing** the museum.

Afraid of	Impressed by	Tired of
Angry about / at	Interested in	Worried about
Bad at	Keen on	**Worth**
Busy	Glad about	
Clever at	Good at	
Crazy about	**Like**	
Disappointed about	**Near**	
Excited about	Proud of	
Famous for	Sick of	
Fond of	Sorry about	

◊ **Nouns** with / **without** prepositions followed by **gerund**.

Example: there is no **point in** wait**ing** any longer.

Advantage of	**Fun**	Possibility of
Alternative of	Hope of	**Problem**
Chance of	Idea of	Reason for
Choice between	Interest in	**Trouble**
Danger of	Opportunity of	Trouble in
Difficulty in	Place for	**Use**
Doubt about	Pleasure in	Way of
Experience in	Point in	Waste of (money / time)

◊ **After expressions**

As well as	Have difficulty in	It's (no) worth
Can't help	Have trouble	It's no use
Can't stand	I'm busy	Not after / after
Have a difficult time	In addition to	There is (no) point in
Have a hard time	It's (no) good	What's the use of

◊ **As a noun**

Running is healthy.

◊ **AFTER** : <u>Hear</u> , <u>Listen</u> , <u>Notice</u> , <u>See</u> , <u>Watch</u>

To express an <u>in</u>complete action or an action in progress. We want to emphasize that the action continued for some time.	I **saw** him throw**ing** rubbish out of the window.	I saw **a part** of the action . I didn't wait until he had finished. Perhaps he threw more rubbish.

◊ **BUT**:

Hear , **Listen** , **See** , **Watch** + infinitive <u>without</u> "To"

Express a **complete** action from beginning to end. We want to emphasize that it lasted for a short time.	I **saw** him <u>throw</u> rubbish out of window.	I saw **all** of the rubbish being thrown out of the window.

■ **Infinitive**

◊ **Forms of the infinitive**

	Active voice	Passive voice
Present	(to) try	(to) **be** tried
Present cont.	(to) **be** trying	rarely used
Perfect	(to) **have** tried	(to) **have been** tried
Perfect cont.	(to) **have been** trying	rarely used

◊ **Forms of the infinitive corresponding to verb tenses.**

Verb tenses	Active voice / Passive voice	Forms of the infinitive Active voice / Passive voice
Present simple Future simple	She cleans... / ...is cleaned... She will clean... / ...will be cleaned...	to clean / to **be** clean**ed** (**Present infinitive**)
Present cont. Future cont.	She is cleaning... /... is being cleaned... She will be cleaning / ...will being cleaned	to **be** clean**ing** / no passive form (**Present continuous infinitive**)
Past simple Present perfect Past perfect Future perfect	She cleaned... / ...was cleaned... She has cleaned... /... has been cleaned She had cleaned... /... had been cleaned She will have cleaned /...will have been cleaned...	to **have** cleaned / to **have been** clean**ed** (**Perfect infinitive**)

Past continuous	She was cleaning / ...was being cleaned	to **have been** cleaning / no passive
Present perfect cont.	She has been cleaning / has been being	form
Past perfect cont.	She had been cleaning / had been being	(**Perfect continuous infinitive**)
Future perfect cont.	She will have been cleaning/...will have been being cleaned...	

◊ **The to - infinitive is used:**

To express purpose

You should take a few days off **to recover**.

After certain verbs (with to)

Example:He refused **to pay** the bill.

Afford	Expect	Promise
Agree	Fail	Refuse
Aim	Guarantee	Resolve
Appear	Happen	Seem
Arrange	Have	Stop
Ask	Help (also without to)	Swear
Attempt	Hesitate	Tend
Be determined	Hope	Threaten
Beg	Learn	Trouble
Care	Long	Undertake
Choose	Manage	Used
Claim	Mean	Volunteer
Condescend	Need (also without to)	Vow
Consent	Neglect	Want
Dare (also without to)	Offer	Wish
Decide	Ought	Yearn
Demand	Plan	
Deserve	Prepare	
Endeavour	Proceed	

After certain adjectives

Example:It was impossible **to go** back.

Amazed	Disappointed	Odd
Amazing	Easy	Rude
Angry	Extraordinary	Selfish
Astonished	Funny	Silly
Astonishing	Generous	Sorry
Awkward	Glad	Strange
Brave	Happy	Stupid
Careless	Hard	Surprised
Clever	Honest	Wicked
Cowardly	Horrified	Wise
Crazy	Impossible	Pointless
Delight	Kind	Relieved
Difficult	Nice	Ridiculous

After

I would like		
I would love	to express **specific preference**.	**I would like to eat** only organic foods.
I would prefer		
I would hate		
After certain nouns		It was such a **mistake to be** with them.

After : "Too"		He's **too** poor **to** buy a car.
After : "Enough"		He is strong **enough to** move the stone.
		There is **enough** food **to** go around.

With: (It+be+adjective+of+noun / pronoun) + to-infinitive	**It was unkind of her** to say that...
With: so+adjective+as	Would you be **so kind as to** give us information.
With "Only" to express an unsatisfactory result.	He won the lottery **only to lose at the casino**.
AFTER: Be + the first / the second / the third , etc Be + the next / the last / the best / the one	She **was the first** to congratulate him.
In the expression: For + noun / pronoun + to-inf	**For him to** lend you his bike was very unusual.
In expressions such : to tell you the truth to begin with to be honest	**To be honest** , I didn't know how to react.
With: Be sure to... / Be certain to... / Be bound to...	**Be sure to** do it later.

The infinitive **WITHOUT** "To" is used:

AFTER : most modal verbs (**Can** , **Could** , **May** , etc)	He **can go** if he wants to.
AFTER : **Had better** / **Would rather** / **Would sooner**	You **had better go** to bed.
AFTER : **Feel / Hear / Help / Let / Make / See** in the active	She **made** her baby **eat** all this soup.
NOTE : **Feel / Hear / Help / Let / Make / See** in the passive voice + to-inf "**LET**" turns into: Was / Were allowed to in the passive.	The baby **was made to eat** all this... She **was allowed to** stay out till midnight.
AFTER : **Need** , **Dare** in some cases.	You **need** not **make** such a fuss. How **dare** you **call** me a liar?
AFTER : And , As , But , Except , Like , Or , Than	It is **as easy** to smile **as frown**. We had nothing to do **except look** at the cinema posters.
AFTER : Do	**Do** you **think** she is ready? I **do admit** that I was wrong.
AFTER : Questions started with **Why** / **Why not** in **present tense**.	**Why pay** more at other shops? **Why not arrange** a party at his honor?
(**NO** noun or pronoun should come after **Why** / **Why not**.)	(**NOT**: Why we pay more at...) (**NOT**: Why not we arrange...)
If **two infinitives** are joined by "**AND**" or "**OR**" the "to" of the second infinitive can be omitted.	"I would prefer **to go** to a disco **and dance** with my friends."

◊ **NOTE**:

The **subject** of the **infinitive** or the "**-ing**" form is omitted when it is the **same** as the **subject** of the **main** verb.	I would like (**me**) **to** help with the preparations.
When it is **different**, however, it is **not** omitted.	I would like **Mary to** help with the preparations.

◊ **Verbs taking to-infinitive or -ing form <u>without</u> a change in meaning.**

Begin **Continue** **Intend** **Start**	(+) to-infinitive (+) -ing form	She **began to** speak. She **began** speak**ing**. (**NOT**: She **is** beginn**ing** speak**ing**.)
Advise **Allow** **Encourage** **Permit** **Require**	(+) <u>object</u> + to-infinitive (+) -ing form	She doesn't **allow** <u>them</u> **to** talk in class. She doesn't **allow** talk**ing** in class.
Be advis<u>ed</u> **Be allow<u>ed</u>** **Be encourag<u>ed</u>** **Be permitt<u>ed</u>** **Be requir<u>ed</u>**	(+) to-infinitive (+) -ing form	They **aren't allowed to** talk in the class. They **aren't allowed** talk**ing** in the class.
Need **Require** **Want**	(+) to-infinitive (+) passive - infinitive (+) -ing form	You **need to** wash your car. Your car **needs to be** wash**ed**. Your car **needs** wash**ing**.

◊ **Verbs taking to-infinitive or -ing form <u>with</u> a change in meaning.**

Forget + <u>to-inf.</u> **Forget** + ing form	**Forget** to do something. **Forget** a past event.	He **forgot** <u>to switch</u> off the T.V. He **forgot** meet**ing** Jane last summer.
Remember + <u>to-inf.</u> **Remember** +ing	**Remember** to do something. **Recall** a past enent.	I'll hope you **remember** <u>to tide</u> your room. I **remembered** play**ing** soccer in the school's yard.
Mean + <u>to-inf.</u> **Mean** + ing form	**Intent** to **Involve**	She **means** <u>to start</u> a new life. I won't take the job if it **means** mov**ing** to Scotland.
Go on + <u>to-inf.</u> **Go on** + ing form	**Finish** doing something and **start** doing something else. **Continue**	She gave up college and **went on** <u>to work</u> as a book seller. She **went on** writ**ing** till the early hours.
Regret + <u>to-inf.</u> **Regret** + ing form	**Be sorry** to **Repent** of something.	I **regret** <u>to inform</u> you that the meeting has been cancelled. He **regrets** misbehav**ing**.

Would prefer + <u>to-inf.</u> Prefer + ing form Prefer + <u>to-inf.</u>+ rather than + inf. <u>without</u> <u>to</u>.	Specific preference General preference Say you **like** <u>one thing</u> instead of <u>another</u>.	I **would prefer** <u>to see</u> you in private. I prefer work**ing** on my own. I **prefer** <u>to eat</u> cooked food **rather than** raw.
Try + <u>to-inf.</u> Try + -ing form	Best attempt / best solution Do something **as an experiment**.	**Try** <u>to eat</u> less cholesterol food. **Try** cutt**ing** down fat. You might get thinner.
Want + <u>to-inf.</u> Want + -ing form	Wish Something needs to be done.	I **want** <u>to stop</u> smoking. This room **wants** tidy**ing** up.
Stop + <u>to-inf.</u> Stop + -ing form	Pause temporarily Finish , cease	He **stopped** at the garage <u>to have</u> the tank filled. He stopped behav**ing** foolishly.
Be sorry + <u>to-inf.</u> Be sorry for + -ing	Feel sad about sth Apologize for	I'm **sorry** <u>to tell</u> you that your flight has been cancelled. He is **sorry for** hurt**ing** her feelings.
Hate + <u>to-inf.</u> Hate + -ing form	Hate one is **about to do**. Feel sorry about **one is doing**.	I **hate** <u>to wake up</u> early tomorrow morning. I **hate** caus**ing** you so much inconvenience.
Be afraid + <u>to-inf.</u> Be afraid of + -ing	Be too frightened to do something. Be afraid that what is referred to **by the** "-**ing form**" may happen.	She was **afraid** <u>to climb</u> the tree. When she goes swimming,she is always **afraid of** be**ing stung by a jellyfish**.
Come + <u>to-inf.</u> Come + -ing form With verbs of <u>motion</u>	End up Describes **the activity** of **the coming**.	John **came** <u>to accept</u> that Mary wouldn't marry him. He **came** <u>rushing</u> into my office.

◊ **NOTE**: Uses of "**Suggest**" & "**Be committed**"

Suggest + (<u>that</u>) cla-<u>use</u>. Suggest + ing form		He suggested **(that) we should go out** **for a walk**. The company suggested tak**ing** an extra day off.
<u>Be</u> committed <u>Be</u> committed	<u>to</u> do**ing** sth (**Refers to energy , effort** and **time** for an **ongoing activity**.) <u>to</u> do sth (Refers to a **binding promise**.)	They **are committed** <u>to</u> work**ing** overtime for many weeks. (**Ongoing activity**) He **is committed** <u>to</u> marry her. (**Binding promise**)

◊ **NOTE: Present participles (Verb+ing)**   **Past participles (Verb+ed)**

Describe what somebody or something **is**. It was a bor**ing** lecture. (**What kind of lecture? Boring**)	Describe what someone **feels**. They were bor**ed** by the lecture.

◊ **NOTE**:

After "**Help**" we can use **either** a **bare infinitive** or "**to-infinitive**".	My schoolmates **helped** me **pass / to pass** the test.

◊ **NOTE:**

In **negative sentences** , the position of "**NOT**" can **influence** the meaning in **active** and **passive** voice.

In the active voice	**In the passive voice**
I **regretted not** buy**ing** this new car.	I **was** allow**ed not** to visit him.
(I did**n't** buy the new car **and I regret it**.)	(…they said I should**n't** visit him.)
I **didn't regret** buy**ing** the new car.	I **wasn't** allow**ed** to visit him.
(I **bought** it and I did**n't** regret it.)	(…they did**n't** say I should**n't** visit him.)

◊ **NOTE:** <u>Perfect</u> form of **gerunds** in the **active voice.**

There is also the <u>**perfect**</u> form of gerunds. The <u>**perfect**</u> form of gerunds, in the **active voice**, is for-med using: "**Having** + **past participle**".This kind of gerund suggests that the **gerund happened** <u>befo-re</u> something else.

With no gerund	I **have** train**ed** hard for the school's competition.
With gerund	<u>**My**</u> **having** train**ed** hard every afternoon, when I was a child, helped me to win the school's competition.
	(This suggests that the speaker **had trained** hard **before** he / she won the scho-ol's competition.)

This rule works **not only** for the **present perfect, but also** for **other** <u>past tense</u> forms using:
"**Having** + **past participle**". Look at the following sentences. The first one (without the gerund) uses the **simple past** tense (**took**).

With no gerund	I <u>**took**</u> a physics class.
With gerund	**Having taken** a physics class helped me in calculus.

This suggests that the speaker **had taken a physics class** <u>**before**</u> he / she took the calculus.

◊ **NOTE:** The **present** and the **perfect** form of **gerunds** in the **passive voice.**

There is also a **passive form of gerunds**. The **passive form of gerunds** is formed using "**Being** + **past participle**" (**for the present form**) and "**Having** <u>been</u> + **past participle**" (**for the Perfect form**).

With no gerund	When I <u>**was**</u> **accepted** to Harvard University **was** the greatest day of my life.
With gerund	<u>**Being**</u> **accepted** to Harvard University **was** the greatest day of my life.
With no gerund	The older students recall**ed** because they <u>**had been**</u> **taught** that **already**.
With gerund	The older students recall**ed** <u>**having been**</u> **taught** that **already**.

◊ The <u>**passive**</u> form of gerunds is also formed by using "**Getting** + **past participle**":

With no gerund	We **got scared** by that movie, so we took the decision to leave before the end.
With gerund	**Getting scared** by that movie made us leave before the end.

◊　**NOTE**: <u>Perfect</u> form of **infinitives** in the **active voice**.

We use forms of the <u>perfect infinitive</u> to talk about an **event** that <u>happened earlier from now</u> or <u>it is completed</u>. **Perfect infinitive** can refer **to** <u>future</u> actions.

■　**Verb** + <u>to have</u> + <u>past participle</u> (**Perfect form** in the **active voice**).	I **knew** him <u>**to have won**</u> the race. (**Happened earlier from now**.) Tom is thought <u>**to have**</u> already <u>**finish-**</u> <u>**ed**</u> his preparation. (**A complete event**)
The **perfect form** of **infinitive** can refer to **future actions**.	I am <u>**to have bought**</u> the car before you come. (**Future reference**)
It is also used when we talk about **actions** that <u>**did not**</u> **happen-ed**.	He promised <u>**to have studied**</u> history and maths. (We know that **he didn't study**.)
■　**Verb** + <u>to have been</u> + <u>present</u> participle (**Perfect continuous form** in the **active voice**). Is used when we talk about **actions** that <u>**may not**</u> have **happe-ned**.	He promised <u>**to have been**</u> speaking Spanish, in six months, fluently. (**Six months was not enough time**.)

◊　**NOTE**:

The **perfect infinitive** is often used **after verbs** like "**Mean**", "**Be**", "**Would like**", **etc**, to talk about <u>**unreal past situations**</u>.	I **meant to have posted** the letter, **but** I **forgot**. (I did **not post** the letter.)

◊　**NOTE**: The **present** and the **perfect** form of **infinitives** in the **passive voice**.

Sometimes there is a little difference in meaning whether "**Be**" & "**Have been**" **passive forms** are used. On other occasions, the **present form** "**To be**" is more clearly associated with **pre-sent time** and the **perfect form** "**To have been**" more clearly associated with **past time**.	Jane Perry **is** the second woman **to be nominated** for the best manager. (**Present time**) Jane Perry **was** the second woman **to have been nominated** for best mana-ger. (**Past time**)

◊　**NOTE**: **Future actions of the infinitives**

Future actions can **also** be indicated using the **present contin-uous infinitive** in the **active** (**To be** + present participle).	I think <u>**to be**</u> try<u>**ing**</u> again. (**Future reference**)
They can **also** be indicated using the <u>**passive infinitive**</u>. (**To be** + past participle)	Less students **are expected** <u>**to be**</u> in-troduc<u>**ed next year**</u>. (**Future reference**)

■　"**Go** + gerund" combinations

Go bird watching	**Go** jogging	**Go** skiing
Go boating	**Go** kayaking	**Go** skinny-dipping
Go bowling	**Go** mountain climbing	**Go** sledding
Go camping	**Go** running	**Go** snorkeling
Go canoeing	**Go** sailing	**Go** swimming
Go dancing	**Go** shopping	**Go** tobogganing
Go fishing	**Go** sightseeing	**Go** window shopping
Go hiking	**Go** skateboarding	
Go hunting	**Go** skating	

- **Expressions with to + ing**

Acclimatize to	Dedicate oneself to	Owing to
Accustomed to	Devote a ... to	Plead guilty to
Addicted to	Devote oneself to	Prefer...to
Adjust to	Face up to	Resign to
Adopt to	Fall to	Resort to
Attribute to	Feel up to	See to
Be close to	Get down to	Settle down to
Be equal to	Get round to	Take to
Be near to	Have an objection to	Turn one's attention to
Be opposed to	It's due to	What do you say to
Be up to	Look forward to	When it comes to
Confess to	Lower oneself to	With a view to
Contribute to	Object to	

From above "To" is a **preposition** <u>not</u> infinitive.

- **Examples with expressions** followed by **gerund**.

Have **a problem**	Debbie had **a problem** understand**ing** his accent.
Have **no problem**	Francis had **no problem** go**ing** from the airport to the hotel.
Have (**some**) **problems**	He had (**some**) **problems** read**ing** without his glasses.
Have **a difficult time**	She had **a difficult time** hik**ing** up the mountain.
Have **a good time**	They had **a good time** danc**ing**.
Have **a hard time**	She had **a hard time** explain**ing** the situation.
Have **an easy time**	She has **an easy time** work**ing** on a new project.
Have **difficulty**	Jane had **difficulty** translat**ing** the letter by herself.
Have **no difficulty**	They had **no** difficul**ty** find**ing** a discount flight to London.
Have **fun**	The had **fun** ski**ing**.
Spend **one's time**	He always **spends his time** work**ing** out at the gym.
Waste **one's time**	She always **wastes her time** play**ing** video games.

4 PASSIVE CAUSATIVE FORM - CAUSATIVE VERBS

◊ **Passive causative form**

■ We use: <u>Subject</u> + "**Have**" / "**Get**" + <u>Object</u> + **past participle** of the main verb to say that we have **assigned** to **someone else to do something for us.**	<u>She</u> **has** her <u>**children**</u> look**ed** after.
■ We use: <u>Subject</u> + "**Have**" / "**Get**" + <u>Object</u> + **past participle** to say that something **unexpected**, and **usually unpleasant** happens **to someone** or **we experience** something.	<u>I</u> **had** my <u>**house**</u> **unlocked.** (**Unexpected**) <u>I</u> **had** my <u>**bag**</u> **stolen last week.** (**Unpleasant / Experience**)
■ "**Get**" can be used instead of "**Have**" to suggest that the <u>subject</u> was **responsible for the event.**	<u>She</u> **got** her <u>**car**</u> **crashed.** (She **is** responsible.)

◊ Present simple Present simple con.	<u>She</u> **looks** after her <u>**children**</u>. <u>She</u> **is** look**ing** after her <u>**children**</u>.	<u>She</u> **has** her <u>**children**</u> look**ed** after. <u>She</u> **is** having her <u>**children**</u> look**ed** after.
◊ Past simple Past continuous	<u>She</u> **looked** after her <u>**children**</u>. <u>She</u> **was** look**ing** after her <u>**children**</u>.	<u>She</u> **had** her <u>**children**</u> look**ed** after. <u>She</u> **was** having her <u>**children**</u> look**ed** after.
◊ Future simple	<u>She</u> **will** look after her <u>**children**</u>.	<u>She</u> **will have** her <u>**children**</u> look**ed** after.
◊ Future continuous	<u>She</u> **will be** look**ing** after her <u>**children**</u>.	<u>She</u> **will be** having her <u>**children**</u> look**ed** after.
◊ Be going to	<u>She</u> **is going to** look **after** her <u>**children**</u>.	<u>She</u> **is going to have** her <u>**children**</u> look**ed** after.
◊ Present perfect	<u>She</u> **has** look**ed** after her <u>**children**</u>.	<u>She</u> **has had** her <u>**children**</u> look**ed** after.
◊ Present perfect con.	<u>She</u> **has** been look**ing** after her <u>**children**</u>.	<u>She</u> **has** been having her <u>**children**</u> look**ed** after.
◊ Past Perfect	<u>She</u> **had** look**ed** after her <u>**children**</u>.	<u>She</u> **had had** her <u>**children**</u> look**ed** after.
◊ Past Perfect cont.	<u>She</u> **had** been look**ing** after her <u>**children**</u>.	<u>She</u> **had** been having her <u>**children**</u> look**ed** after.
■ **Infinitive**	<u>She</u> can **look** after her <u>**children**</u>.	<u>She</u> can **have** her <u>**children**</u> look**ed** after.
■ **ing form**	<u>She</u> likes look**ing** after her <u>**children**</u>.	<u>She</u> likes having her <u>**children**</u> look**ed** after.
■ **In questions & negations**	With "**Do**" / "**Does**" in **Present simple**.	**Does** <u>she</u> **have** her <u>**children**</u> look**ed** after? <u>She</u> **doesn't have** her <u>**children**</u> look**ed** after.
	In the **present continuous** tense we put the subject **after** the **verb** "**Be**" and in negations we add "**Not**" **after** the **verb** "**Be**"	**Is** <u>she</u> having her <u>**children**</u> look**ed** after? <u>She</u> **is not** having her children look**ed** after.

With "**Did**" in **Past simple**.	**Did** <u>she</u> **have** her <u>**children**</u> look**ed** after? <u>She</u> **didn't have** her <u>**children**</u> look**ed** after.
With "**Will**" in **Future simple-continuous**.	**Will** <u>she</u> **have** her <u>**children**</u> look**ed** after? <u>She</u> **will not have** her <u>**children**</u> look**ed** after. **Will** <u>she</u> **be** having her <u>**children**</u> look**ed** after? <u>She</u> **will not be** having her <u>**children**</u> look**ed** after.
With "**Have**" in **Present perfect**	**Has** <u>she</u> **had** her <u>**children**</u> look**ed** after? <u>She</u> **has not had** her <u>**children**</u> look**ed** after.
With "**Had**" in **Past perfect**	**Had** <u>she</u> **had** her <u>**children**</u> look**ed** after? <u>She</u> **had not had** her <u>**children**</u> look**ed** after.

◊ **Causative Verbs**

■ <u>Get</u> + object + <u>to-inf</u>

Is used to show that someone **persuades** someone **to do something**.	She <u>**got**</u> her husband <u>**to cut**</u> the grass.

■ <u>Let</u> + object + <u>bare infinitive</u>

The structure is closer to "**Allow + somebody + to-infinitive**".	I <u>**let**</u> Jim <u>**clean**</u> up the mess.

■ <u>Make</u> + object + <u>bare infinitive</u>

The structure implies that other persons **did not really want** to do something but they **were forced**.	The teacher **made** Jack <u>**rewrite**</u> the composition. (**Active voice**)
When we transform this structure into **passive** we insert (**to**) between "**Make**" and the **infinitive**.	I **was** <u>**made**</u> to <u>**rewrite**</u> the composition. (**Passive voice**)

■ <u>Have / Had</u> + object + <u>bare infinitive</u>

The structure is **not** as strong as: "**Make + object + bare infinitive**", and the is closer to: "**Ask + somebody + to-infinitive**". <u>The **infinitive** refers **to one specific event**</u>.	I'll <u>**have**</u> her <u>**copy**</u> the document. (I'll <u>**ask**</u> her <u>**to copy**</u> the document.)

■ <u>Have / Had</u> + object + <u>gerund</u>

If you **have** someone do**ing** something the sense is that the action is **ongoing**.	I <u>**have**</u> him water**ing** all the flowers **today**.

- **Have / Get** + object + **present** participle

Start something	Don't worry , we will soon **have** your car go**ing**.
Experience something that is happening to someone **as a result of something else**.	We will **have** my **brother** stay**ing** with us **until he finds a new apartment**.
To express a **repeated action**.	His health problems **have** / **got** him go**ing** to hospital for many times this year.

◊ **NOTE**: "I won't have" / "I wouldn't have"

When we use the expression "**I won't / wouldn't have**...", it means "**I won't allow + to-infinitive**" / "**I wouldn't allow + to-infinitive**". Here the "**-ing**" form works best.	**I won't have** you smok**ing** in the bedroom. **She wouldn't have** letting him to go on vacation with his friends.

◊ **NOTE: Causative form** of the **Modal verbs**.

- **Modal verbs**

Modal verbs	Present / Future	Present / Future Causative form
Can	He **can make** Sushi.	He **can have** Sushi **made**.
Could	He **could make** Sushi.	He **could have** Sushi **made**.
Must	He **must make** Sushi.	He **must have** Sushi **made**.
Should	He **should make** Sushi.	He **should have** Sushi made.
Ought to	He **ought to make** Sushi.	He **ought to have** Sushi **made**.
May	He **may make** Sushi.	He **may have** Sushi **made**.
Might	He **might make** Sushi.	He **might have** Sushi **made**.
Will	He **will make** Sushi.	He **will have** Sushi **made**.
Would	He **would make** Sushi.	He **would have** Sushi **made**.
Have / Has (got) **to**	He **has** (got) **to make** Sushi.	He **has** (got) **to have** Sushi **made**.
Need to	He **needs to make** Sushi.	He **needs to have** Sushi **made**.
Needn't	He **needn't make** Sushi.	He **needn't have** Sushi **made**.
Had better	He **had better make** Sushi.	He **had better have** Sushi **made**.

- **Modal verbs**

Modal verbs	Past	Past Causative form
Can't have	He **can't have made** Sushi.	He **can't have had** Sushi **made**.
Could have	He **could have made** Sushi.	He **could have had** Sushi **made**.
Must have	He **must have made** Sushi.	He **must have had** Sushi **made**.
Should have	He **should have made** Sushi.	He **should have had** Sushi **made**.
May have	He **may have made** Sushi.	He **may have had** Sushi **made**.
Might have	He **might have made** Sushi.	He **might have had** Sushi **made**.
Would have	He **would have made** Sushi.	He **would have had** Sushi **made**.
Had to	He **had to make** Sushi.	He **had to have** Sushi **made**.
Used to	He **used to make** Sushi.	He **used to have** Sushi **made**.

5   CONDITIONALS / WISHES / UNREAL PAST

◊   **Real Conditionals**

■   **Real Conditionals in the Present and in the Future**

If clause	Result clause
Present perfect	**Bare** infinitive / **Present simple**

If you **have finished** your job , **take** this things out of the room.	True or **likely to happen** in the **present**.
If you **have done** your homework , you **can** watch T.V.	True or **likely to happen** in the **present**.

Present simple **Present continuous**	(**will / can / may / might / must / should**) + **bare infinitive**

If the weather **is** nice , we **will go** on excursion.	True or **likely to happen** in the **future**.
If I **am** going out **tonight** , I **will go** to the cinema.	True or **likely to happen** in the **future**.

When clause	Result clause
When / If clause	**Present simple**

When I get up late, I **miss** the bus.	General truth.
If you **heat** ice, **it melts**.	General truth.

■   **Real Conditionals in the Past**

If clause	Result clause
Past simple	**Past simple**

If I **went** to a friend's house for dinner, I usually **took** a bottle of wine or some flowers.

◊   **Unreal Conditionals**

■   **Unreal Conditionals in the Present / Future**

If clause	Result clause
Past simple **Past continuous**	(**would** / **could** / **might**) + **bare infinitive** (Unreal in the Present)

If he **didn't** eat so many sweets, he **wouldn't** have problem with his teeth.	Unreal in the **present**. (He eats a lot of sweets).
If I **were** you, I **wouldn't** speak to him again.	Unreal in the **present**. (Give advice)
If the sun **was** shining, I **would** go to the beach.	Unreal in the **present**.

Past simple	(**would** / **could** / **might**) + **be** + **ing form** (Unreal in the Future)

If I **was** alone, I **would be going** to the cinema.	Unreal in the **future**. (Possible plan)

■ **Unreal Conditionals in the Past**

If clause	Result clause
Past perfect	(would / could / might) + have + past participle (would / could / might) + have been + present participle

If she **had known** how to use the mixer, she **wouldn't have broken** it.	Unreal in the **past**. (She **didn't** know how to use the mixer.)
If she **had missed** the train, he **wouldn't have been** waiting for her at the station **for** hours.	Unreal in the **past**. (She **didn't** miss the train.)

If clause	Result clause
Past perfect cont.	(would / could / might)+ have + past participle

If he **had been** standing near the house when the wall collapsed , it **would have killed** him.	Unreal in the **past**. (He **wasn't** standing near the house.)

◊ **Mixed conditions**

If clause	Result clause
If they **were working** all day (**Perhaps** they were working all day	they **will be** tired now. so they are tired now.)
If I **were** you (You are **not** me	I **would have** accepted the job. so you **didn't** accept the job.)
If she **had finished** earlier (She **didn't** finished earlier	She **would** <u>be going</u> to the party. so she is**n't** going to the party.)

◊ **NOTE**:

■ We can use "**If**...**were** + **to-infinitive**" rather than "**If** + **past simple**" to talk about <u>unreal future situations</u>.	If the team **were to win** the championship it **would be** the greatest success in its history. (The team didn't win.)
■ We **don't** usually use this pattern with **stative** verbs: (**Belong** , **Doubt** , **Know** , **Understand**)	If it **belonged** to us we **would sell** it. (<u>NOT</u>: If it **were to belong** to us we...)

◊ "**Unless**" and "**If**...**not**"

■ In <u>real</u> **conditional sentences,** we can often use either "**Unless**" or "**If**...**not**" when the meaning is "**Except if**". We also use "**Unless**" to say that something **will happen** or be **true** if something else **does not happen** or **is not true**.	If we **don't** improve our productivity we will **not** succeed our goals. **Unless** we improve our productivity we will **not** succeed our goals.
■ We use "**Unless**" <u>but not</u> "**If**...**not**" when we introduce an <u>afterthought</u>.	We should leave the island in two days <u>**unless** we take the decision to stay for at least a week</u>.

◊ **We usually use "If...not" but not "Unless"**

■ When we say that an **event** or **action** in the "**If-clause**" is **unexpected**.	**If** I do**n't** pass the exams, I will be shocked. (He **expects** to pass the exams , and will not be shocked.)
■ In **questions**	How can you buy this car **if** you are **not** able to afford?
■ When the meaning is **different to "Except if"** or when we **know** that something **did not** or **will not** happen.	**If** John and Mary decide **not** to help us we will turn to other sponsors. (We believe that they **will not** help us. Meaning different to "**Except if**".)
■ In **unreal** conditional sentences.	**If** he did**n't** study hard he **would** never pass the exams. (Of course he studied hard.)

◊ **Conditionals are usually introduced with "IF". Other expressions are:**

As long as **But for** **Even if** **For + ing / noun** **In case of** **On condition (that)** **Only if** **Or else** **Otherwise** **Provided / Provided that** **Supposing** **Unless (= if not)** **What if**	You **can** be successful **only if** you study hard. **Unless** you work more efficiently , you **will** be fired.

◊ **NOTE:**

We do **not** normally use "**Will**" , "**Would**" , or "**Should**" in "**If-clauses**".	**If** you **want** this, you can have it. **NOT**: If you **will** want this…

◊ **"Will" , "Would" , "Should" can be used in if clauses:**

■ To make a **request**.	**If** you **will / would** stop talking with the others, then I**'ll** give you information. (**Request**: **Will** you please stop talking with the others?)
■ To express: **Annoyance** , **Doubt** , **Uncertainty** , **Insistence**.	**If** he **will** come, show him his room. (**Doubt / Uncertainty**: We doubt that he will come.)
■ We **can** use "**Will**" when we **talk about a result** of something in the **main clause**, or when we **want to show** that we **strongly disapprove** something.	**If** this food **will** help you to feel better, then you **can eat more**. ("**Eat more**"= result in the **main clause**.) **If** you **will tell the secret** to everyone, you will make your greatest mistake! ("**Tell the secret**" = Something that we disapprove.)
■ We **can** use "**Would**" when we talk about a **desired outcome**.	**if** I **would** buy this new house, my life would be more comfortable.

◊ "IF" can be omitted in **if-clauses**. In this case "**Should**" , "**Were**" , "**Had**" come **before** the <u>subject</u>.

If **he should** stay , show him his room.
Should <u>he</u> stay , show him his room.

If <u>I</u> **were** you , I wouldn't tell you.
Were <u>I</u> you , I wouldn't tell you.

If <u>I</u> **had** known the truth , I would have called the police.
Had <u>I</u> known the truth , I would have called the police.

◊ **Conditional questions**

If you **had to** change a part of your body <u>**which**</u> part **would** you change**?**
If you **had** one wish <u>**what**</u> would it be**?**
If you **had been** married in Switzerland , <u>**which**</u> city **would you have been** lived in**?**
<u>**What**</u> **will** happen **if** you **don't** study hard enough**?**

◊ **NOTE**:

If he **had been** more careful , he **didn't** cause**d** the accident.
He **didn't** cause**d** the accident If he **had been** more careful.

Separate two clauses with a **comma**.
No comma.

After "**If**" we normally use "**were**" instead of "**was**" for all persons in **unreal conditionals** in **present /future**, in formal English.

If I **were** you, I will tell her everything.

◊ **NOTE**: "**IF**" and politeness

Apart from **conditionals**, "**If-clauses**" are also used to tell or ask people to do things **in a polite way**.

If you could repeat this question again?

◊ **Wishes**

■ **About present**

Wish (If only) + **past tense**.

I wish we **were** in Paris now.
(**Wish / regret** about the **present situation** that we want to **be different**.)

Wish (If only) + <u>**could**</u> + bare infinitive

I wish I <u>**could** swim</u>.
(**Wish / regret** about the **present** concerning <u>lack of ability</u>.)

■ **About past**

Wish (If only) + **past perfect**.

I wish you **had told** me earlier.
(**Regret** about something happened or didn't happen in the **past**.)

■ **About** <u>impossible</u> **wish for a** <u>future change</u>.

Wish (If only) + <u>**would**</u> + **bare infinitive**

I wish he <u>**would** stop</u> smoking.
(**Wish** for a **future** change **unlikely** to happen.)

■ **Dissatisfaction / Disappointment**

Wish (If only) + <u>would</u> + **bare infinitive**	I wish students **would pay** more attention. (**Dissatisfaction**)
Wish+ <u>inanimate subject</u> + <u>would</u> + **bare infinitive**	I wish **the wind would** stop blowing. ("**Wish**" implying **disappointment**.)

■ **Wish implying <u>lack of hope</u>.**

Wish+ <u>subject</u> + would + **bare infinitive**	I wish **you would find** your stolen car. (**Lack of hope**.)

◊ **NOTE**: "Wish" & "Hope"

If we want something **to be true** or **to happen** in the **future** and we **believe it is possible**, then a structure such as "**I hope**" , "**I do hope**" , "**hoping**" is required. "**Wish**" is used **for things** which we **want to happen**, but we **think** that they may **not** happen.

◊ **Unreal Past**

When we talk about **imaginary**, **unreal** , **improbable** situations in the **present** or **future** we use the **Simple Past**. When we talk about **imaginary**, **unreal** , **improbable** situations in the **past** we use the **Past Perfect**.	This is called **unreal past**.

Imaginary , unreal , improbable situations in the present or **future.**	**Imaginary , unreal , improbable situations in the past.**
Simple Past	**Past Perfect**
If I **were** you , I **wouldn't** do that.	**If** he **had warned** me , this **wouldn't have** happened.
Wish I wish she **were** more cooperative.	**Wish** **If only** I **hadn't** lost all my money last night.
I'd rather , I'd sooner I **would rather / I would sooner pay** me today.	**I'd rather , I'd sooner** **I'd rather** you **had** not **told** to everyone.
Suppose / Supposing **Suppose** your father **caught** you smoking , what **would** you do? (**Future situation**)	**Suppose / Supposing** **Suppose** he **had left** before the boss came , what **would have** happened?
As if / as though She behaves **as if** she **were** the queen.	**As if / as though** Soon after being introduced, they were talking to each other **as if** they **had been** friends for years.
It is (**about / high**) **time + past tense** It's (**about**) **time** we **left**.	-
It is (**about / high**) **time + <u>infinitive</u>** It's (**about**) **time <u>to leave</u>**. (When making a **general statement**)	-

◊ **NOTE** : "I would rather" = "I would sooner" = "I would prefer" <u>in meaning</u>

◊ **Unreal past with**: "**Would rather + bare infinitive**"

■ **When** the **subject** of **would rather** <u>is also</u> the subject of the **infinitive** then:

I would rather + **Present bare infinitive** (**Present / Future reference**)	I'd rather **play** tennis.
I would rather + **Perfect bare infinitive** (**Past reference**)	I'd rather not **have gone** out with him yesterday.

◊ **Unreal past with**: "**Would rather + Past simple / Past Perfect**"

■ **When** the **subject** of "**Would rather**" is **different from** the **subject** of the **main verb** then:

I would rather **sb** + **Past Simple** (**Present / Future reference**)	I'd rather **you** stopp**ed** smoking.
I would rather **sb** + **Past Perfect** (**Past reference**)	I'd rather **you had** mention**ed** that before.

◊ **Unreal past with**: "**Would rather / Would sooner + <u>bare infinitive</u> + than + <u>bare infinitive</u>**"

Would rather / Would sooner + <u>bare infinitive</u> + **than** + <u>bare infinitive</u>	I'**d rather** <u>listen</u> to music **than** <u>watch</u> TV. (**General preference in the present**).

■ "**Would rather**" is very common in **spoken** English and is often abbreviated to "**'d rather**".

When we are talking about **specifics**, "**Would rather**" is used as an alternative to "**Would prefer to**" followed by an <u>infinitive</u>.	Would you like to go out for dinner tonight? No, I think **I'd rather** <u>eat</u> at home. (**I would prefer to** <u>eat</u> at home.)

◊ **Unreal past with**: "**Would prefer...rather than... , Prefer...rather than... , Prefer...to...**"

■ **Would prefer** + <u>full infinitive</u> + **rather than** + <u>bare infinitive</u>

Would prefer + <u>full infinitive</u> + **rather than** + <u>bare infinitive</u>	I'd **prefer** <u>to live</u> in London **rather than** <u>live</u> in Paris. (**Specific preference in the present**).

■ **Prefer** + <u>full infinitive</u> + **rather than** + <u>bare infinitive</u> / **noun**

Prefer + <u>full infinitive</u> + **rather than** + <u>bare infinitive</u>	I **prefer** <u>to drink</u> coffee **rather than** <u>drink</u> tea. (**General preference in the present**).
Prefer + <u>full infinitive</u> + **rather than** + <u>noun</u>	I **prefer** <u>to drink</u> coffee **rather than** <u>tea</u>. (**General preference in the present**).

■ **Prefer + gerund / noun + to + gerund / noun**

Prefer + gerund + to + gerund	I prefer drink**ing** tea **to** drinking coffee. **(General preference in the present)**.
Prefer + noun + to + noun	I prefer **tea to coffee**. **(General preference in the present)**.

◊ **NOTE: Unreal past with**:

■ **Had better / Should + present bare infinitive**

Had better / Should + <u>present bare infinitive</u> **(Present / Future reference)**	You **had better / should** <u>consult</u> a lawyer.

■ **It would have been better if + Past Perfect**

It would have been better if + <u>Past Perfect</u> **(Past reference)**	**It would have been better if** you **had**n't talk**ed** to James last night.

6   EMPHATIC STRUCTURES / INVERSION

◊   **Emphatic Structures**

◊   **Fronting**

We can **emphasize** a <u>particular part</u> of a sentence **moving it to the front** of the sentence.

| <u>On the table</u> **stood** a vase of flowers.
A vase of flowers **stood** <u>on the table</u>.

<u>Learning English</u> **I think** is a basic educational qualification.
I think <u>learning English</u> is a basic educational qualification.

◊   **Cleft sentences**

■   **"It"**

It + is / was (not) + **subject / object** + that / who(m)
Statement

| **It** was **Mary** that / who called you.
It was the **manager** that / who(m) I wrote to.
It was in the **mid-1980s** that you first met me.

Negation

| **It** wasn't me that / who called the police.

Questions

| Is **it** the car that / which you are going to buy ?

■   **"That"**

That + is / was + <u>question word</u>
(**Statement**)

| **That** is <u>what</u> most of us know about him.

Is / was + **that** + <u>question word</u>
(**Questions**)

| Is **that** <u>why</u> she leaves the house?

■   **"What"**

<u>What</u> + <u>subject</u> + **verb** + is / was

| <u>What</u> he **needs** is a long holiday.
(A long holiday is <u>what</u> he **needs**.)

To express **admiration / anger / concern** we use question words with **ever**.

| What**ever** you are thinking about.

Sometimes we use "**All**" instead of "**What**"

| <u>All</u> she **wants** is to win the contest.

◊ **NOTE:**

■ After the "What" we **usually** use a **singular form** of "**Be**" ("**Is**" or "**Was**").

What she wants / they want **is** to talk to the manager.

■ We can sometimes put a "**Wh-cleft**" at the **end**.

The technological evolution **is what th-ey discussed**.

◊ **NOTE:**

■ To **emphasize an ACTION** we can use :

"**Wh-cleft**" with "**What**" + **Subject** + form of "**do**" + form of "**be**" + **(to)-infinitive**.

What **they do is to play** tennis every Saturday. (**Action = tennis**)

■ To **emphasize** a **whole sentence** we can use:

"**Wh-cleft**" with "**Happen**"

What **happened** to John and Mary **w-as** too strange for the most of us.

■ "**Do**" / "**Does**" / "**Did**" + **bare infinitive** used in the **Present simple**, **Past simple**, **imperative** to gi-ve **emphasis**.

Present simple	I **do promise** to keep your secret.
Past simple	He **did buy** a diamond ring.
Imperative	Do **have** some more coffee.

◊ **Inversion**

We can invert the **subject** and the **auxiliary verb** in the sentence **to give emphasis**.

Where **no auxiliary** is present "**Do**", "**Does**" or "**Did**" is used. **This happens**:

◊ **After certain expressions** placed at the **beginning** of a sentence :

At no time	Not only... but also	Only in
Barely	Not since	Only in this way
Hardly (ever)	Not till	Only then
In no circumstances	Not until	Only when
In no way	Nowhere	Rarely
Little	On no account	Scarcely (ever)
Never (before)	On no occasion	Seldom
Neither / Nor	Only after	Under no circumstances
No sooner...than	Only by	...when
Not even once	Only if	

◊ **Before the inversion** / **After the inversion**

He **said little** about the accident.

Little did he **say** about the accident. ("**Did**" is used.)

He **visits** us **rarely**.

Rarely does he **visit** us. ("**Does**" is used.)

Elda **will** leave the house **under no circumstances**.

Under no circumstances will Elda **leave** the house. (**Auxiliary "Will"** is used.)

◊ **NOTE:**

■ **When:**Only after / Only by / Only if / Only in / Only when and Not since / Not till / Not until clauses are put at the <u>beginning</u> of a sentence we **use inversion** in the <u>main</u> clause, **neither** in "Only clause" **nor** in the "**Not clause**".

Only when you see him **will you** realise how much he had suffered.
Not until hours later **did I** find him.

NOT:
Only when will you see him you realize how much he had suffered.

◊ **In conditionals when:** "**Should**" , "**Were**" , "**Had**" are placed at the **beginning** of the sentence.

If <u>you</u> **should** go out , leave the key under the mat.
(**Type 1**)

Should <u>you</u> go out , leave the key under the mat.

If <u>I</u> **were** you , I would apologize.
(**Type 2**)

Were <u>I</u> **you** , I would apologize.

If <u>he</u> **had** been invited , he would have come.
(**Type 3**)

Had <u>he</u> **been invited** , he would have come.

◊ **After** <u>adverbs of place</u> we **invert** the <u>subject</u> and the **main verb**. (**Adverb** + **Verb** + <u>Subject</u>)

Before the inversion	Inversion after the adverb of place	BUT:
The <u>bus</u> **goes** <u>there</u>.	**There goes** the <u>bus</u>.	<u>**There**</u> it goes! (**NOT**: <u>**There**</u> goes <u>it</u>!)
Your <u>pen</u> **is** <u>here</u>.	**Here is** your <u>pen</u>.	<u>**Here**</u> it **is**! (**NOT**: <u>**Here**</u> **is** it!)

◊ **NOTE: Inversion** also occurs **after:**

■ <u>Prepositional phrases</u> of **place** or **movement** and <u>**adverbs**</u> describing **a movement in a particular direction**.

<u>Into</u> the classroom walked **John**.
(**John** walked <u>into</u> the classroom.)
<u>**Outside**</u> he walked to find his lost wallet.
(**He** walked <u>**outside**</u> to find his lost wallet.)

■ **Verbs** describing **place** and **movement**: "<u>Be</u>" , "<u>**Come**</u>" , "<u>**Fly**</u>" "<u>Go</u>" , "<u>**Hang**</u>" , "<u>**Lie**</u>" , "<u>**Live**</u>" , "<u>**March**</u>" , "<u>**Roll**</u>" , "<u>**Run**</u>" , "<u>**Sit**</u>" , "<u>**Stand**</u>" , "<u>**Swim**</u>" , "<u>**Walk**</u>" are commonly used with **inversion**.

Out of the theatre **walked** John.
(**John** <u>walked</u> out of the theatre.)

■ We **do** <u>not</u> usually invert **subject** and a **verb** when the **subject** is a <u>**pronoun**</u>.

<u>Into</u> the classroom **she** walked.
(**She** walked <u>into</u> the classroom.)
(**NOT**: <u>Into</u> the classroom **walked** <u>she</u>.)

■ We invert <u>time sequence adverbs</u> such as: "**First**" , "**Next**" , "**Now**" , "**Then**" with "<u>**Be**</u>" or "<u>**Come**</u>".

And **then came** <u>a message</u> to be a referee at school's match.
(And <u>a message</u> **came** to be a referee at school's match **then**.)

The **first was** the most difficult exercise.
(The most difficult exercise **was** the **first**.)

Then, <u>a message came</u> to be a referee at school's match.

If there is a **comma after** the **adverb**, <u>normal word order</u> is used.

■ "**So** + <u>adjective</u>...**that**" emphasizing the <u>adjective</u>.	**So** <u>beautiful</u> **was** Mary **that** everyone looked at her. (Mary **was so** <u>beautiful</u> that everyone looked at her.)
■ "**Such** + <u>be</u> + **that**" , emphasizing the **extent** or **degree** of <u>something</u>.	**Such was** their <u>excitement</u> **that** they began to jump up and down. (Their <u>excitement</u> **was** **such that** they began to jump up and down.)
■ **After** <u>adjectives</u> or after <u>past participle</u> used as an <u>adjective</u>.	<u>Blessed</u> **are the children** who are still unaware of what the future holds. (**The children** who are unaware of what the future holds **are** <u>blessed</u>.) <u>Gone</u> **are the days** when I could have been happy. (**The days** when I could have been happy **are** <u>gone</u>.) (Here the **past participle** "**Gone**" is used as an **adjective**.)
■ After "**As**"	She decided to leave early , **as did Gerald**. (She decided to leave early , **as** Gerald **did**.)

7 REPORTED SPEECH

◊ **Direct speech**: Gives the **exact words** of what someone has said. **We use commas** in direct speech.

"it**'s** quite warm", **she** said.

◊ **Reported speech: Gives the exact meaning of what someone** has said but **not** the **exact** <u>words</u>.We **do not** use commas in reported speech.

She said it **was** quite warm.

■ <u>Say - Tell - Ask</u>

◊ **"Say"**:
We use **"Say"** in **direct** speech. We use **"Say"** in **reported** speech when is <u>not</u> **followed** by the person the words were spoken to.

Direct speech	**Reported speech**
"I can't help you," **said John**.	**John said** he couldn't help me.

◊ **"Tell"**:

We use **"Tell"** in **reported** speech when **is followed** by the <u>person</u> the words were spoken to.

Direct speech	**Reported speech**
"I can't help you," he **said** <u>to me</u>.	He **told** <u>me</u> he couldn't help me.

◊ **"Ask"**:

■ We use **"Ask"** in <u>reported</u> questions and **commands**.

Direct speech	**Reported speech**
"Where are you going**?**" She said	She **asked** me where I was going. (**Reported question**)
He said to me, "**Help me !**"	He **asked** me to help him. (**Reported command**)

■ **If** we use **"Ask"** in <u>direct</u> **questions then** we should use **"Ask"** in <u>reported</u> **answers**.

Direct speech	**Reported speech**
He **asked** ,"Are you OK **?**" (**Direct question**)	He **asked** me **if** I was OK. (**Reported answer**)

◊ **We use**:

Say	+ <u>to-infinitive</u> (BUT NEVER: Say about)	Mun **said** <u>to be</u> home by 10 o'clock.
Tell	+ <u>sb</u> <u>about</u>	She **told** <u>us</u> <u>about</u> her adventures.
Speak + <u>about</u>		She **spoke** <u>about</u> her adventures.
Talk	+ <u>about</u>	She **talked** <u>about</u> her adventures.

◊ **Expressions with "Say" , "Tell" , "Ask"**

■ **With "Say"**

Say good morning / evening , etc
Say something
Say one's prayer
Say a few words

Say so
Say no more
Say for certain / sure , etc

■ **With "Tell"**

Tell the truth
Tell a lie
Tell (sb) the time
Tell (sb) one's name
Tell a story
Tell (sb) a secret

Tell one from another
Tell sb's fortune
Tell sb so
Tell the way
Tell the difference, etc

■ **With "Ask"**

Ask a favor
Ask the time

Ask a question
Ask the price , etc

◊ **Reported statements**

■ **The tenses change as follows:**

	Direct speech	Reported speech
Present Simple	"He **plays** well," she said.	She said (that) he play**ed** well.
Present Continuous	"He **is playing** well," she said.	She said (that) he **was** playing well.
Past Simple	"He **played** well," she said.	She said (that) he **had played** well.
Past Continuous	"He **was** playing well," she said.	She said (that) he **had been** playing…
Future Simple	"He **will play** well," she said.	She said (that) he **would play** well.
Future Continuous	"He **will be playing** well," she said.	She said(that) he **would** be playing…
Future Perfect	"He **will have played** well," she said.	She said(that) he **would** have played…
Be going to	"He **is going to** play well," she said.	She said (that) he **was** going to play…
Present Perfect	"He **has** played well," she said.	She said (that) he **had** played well.
Present Perf. Cont.	"He **has** been playing well," she said.	She said(that) he **had been** playing…

◊ **NOTE:**The **Past Perfect** and the **Past Perfect Continuous** remain **the same** in **reported speech**.

■ **Tenses do not change in reported speech when:**

◊ The **reporting verb** is in the:

	Direct speech	Reported speech
Present	"The weather **is** hot," she **says**.	She **says** (that) the weather **is** hot.
Future	"The weather **is** hot," she **will** say.	She **will** say (that) the weather **is** hot.
Present Perfect	"The weather **is** hot," she **has** said.	She **has** said (that) the weather **is** hot.

◊ The **speaker** expresses:

	Direct speech	Reported speech
General truth **Permanent states**	"Water **freezes** at 0°C," he said "**I spent** all **my** life in this place," he said	He said (that) water **freezes** at 0°C. He said (that) **he spent** all **his** life in...

◊ The **speaker** is reporting something **immediately after** it was said (**Up**-to-**date**)

Direct speech	Reported speech
"The hotel **is** awful," she said.	She said (that) the hotel **is** awful. (Reported **after it was said**.)
"**I am** going to the cinema tonight," she said.	She said **she is** going to the cinema tonight. (Reported **after it was said** , **before she goes** to the cinema.)

◊ The **reported** sentence deals with:

Conditionals
Unreal past
Wishes

Direct speech	Reported speech
"**If I** <u>did</u> **my** homework, **my** teacher **would**n't be angry with **me**," he said. "**I would rather** play golf," she said. "**I wish I** <u>were</u> rich," she said.	He said that **if he** <u>did</u> his homework **his** teacher **would**n't be angry with **him**. She said **she would rather** play golf. She said **she** wish**ed she** <u>were</u> rich.

◊ When the **reported sentence** contains <u>time clause</u> , the <u>past</u> tense of the <u>time clause</u> **DO NOT** **change**.

Direct speech	Reported speech
"The car **broke** down <u>while I was</u> driving to work," he said	He said the car **had** broken down <u>**wh**</u><u>**ile he was** driving</u> to work.

■ **Tenses** <u>change</u>:

■ If the **reported** sentence is **out-of-date**.

Direct speech	Reported speech
"He mov**ed** out a month **ago**," he said.	He said that he **had** moved out a month **before**. (Speech reported **after he had moved**. **Out** -of-**date**)

■ The **speaker** expresses something **which is believed to be untrue**.

Direct speech	Reported speech
"China **is** a small country," she said.	She said (that) China **was** a small country. (**Untrue**)

◊ **NOTE: Certain words** change as follows **depending to context**.

Direct speech	Reported speech
This / These	That / Those
Here	There
Come	Go
"**Will** you **come** to **my** house for dinner**?**", she said.	She **asked** me to **go** to **her** house for dinner.

◊ **NOTE: Personal pronouns** and **possessive adjectives** change according to context.

Direct speech	Reported speech
"No, **I** won't lend **you** my new car!" He said.	He said **he** wouldn't lend **me** **his** new car.

◊ **NOTE: Time words** can **change** or **remain the same** depending on the **time reference**.

Direct speech	Reported speech
Tonight	That night
Today	That day
This week / month / year	That week / month / year
Now	Then, at the time, at once, immediately
Now that	Since
Yesterday	The day before
Last night / week / month / year	The previous night / week / month /...
Tomorrow	The following day , the day after
Next week / month / year	The following week / month / year
Two days / months / years / etc ago	Two days / months / years / etc before
"**I'm** sitting an exam **tomorrow**," he said	He said **he was** sitting an exam **the following day**. (**Out**-of-**date** reporting.)
"**I'm** sitting an exam **tomorrow**," he said	He said **he is** sitting an exam **tomorrow**. (**Up**-to-**date** reporting.)

◊ **Reported Questions**

Reported Questions: Are used to report **someone else's questions** , **suggestions** , **offers** , or **requests**.
In reported questions we use **affirmative word order** and the **question mark** becomes **full stop**.

◊ To **report** the question we use:

■ **Ask + question word** ("Who" , "Which" , "Where" , "How" , "What" , etc) when the **direct question begins** with a **question word**.

Direct speech	Reported speech
He **asked** her, "**What is** your name?"	He **asked** her **what** her name **was**.

- **Ask + "If" / "Weather"** when the **direct question** begins with the **auxiliary verb** ("Do" , "Can" , "Have" , "Be" , "Will" , etc.)

Direct speech	Reported speech
He asked her, "Do you like tea?"	He asked her **if / weather** she liked tea.

◊ **Indirect Questions** in **reported speech**

- **Indirect Questions**: are used to **asked for INFORMATION / ADVICE**. They introduced **with**:

"**Do you know?**" "**I want to know**" "**I doubt**" "**I have no idea**" "**I wonder**"	and the **verb** is in the **affirmative**.

◊ **NOTE**:

With: "**I want to know**" , "**I doubt**" , "**I have no idea**" , "**I wonder**" the **question mark** is **omitted**.

Direct Questions	Indirect Questions
He asked me,"**How** old **is** Tom?" (**Ask for information**)	**Do you know** how old Tom **is** ? (**Information**)
He asked me,"**Where can** I leave it ?" (**Ask for information**)	**He wanted to know** where he **could** leave it. (**Information**)
He asked me,"**Is** it correct?" (**Ask for advice**)	**He wonder** whether it **is** correct. (**Advice**)

- **"Wh - question words"** in **indirect questions**.

"**What**" , "**Who**" , "**Where**" , "**Whether**" can be followed by an **infinitive** in the **indirect question** if the **subject** of the **question is the same** as the **subject** of the **introductory verb**.

Direct question	Indirect question
He asked me, "**Where** can **I** leave it ?"	**He** wanted to know where **to** leave it.

◊ **Reported Questions with the introductory verb "WONDER"**

■ **"Wonder-ed" + question words ("Where" / "What" / "Why" / "How") + subject + clause**

	Direct questions	Reported questions
(When the **subject** of the **introductory verb is not the same** as the subject of the **reported** question).	He asked himself,"**How can she** do that?" He asked himself,"**Where have they** gone?" He asked himself,"**Why is Tom** so rude?" He asked himself,"**What will they** do?"	He wondered how **she could** do that. He wondered where **they had** gone. He wondered why **Tom was** so rude. He wondered what **they would** do.

■ **"Wonder" + ("Where" / "What" / "How") + to-inf**

	Direct questions	Reported questions
(When the **subject** of the **infinitive** is the **same** as the subject of the **introductory verb**).	He asked himself,"**Where can I** find food?" He asked himself,"**What shall I** do next?" He asked himself,"**How can I** break the news?	He wondered where **to find** food. He wondered what **to do** next. He wondered how **to break** the news.

■ **"Wonder" + "Whether" + to-infinity / clause**

	Direct questions	Reported questions
(When the **subject** of the **infinitive** is the **same** as the subject of the **introductory verb**).	He asked himself, "**Shall I** take the job?"	He wondered **whether to take** the job. He wondered **whether he should take the job**.

◊ **NOTE**:

To report a **question** with "**Should**" asking for **advice** or **information** , we can also use "**to-infinitive**".

Direct questions	Reported questions
"**What should** we buy first?" He asked. (**Advice**)	He asked **what to buy** first. (**Advice**)

◊ **NOTE**: We do **not** use "to-infinitive" to report "**Why**" questions.

Direct questions	Reported questions
Why should we go there?	He wanted to know **why** we **should** go there. (**NOT**: ...**why** to go there.)

◊ **NOTE**:

To report : **commands** , **requests** , **suggestions** , etc we use an **introductory verb** followed by:
"**to-infinitive**" , "**ing form**" , "**that clause**" depending on the introductory verb.

◊ **Special introductory verbs**:

■ **Verb + to-infinitive**

	Direct speech	Reported speech
Apply **Offer** **Refuse** **Swear** **Volunteer**	He said ,"**Shall I** take **you** home?"	**He offered to** take **me** home.

■ **Verb + to-infinitive / that clause**

	Direct speech	Reported speech
Agree to **Claim to** **Decide to** **Demand to** **Expect to** **Guarantee to** **Hope to** **Promise to** **Request to** **Swear to** **Threaten to** **Vow to**	"**Yes I will** be happy to help **you**,"she said. "**I saw** him steel the car." "**We decide** to go to Greece," they said.	**He agreed to** help **me**. **He claimed to have seen** him steel... **They** decided **to** go to Greece. or **They** decided **that they go to Greece**.

■ **Verb + (Object) + to-infinitive**

	Direct speech	Reported speech
Ask (sb) to **Beg (sb) to** **Expect (sb) to**	"**Would you like** to stay with **us**?", she sa-id.	She **asked** me **to stay** with **them**. or She **asked to stay** with **them**.

■ **Verb + Object + to-infinitive**

	Direct speech	Reported speech
Advise sb to **Allow sb to** **Ask sb to** **Beg sb to** **Call on sb to** **Command sb to** **Encourage sb to** **Forbid sb to** **Force sb to** **Instruct sb to** **Invite sb to** **Order sb to** **Permit sb to**	"**Leave** the room!", he said. (**Imperative**) "**Close** the door immediately", he said.	He **commanded us to** leave the room. He **ordered me to** close the door...

Remind sb to
Request sb to
Teach sb to
Tell sb to
Urge sb to
Warn sb to

- ### ing form

	Direct speech	Reported speech
Accuse sb of	"**You steal** my money!", she said.	She **accus<u>ed</u> me of** steal**ing** her…
Admit	"Yes, **I broke** the window", he said.	**He admit<u>ted</u>** hav**ing** brok**en** the window.
Advise		
Apologize for		
Boast about		
Complain to sb abou-	"**You always leave** the door open," she	She **complain<u>ed</u> to me about <u>my</u>**
t + ing	said.	always leav**ing** the door open.
Deny		
Insist sb (on)	"**You** must take all the medicine," he sa-	He **insis<u>ted</u> <u>my</u>** tak**ing** all the medicine.
Mention	id.	
Propose		
Recommend		
Report		
Suggest	"**Let's go out** for a walk," he said.	He **sugges<u>ted</u> us** go**ing** out for a walk.

- ### Verb + <u>that clause</u>

	Direct speech	Reported speech
Add that		
Agree that	"**Yes**, it**'s** a great idea," he said.	He **agre<u>ed</u> <u>that</u></u> it <u>was</u> a great idea</u>.
Announce that		
Answer that		
Argue that		
Boast that		
Claim that		
Comment that		
Confirm that		
Complain that		
Deny that		
Emphasize that		
Exclaim that	"It **is** a success!" He said.	He **exclaim<u>ed</u> <u>that</u></u> it <u>was</u> a success</u>.
Explain that		
Grumble that		
Guarantee that		
Insist that		
Note that		
Object that		
Observe that		
Point out that		
Predict that		
Protest that		
Remark that		
Repeat that		

Reply that
State that
Suggest that
Swear that
Think that

■ **Verb + Object +** that clause

	Direct speech	Reported speech
Assure sb that **Convince sb that** **Inform sb that** **Notify sb that** **Persuade sb that** **Reassure sb that** **Remind sb that** **Tell sb that**	"**I think** it **is** the best thing **we can** to do," he said.	He persuad<u>ed</u> us <u>that it was</u> the best <u>thing we **could**</u> do.

■ **Verb + (Object) +** that clause

	Direct speech	Reported speech
Advise (sb) that **Promise (sb) that** **Show (sb) that** **Teach (sb) that** **Warn (sb) that**	"**Please** do not sell **your** car," he said.	He **advised me** <u>that I should</u> not sell <u>my</u> car. or He **advised** <u>that I should</u> not sell **my** car.

■ **Verb +** that clause **/** Object **+ to-infinitive**

	Direct speech	Reported speech
Acknowledge **Advise** **Assume** **Believe** **Claim** **Consider** **Declare** **Expect** **Feel** **Find** **Order** **Presume** **Suppose** **Think** **Understand**	"**You** should think carefully," he said. "**I am sure** that the **competition** would be postponed," he said.	He advis<u>ed</u> <u>that I should think</u> carefully. or He advis<u>ed</u> <u>me</u> **to think** carefully. He believ<u>ed</u> <u>that the **competition**</u> would be postponed. or He believ<u>ed</u> <u>the **competition**</u> to be post-poned.

■ **Verb + <u>that clause</u> / <u>to</u> + Object + <u>that clause</u>**

	Direct speech	**Reported speech**
Admit **Announce** **Complain** **Confess** **Explain** **Indicate** **Mention** **Purpose** **Recommend** **Report** **Reveal** **Say** **Whisper**	"I must **confess this is** an excellent job," he told me.	He confess**ed** <u>that this was an excellent</u> job. **or** **He** confess**ed** <u>to</u> me <u>that this was an excellent job</u>.

■ **"How" & "Let's"**

	Direct speech	**Reported speech**
How	"**That's how** I crash**ed** the car," he said.	He explain**ed** <u>to me</u> **how** he **had** crash**ed** the car.
Let's	She said, "**Let's** go to the restaurant."	She suggest**ed going** to the restaurant. She suggest**ed that** they / we should go to the restaurant.

◊ **<u>Modal Verbs in Reported Speech</u>**

■ <u>Some</u> modal verbs **change** in **reported speech** when the **reported speech** is **OUT OF DATE**.

	Direct speech	**Reported speech**
Will	He said,"**I will** phone you **this** evening."	He said that **he would** phone me **that** evening.
Can	He said,"**I can** speak French."	He said (that) **he could** speak French. (**Real fact**)
	He said,"**I can** join **you** soon."	He said that **he** <u>would be able to</u> join **us** soon. (**Future reference / ability**)
May	He said,"**I may** be late home."	He said that **he might** be late home.
Shall	He said,"**How** <u>shall</u> I solve this problem?"	He asked **how he** <u>should</u> solve **that** problem. (**Advice**)
	He said,"**Where** <u>shall</u> we find the store?"	He asked **where they** <u>would</u> find the store. (**Information**)
	He said,"**I** <u>shall</u> phone **you** later."	...he <u>would</u> phone me later. (**Future**)
	He said,"<u>**Shall**</u> I take you home?"	He <u>**offered to**</u> take **me** home. (**Offer**)

Must	He said,"**You must** follow the rules."	He said that **I had to** follow the rules. (**Obligation**)
	He said,"**You must** find another job."	He said that **I must** find another job. (**Deduction**)
Mustn't	"**You mustn't** stay out until midnight,"he said.	He said **I was not to** stay out until midnight.
Should	He said,"**You should** take a holiday."	He said that **I should** take a holiday.
Had better	He said,"She **had better** tidy her room."	He said that she **had better** tidy her room.
Need	"**You need** an operation,"the doctor told me. ("**Need**" is used as a **main verb**.)	The doctor told me that **I need**ed an operation.
	"I **need to go** to a toilet,"he said. ("**Need**" as a **modal verb**.)	He said that **he had to go to** a toilet.
Needn't	He said,"She **needn't** know who he was."	He said that she **didn't need to** know who he was. (She **didn't** know.) **Or** He said that she **didn't have to** know who he was. (She **didn't** know.)
	He said,"**You needn't meet me** tomorrow."	He said that **I wouldn't have to** meet **him** the **next day**. (**Future reference**)

◊ **NOTE:**

▪ "**Must**" remains the **same** when it expresses **Possibility**, **Deduction**, **Laws** or **General truth**.

"You **must not** go more than 50 km/h", he said (**Law / Direct speech**)
He said we **must not** go more than 50 km/h (**Law / Reported speech**)

▪ "Could", "Should", "Would", "Ought to", "Might", "Used to", "Hed better" do **not change** in **reported speech**.

◊ **NOTE: COULD or WOULD ?**

"Could" and "Would" are "**first cousins**" to "**Can**" and "**May**".

<u>Could</u> is used **to determine** one's **capability** or **ability** to do something.

Could you open the door for me? (The person **is there** and has the **ability** to do the door-opening)

<u>Would</u> is used when the speaker ask "**permission**" (**help**) from somebody to **do sth for him / her**.

Would you open the main door please? (The person is **not** there. It is a question of person's **willingness** to perform the act of door-opening.)

◊ **Exclamations - Yes / No short answers - Question tags in Reported speech**

◊ **Exclamations** are <u>replaced</u> in **reported speech** with:

Cry out in pain, etc	**Thank**	The **exclamation mark** becomes **full stop.**
Exclaim	**Wish** , etc	
Say		

◊ **Exclamatory words** such as: **Oh!** , **Eek!** , **Wow! are omitted** in **reported** sentence.

Direct speech	Reported speech
"Wow!" <u>She</u> said <u>when she</u> **saw** <u>the huge cake.</u>	She **cried out in surprise** <u>when she</u> **had seen** <u>the huge cake.</u>

◊ **"Yes" / "No" short answers** are expressed in **reported** speech with:

■ <u>**Subject**</u> + appropriate <u>**auxiliary**</u> verb.

Direct speech	Reported speech
"<u>Can</u> you help me?"**She** said. **"<u>No</u>."** **he** said.	**She** asked **him** if he **could** help **her** but **he** said <u>**he** couldn't</u>.

■ <u>**Subject**</u> + appropriate <u>**introductory verb**</u>.

Direct speech	Reported speech
"Can you help me?"**She** said. **"No."** he said.	**She** asked **him** if he **could** help **her** but <u>**he** refused</u>.

◊ <u>**Question tags**</u> are **omitted** in **reported** speech. We can use appropriate <u>**introductory verb**</u> to retain their effect.

Direct speech	Reported speech
"They **haven't made** up their minds yet, <u>**have they**</u>? "She said.	She <u>**wondered if**</u> they **had already made** up their minds.

◊ **NOTE: Commas with <u>direct</u> speech**

If the <u>direct speech</u> is at the **beginning** of the sentence, we put the comma **before** the **final quotation mark (" ")**.	"<u>Let's go out for a walk</u> ," he said.
If the <u>direct speech</u> is at the **end** of the sentence, we put the comma **before** the **first quotation mark (" ")**.	He said ,"<u>Shall I take you home</u>?"

8   SUBJUNCTIVE

◊   **The structure** of the subjunctive is very simple. For **all verbs**, except the **past tense** of the verb **"Be"**, the subjunctive is the **same** in all persons as **the bare infinitive** of the verb.

"Be" In the present	"Be" In the past	All other verbs (past & present) (We use verb "Work" as an example)
I **be**	I **were**	I **work**
you **be**	you **were**	you **work**
he, she, it **be**	he, she, it **were**	he, she, it **work**
we **be**	we **were**	we **work**
you **be**	you **were**	you **work**
they **be**	they **were**	they **work**

■   **We use** the subjunctive mainly when we talk about:

Events that are **not** **certain to happen**.

It is desirable that you be present at the contest.

■   **We use** the subjunctive when we talk about **events that somebody**:

Wants to happen:

The President **requests that** you **be** present at the meeting.

Hopes will happen:

It is vital that you **be** present at the meeting.

Imagines happening

If you **were** at meeting, the President would be happy.

◊   **The subjunctive** is typically used **after two structures**:

The expressions	The verbs	
It is a bad idea	**Advise** (that)	**Request** (that)
It is a good idea	**Ask** (that)	**Require** (that)
It is best	**Beg** (that)	**Suggest** (that)
It is crucial	**Command** (that)	**Stipulate** (that)
It is desirable	**Demand** (that)	**Urge** (that)
It is essential	**Direct** (that)	**Warn** (that)
It is high time	**Insist** (that)	
It is imperative	**Instruct** (that)	
It is important	**Intend** (that)	
It is necessary	**Order** (that)	
It is recommended	**Prefer** (that)	
It is urgent	**Propose** (that)	
It is vital	**Recommend** (that)	

◊ **NOTE:**

We can also use "**That clause**" with modal verb "**Should**" after **nouns** related to these **verbs** such as:

"**Advice**" , "**Command**" , "**Demand**" , "**Direction**" , "**Insistence**" , "**Instruction**" , "**Proposal**".

◊ **Here are some examples with subjunctive:**

The board of directors **recommended that** he **join** the company.
It is crucial that you **be** there before Tom arrives.
It is important she **attend** the meeting.
The **commands that should** be followed will be given to you immediately.

◊ **NOTE:**

■ Sometimes we use "**Should + bare infinitive**" or "**Should + be + past participle**" (passive) in a "**that clause**" to report **advices** , **orders** , **requests** , **suggestions** about things that are **desirable** or **need to be done**.	He **suggested** that you **should see** the doctor. (**Suggestion**) I **demand** that he **should be** invited to speak. (**Passive subjunctive**) (**Order**) I **ugred that** the meeting **should be** postponed. (**Passive subjunctive**) (**Advice**)
■ We **don't use** this pattern to report **statements** with **other functions**.	it is a bad idea that you **be** there with them. **NOT** it is a bad idea that you **should be** there with them.
■ In **formal** contexts, we can often **leave out** "**Should**" and we use only the **bare infinitive** or "**Be + past participle**".	I **suggested** that we **contact** him. They **demanded** that the project not **be** postponed.

◊ **NOTE:**

In **these structures** the subjunctive is **always the same**. It is not matter whether the **sentence** is in the **past** or in the **present**.

Present	Past
The President **requests** that they **stop** occupation.	The President request**ed** that they **stop** occupation.
It **is** essential that she **be present**.	It **was** essential that she **be present**.

◊ **"Were" Subjunctive**

Sometimes we hear things like "if **I were** you, I would go" or "if **he were** here, he would tell you".
Normally, the past tense of the verb "**to be**" is: **I was / he was**. But the "**if I were you**" structure does **not** use the **past simple tense** of the verb "**to be**". It uses the **past subjunctive** of the verb "**to be**".
In the following examples, we can see that we often use the subjunctive form "**were**" instead of "**was**" after:

As if **If** **Suppose** **Wish**	If **I were** younger, I would go. I **wish it were** longer.

We **do not** normally say "if I **was** you", even in **familiar conversation**.

◊ **Examples of Passive Subjunctive**

I request that he <u>should be</u> invited **to** speak.
Christine demand<u>ed</u> that I <u>should be allow<u>ed</u></u> to take part in negotiations.
We suggest<u>ed</u> that you **should be** admitt<u>ed</u> to the organization.

◊ **Examples of Continuous Subjunctive**

It is important that you <u>be</u> standi**ng** here **while** they are still out of the office.
It is necessary that you <u>be</u> study**ing** hard for the exams.
I propose that we should **be** wait**ing** , until my brother comes , in Tim's apartment.

◊ **Present Subjunctive**

The term **present subjunctive** can be misunderstood, as it describes a **form** rather than a **meaning**.
The **present** subjunctive **is so named** because it **resembles the present indicative <u>in form</u>**, but it
may refers in <u>past</u> **situations**.

For example:

"**Be done**" (a **present subjunctive** form) has **no** present-tense sense , as it refers to the <u>**past**</u>.	She ask<u>ed</u> that it **be done** <u>**yesterday**</u>.

■ The **present subjunctive** is used in <u>**that clauses**</u> expressing **Desire**, **Demand**, and **Emotions**.

For example:	I **insist that** he **be** here. (**Demand**) I **prefer that** she **go** to work now. (**Desire**)
■ The **present subjunctive** also appears in "**Lest**" clauses.	I am running faster **lest** she **catch** me. ("**Lest**" means: "**The event in the de-pendent clause won't happen**").

◊ **Past Subjunctive**

The term **past subjunctive** can be misunderstood, as it describes a **form** rather than a **meaning**.
The **past subjunctive** is so named because **it resembles the past indicative <u>in form</u>**, but it **may** re-fers in <u>**present**</u> situations.

For example:

The word "<u>**Were**</u>" (a **past** subjunctive form) has **no past-tense** sense and it describes a **counterfactual condition** in the pre-sent.	If that <u>**were**</u> true, I **would** know it. (**It isn't true for the time being**.)

■ The <u>**past subjunctive form**</u> also appears in **that clauses** expressing **a wish** that is **unlikely to be fulfilled**. Usually the **main-clause** verb in this circumstance is "**Wish**".

For example:	I **wish that** he **were** here now. (**Unlikely to be fulfilled**)

■ **But occasionally** the <u>past subjunctive form</u> also appears with some **other expressions** implying an **unlikely** wish.

| For example: | It is **a good idea** <u>that</u> we **bought** a big house. (**Unlikely wish**) |

◊ **Past Perfect ("Had") subjunctive**

The **Past Perfect** (or **pluperfect**) **subjunctive** is used **like the past subjunctive**, except that it expresses a **past**-tense sense. it is formed using "**Had**" (the **Past Perfect form** of "**Have**") plus the verb's **past participle**.

| For example: | **If I had known**, I would have gone with you. |

◊ **Future Subjunctive**

The **future subjunctive** is constructed using the **past subjunctive form** of the verb "**to be**" plus the <u>to-infinitive</u> of the verb **whose action is doubtful** or **unreal**, or using "**Should** + <u>bare infinitive</u>".

| For example: | If you **were** <u>to give</u> the money to me, then I would say no more about it. (He **does not** intend to give the money to him. **Doubtful / Unreal future action**.) **It is important** that you **should** <u>leave</u> tomorrow. (**Future action**.) |

◊ **Some fixed expressions use the subjunctive**:

Be that as it may, he still wants to see her.
Come what may, I will never forget you
Far be it from (or for) me
God bless America!
Heaven forbid!
If need be
Long live the King!

So be it.
Suffice it to say (that)...
The powers that be
Truth be told
Woe betide!
Would that it were...

9 IMPERATIVES

◊ We use **imperatives** for different reasons such as: **To tell people what to do** , **to give instructions** and **advices** , **to make recommendations** and **suggestions** , and **for making offers**.

Come in and sit down , please.
Don't open the window - it's cold outside.
Put the coin in the slot and **press** the button.

Don't ask her - she doesn't know.
See the doctor - it's the best solution.
Have a bit more wine.

NOTE: The **affirmative** form of the **imperative** is the same as the **infinitive without "to"**. The **negative imperative** uses "Don't" + **bare infinitive**".

◊ **Emphatic imperative**

We can make **emphatic imperative** with "**Do + imperative**". This is common in **polite requests** , c-omplaints and **apologies**.

Do sit down.
Do forgive me - I didn't mean to interrupt.

Do be a bit more careful.

◊ **"Don't + be"**

Although "**Do**" is <u>not</u> normally used as an auxiliary with "**Be**" , "**Do**" is used before "**Be**" in **negative imperatives**.

Don't be silly!

◊ **Passive imperative**

To tell people **to arrange for things to be done to them** we often use "**Get + past participle**".

Get vaccina<u>ted</u> as soon as you can.

◊ **Subject with imperative**

The imperative **does not usually have a subject** , but we can use a **noun** or <u>pronoun</u> to make it clear to whom we are speaking.

Mary come here, <u>**everybody**</u> else stay where you are.
<u>**Nobody**</u> move.

Relax <u>**everybody**</u>.
<u>**Somebody**</u> answers the phone.

◊ "**You**" before an imperative can suggest **emphatic persuasion** or <u>anger</u>.

You just sit down and **relax** for a bit.

You take your hands off me<u>!</u>

◊ "**ALWAYS**" and "**NEVER**" come **before** the **imperatives**.

Always remember what I told you.
(<u>**NOT**</u> remember always...)

Never speak to me like being a kid!

◊   **Question tags**

After imperatives the normal question tags are: "**Will**" / "**Won't**" / "**Would you**"? , "**Can**" / "**Can't**" / "**C-ould you**"? After **negative** imperatives, "<u>**Will you**</u>?" Is used.

Give me a hand , **will you?**   **Be** quite , **can't you?**
Sit down , **won't you?**   **Don't** tell anybody , <u>**will you**</u>?

10 CONNECTORS & CONJUNCTIONS

◊ INTRODUCTION: "SENTENCES" , "CLAUSES" , "PHRASES"

■ **Sentences**

A **sentence** is a **group of words** that makes **complete sense**.

Sentences are made of **two parts**: the **subject** and the **verb**.	**John is** the most intelligent student in class. (**Complete sense**) ("**John**": is the **subject**.)
The **subject** is **the person** or **thing** <u>that acts</u> or <u>is described</u> in **the sentence**. The **verb**, on the other hand, is "<u>that action</u>" or "<u>description</u>".	("**Is**": is the **verb** of the sentence.)

■ **Clauses**

A **clause** is a **group of words** that contains a **verb**, and usually <u>other components too</u>. A **clause may form part** of a **sentence** or it may be a <u>complete sentence</u> <u>in itself</u>. For example:	**He was** eating a bacon sandwich.
Sentences can be **broken down** into <u>clauses</u>. For example:	<u>**The boy is going to the school**</u>, **and** <u>**he is going to eat there**</u>. (**Two clauses** connected with the conjunction "**and**")
There are mainly **two types** of **clauses**: **Independent** (or **main** or **defining**) clauses, and **subordinate** (or **non defining**) clauses. **Independent clauses** act as **complete sentences**, while **subordinate** clauses **cannot stand**. **For example**:	The boy went to the school. (**Independent clause**) ...after all that he said... (**Subordinate clause**)

■ **Phrases**

A **group** of **two or more** <u>grammatically linked</u> words that <u>**do**</u> <u>**not**</u> have **subject** and **verb** is a **phrase**. **For example**:	The girl is at home, and tomorrow she is going **to the amusement park**. "**to the amusement park**" is a phrase **located** in the **second clause** of the **complete sentence** above.

◊ **SENTENCE CONNECTORS & CONJUNCTIONS IN GENERAL**

■ A <u>sentence connector</u> links **the contents** of **two sentences**. "**However**" is connecting the sentences. Other connectors include: "**Therefore**" , "**This**" , "**Moreover**" , "**Besides**" , "**Consequently**" , **etc**	John went to school as usual. **However** , the school was closed, so he returned to his home.
■ **Sentence connectors** usually come at the **beginning** of the sentence. "**Too**" and "**As well**" can <u>**not**</u> come at the beginning.	He spent his time studying, **as well**.
■ We usually **put a comma after** a <u>sentence connector</u> at the **beginning** or at the **end** of a sentence.	John had planned to visit us today. **However,** it was cancelled due to the rainy weather. There are a lot of activities for every member. Track sports, <u>**for instance**</u>.

- Sentence connectors can be used to link clauses in a sentence if the clauses are join with: "And" , "But" , "Or" , "So" or "a semicolon (;)" , "Colon (:)" or "Dash (-)"

  I couldn't find my ticket and, as a result I will stay at home tonight ("As a result" = a sentence connector.)

- Conjunctions are used to join two clauses of a sentence that are grammatically equal.

  The water was warm, but I didn't go swimming. (Was & Didn't = past forms) "But" is the conjunction linking the two grammatically equal parts together.

- To link two clauses, we use only one conjunction, not two. We usually put a "comma" between clauses linked by a conjuction.

  Although it is too far from here, I would like to go.
  NOT
  Although it is too far from here, but I would like to go.

◊ **SENTENCE CONNECTORS**

- "First(ly)" / "At first" , "Last(ly)" / "At last" , "Finally"

We use "First" or "Firstly" to label the first point in a list.	Firstly, Tom visited Jane when she was in hospital.
We use "At first" to indicate that there is a contrast between two past situations.	At first, I couldn't learn how to use it. Then John showed me the way.
We use "At last" to show that something happened later than hoped or expected.	She took her promotion at last, after having waited for five years.
Often "At last" suggests annoyance or some inconvenience that results from the delay.	He found the last component at last, after having searched for seven days.
We don't use "At last" to label the last point in a list, but we use "Finally" / "Lastly".	First, I had to see the manager. Finally / Lastly my colleagues told me that it wasn't necessary. NOT First, I had to see the manager. At last my colleagues told me that it wasn't necessary.

- "However"

  "However" is often a sentence connector, but it can also be used:

As an adverb when it is followed by an "adjective" , "adverb" or "much" , "many".	I will buy this vintage car, however reliable cars are not the used ones.
"However" can be used as a conjunction when it means "In whatever way".	You can do this however you like. ("However" = subordinate conjunction)

- "On the other hand" , "On the contrary"

We use "On the other hand" when we compare or contrast two statements.	I have to go; on the other hand, I would like to stay a little bit more. (Contrast two statements "go" & "st-)ay")

Sometimes we **introduce** the **first statement** with "**On the other hand**".	**On the other hand** they weren't ready to win the competition.
"**On the contrary**" is used similarly, but **emphasizes** that we **reject** the **first statement** and **accept** the **second**.	Young students say that song contest should be postponed for the next semester. **On the contrary** others say that this semester is the right period of time.

- **Other Sentence Connectors**

TIME	"**After**" , "**As**" , "**As long as**" , "**Hardly**" , "**No sooner...than**" , "**Once**" , "**Since**" "**When**" , "**While**" , "**Until**" , "**Till**" , "**Whenever**"
CONDITION	"**Assuming (that)**" , "**Considering (that)**" , "**Even if**" , "**Given that**" , "**Provided (that)**" , "**Providing**" , "**Unless**"
CONCESSION	"**Although**" , "**Even though**" , "**No matter how / what / ...**" , "**Whatever**" , "**Whereas**" , "**Yet**" , "**Even so**"
EXCEPTION	"**Except (that)**" , "**Only**"
PURPOSE	"**In order (not) to**" , "**In order that**" , "**So as (not) to**" , "**So (that) to**"
REASON	"**As**" , "**Because**" , "**For**" , "**In case**" , "**In that**" , "**Insofar as**" , "**Seeing that**" , "**Since**"
RESULT	"**As a result**" , "**So that**" , "**In such a way that**" , "**Such that**"

◊ **CONJUNCTIONS**

- **Conjunctions** have two basic functions:

Coordinating conjunctions are used to **join two parts** of a sentence that are **grammatically equal**, as it mentioned above. **Coordinating conjunctions** always come **between the words** or **clauses** that they join.	The water <u>**was**</u> warm, <u>**but**</u> I <u>**didn't**</u> go swimming. (**Was** & **Didn't** = **past forms**) "<u>**But**</u>" is the **conjunction** linking the **two grammatically equal parts together**.
Subordinating conjunctions are used **to join a subordinate clause** to a **main clause**. **Subordinating conjunctions** usually come at the **beginning** of the <u>**subordinate clause**</u>.	I went swimming **although** <u>**it was cold**</u>.

- "**Before**" , "**Until**"

Sometimes we can use either "**Before**" or "**Until**" with **little difference** in meaning."**Until**" means "**up to that time**". "**Untill**" also **indicates** a **state** or **process** , while "**Before**" an **instant action**.	There is only a month **until** summer vacation. He worked **until** noon. (**Process**) He left **before** sending a message. (**Instant action**)
We use "**Until**", **not** "**Before**", to highlight that an action **continues** up to a **particular time** <u>**and then stops**</u>.	I was studying for a few weeks **until** my teacher told me that I was ready for the final exams.

- **"Hardly" , "No sooner" , "Scarcely"**

After **"Hardly"** and **"Scarcely"** the **second clause** usually begins with **"When"** or **"Before"**.	I had **hardly** arrived home **when** my phone rang. She had **scarcely** finished reading **before** she fell asleep.
After **"No sooner"** the **second clause** usually begins with **"Than"** or **"When"**.	**No sooner** did I arrive at the station **than** the train left. **No sooner** did she come into the room, **when** she heard an explosion.

- **Other Conjunctions**

TIME	**"After"** , **"Afterward(s)"** , **"Before"** , **"Earlier"** , **"Later"** , **"Meanwhile"** , **"In the mean time"** , **"Previously"** , **"Simultaneously"** , **"Subsequently"**
CONDITION	**"If not"** , **"If so"** , **"Otherwise"**
CONCESSION	**"All the same"** , **"Alternatively"** , **"Anyway"** , **"By / In contrast"** , **"Even so"** , **"However"** , **"In any case"** , **"Instead"** , **"Nevertheless"** , **"Nonetheless"** , **"Still"** , **"Though"**
RESULT	**"As a result"** , **"Because of this"** , **"In consequence"** , **"Consequently"** , **"Hence"** , **"Therefore"** , **"Thus"**
ADDING	**"Above all"** , **"In addition"** , **"After all"** , **"Also"** , **"As well"** , **"Besides"** , **"Furthermore"** , **"Indeed"** , **"Likewise"** , **"Moreover"** , **"Similarly"** , **"Too"** , **"What is more"**
GIVING EXAMPLES	**"For example"** , **"For instance"**
REWORDING	**"In other words"** , **"Namely"** , **"That is"** , **"That is to say"**
LISTING	**"First(ly)"** , **"First of all"** , **"To start with"** , **"To begin with"** , **"Last(ly)"** , **"Finally"** , **"Next"** , **"Then"**
ENDING	**"In all"** , **"All in all"** , **"In conclusion"** , **"To conclude"** , **"To sum up"**

◊ **PREPOSITIONS vs CONJUNCTIONS**

Prepositions are connecting **words**. In general, prepositions show the **relation** of **a** <u>noun</u> or <u>pronoun</u> to **other words** in a sentence.	AFTER <u>the lecture</u>, we went to the movie. (**"After"** as a **preposition** , "<u>the lecture</u>" is a **noun** that is the **object** of a **preposition**.) The pilot landed the plane **BECAUSE OF the bad** <u>weather</u>. (**"Because of"** as a **preposition**, "<u>weather</u>" is a **noun** that is the **object** of a **preposition**.)
Conjunctions are also connecting **words**, but they can do **much more** than a preposition. In contrast to a preposition a **conjuction** can connect **two elements** together. This means that **conjunctions** can connect **two clauses** together.	AFTER <u>we ate</u>, we get out. (**"After"** as a **conjunction** , "<u>we ate</u>" is the <u>clause</u> connected to another **clause** via **conjunction**.) The pilot landed the plane **BECAUSE** <u>the weather was bad</u>.

("**Because**" as a **conjunction** , "the <u>weather was bad</u>" is the <u>clause</u> connected to another **clause** via **conjunction**.)

◊ **NOTE: The following connectors and conjuctions:**

■ "**Even if**"

We can use "**Even if**" to mean "**Whether or not**" and **introduces** a <u>hypothetical</u> condition that is **not** <u>yet</u> true.

Even if he loses his job as Arts Minister, I think he'll continue to be a member of the government.
(He **is still** Arts Minister.)

■ "**Even so**"

"**Even so**" has a meaning similar to "**However**". We use it to <u>introduce a fact</u> that **is surprising** after what **has been said** before.

The bed is extremely **large** and **heavy**. **Even so**, <u>Jim managed **to carry it** into the house by himself</u>.

■ "**Even though**"

We can use "**Even though**" to mean "**Despite the fact that**". Is used to **introduce a condition** which is <u>currently in use</u>.

Even though the <u>injury was serious</u>, he decided to carry on playing.

■ "**Even when**"

"**Even when**" is used for **emphasizing** that <u>although something happens on a regular basis</u>, **the situation** does not change.

He **never stops talking** and goes on and on **even when** <u>his colleagues are talking</u>.

◊ **PREPOSITIONS CONFUSED WITH CONJUNCTIONS AND CONNECTORS:**

The following **prepositions** <u>can not</u> be used as **conjunctions** and **connectors**.

As well as

Peter knows what is happening, **as well as John**.
<u>NOT</u>
Peter knows what is happening, **as well as John knows**.

Apart from

On holiday he eats nothing **apart from hamburgers** and **French fries**.
<u>NOT</u>
Apart from he eats hamburgers and French fries, on holidays he eats nothing else.

Besides

You can choose any topic you want **besides English** and **maths**.
<u>NOT</u>
You can choose any topic you want, **besides** you **can study** English and maths.

Despite / In spite of

She had difficulty communicating in French **despite / in spite of** all her **years** of study.
<u>NOT</u>
She had difficulty communicating in French **despite / in spite of** she **had studied** for many years.

| **Due to** | His defeat was **due to** rain.
NOT
His defeat was **due to** it **was** rain**ing**. |

| **During** | I saw neither one duck on the lake **during our vacation**.
NOT
I saw neither one duck on the lake **during we were** on vacation. |

11 CLAUSES / LINKING WORDS

Sentences can consist of **main** (or **independent** or **defining**) and **subordinate** (or **non defining**) clauses.

<u>Clauses</u> can be:

■ **Noun Clauses**	I know **that** he will come back.
■ **Relative Clauses**	Show me the pictures **which** you took.
■ **Participle Clauses**	The problem is the noise **produced** by the cars.
■ **Reduced Clauses**	**While** on vacation, I worked two hours a day.
■ **To-infinitive Clauses**	She was the first **to win** the game.
■ **Adverbial Clauses:** (**Clauses of time** , **Clauses of result** , **Clauses of reason** , **Clauses of concession** , **Clauses of manner** ,**Clauses of purpose**)	He left early **so as not to** miss the bus.

◊ <u>**Noun Clauses**</u>

◊ A **noun clause** is a **subordinate clause**, containing a **subject** and a **verb**, that can **replace** a <u>noun</u> , a <u>pronoun</u> , an <u>adjective</u>.	I don't know <u>her</u>. (**Not** a noun clause) I don't know **who she is**. (**Noun clause**) ("**who she is**" can replace a pronoun like "**her**".)

■ **"THAT" Noun Clauses**	
In **informal** contexts we often **leave out** "**That**" at the beginning of "<u>That</u>" noun clause.	She said <u>that</u> she was sick. **or** She said <u>she was sick</u>.
■ We use "**The fact that**" rather than "**That**" when:	
The **noun clause** is <u>a subject</u>.	<u>The fact that</u> you are not able to perform this action makes no difference.
■ **Verb + "The fact that"**	
After **preposition** or after **verbs** such as: "<u>Change</u>" , "<u>Discuss</u>" , "<u>Disguise</u>" , "<u>Face</u>" , "<u>Hide</u>" , "<u>Highlight</u>" , "<u>Ignore</u>" , "<u>Overlook</u>" , "<u>Reflect</u>" , "<u>Welcome</u>", etc.	We have to <u>overlook</u> the fact that we lost the opportunity.

◊ **NOTE:**	
Depending on **meaning**, we can use words like: "<u>Argument</u>" , "<u>Assumption</u>" , "<u>Belief</u>" , "<u>Claim</u>" , "<u>Idea</u>" , "<u>Notion</u>" instead of the word "**Fact**".	The <u>argument</u> that we had made mistakes is wrong.

- **"WH-" Noun Clauses**

- **Noun + Of + "Wh - Noun clause"**

When a "**Wh**-" noun clause **follows** certain **nous** like: "**Account**" , "**Description**" , "**Discussion**" , "**Example**" , "**Idea**" , "**Issue**" , "**Knowledge**" , "**Problem**" , "**Question**" ,"**Reminder**" ,"**Understanding**" we often have to include "**OF**" before the "**Wh-word**"

He gave us a **description of wh**at he saw last night.

- **Verb + Object + "Wh - Noun clause"**

Some **verbs** like: "**Advise**" , "**Ask**" , "**Assure**" , "**Convince**" , "**Inform**" , "**Instruct**" , "**Persuade**" , "**Remind**" , "**Show**" , "**Teach**" , "**Tell**" ,"**Warn**" **must have** an **object before** the "**Wh-word**"

I want to **ask you wh**ere you had been.

- **Verb + "How - Noun clause"**

Noun clauses **beginning** with "**How**" are commonly used **after** certain **verbs**: "**Ask how**" , "**Consider how**" , "**Decide how**" , "**Describe how**" , "**Discover how**" , "**Explain how**" , "**Know how**" , "**Remember how**" , "**Reveal how**" , "**Show how**" ,"**Tell how**" , "**Understand how**" , "**Wonder how**".

I can't **explain how I felt that day**.

◊ **NOTE**:

We **can** use a "**Wh-noun clause**" but **NOT** a "**That-noun clause**" **after** a **preposition**.

If you want to talk **about wh**at I intend to do call me in an hour.

We can also use **noun** clauses **beginning** with:

Whatever   (Anything / It doesn't matter what)

Take **whatever** you want.

Whoever   (The person / group who)
        (Any person / group who)

Whoever comes will be welcomed.

Whichever (One thing / person) from a **limited number** to talk about: **Things** , **People** or **Times** that are **indefinite** or **unknown**.

Take **whichever** you like.

◊ **NOTE**:

Instead of a "**Wh-noun clause**" we can often use a **noun** or a **pronoun** which has a meaning related to the "**Wh-**" word.

Why most people didn't come to our meeting is that they...
Or
The reason most people didn't come to our meeting is that they...

Staying at his home is **what** they had to do.
Or
Staying at his home is **something** they had to do.

Other words used in this way :

"**The place**"	rather than "**Where**"
"**The time**"	rather than "**When**"
"**The way**"	rather than "**How**"
"**Somebody**"	rather than "**Who**"
"**Someone**"	rather than "**Who**"

■   "WHETHER" and "IF"   Noun Clauses

We can use "**Whether**" as the "**Wh**" word in a **noun clause** when we talk about **possible choices**.	We discussed **whether it should be sold**. (**Possible choice**)

■   **Differences** between sentences with "**Whether**" / "**If**" and "**That**" **noun clauses**.

I didn't know **whether / if** the contest had been postponed.	(It **may** or **may not** had been postponed.)
I didn't know **that** the contest had been postponed.	(**It was postponed**; now I know.)

◊   **NOTE**:

In **written formal contexts**, we can use "**As to**" with the meaning similar to "**About**" or "**Concerning**" before a "**Whether-noun clause**".	The question arose **as to whether this behavior was unlawful**.

◊   **NOTE**: We can use "**Whether**" **but not** "**If**"

Before "**or not**"	I didn't know **whether or not** I had to follow them. **or** I didn't know **whether** I had to follow them **or not**.
Before a "**to-infinitive**"	I can't decide **whether to move** left or right.
After a **preposition**.	I can't decide **about** whether I have to invite them.
After the verbs: "**Advise**" , "**Choose**" , "**Consider**" ,"**Debate**" , "**Discuss**" , "**Enquire**" , "**Question**".	You can **choose** whether to stay at work or resign.
In a **clause** acting as a **subject** or **complement**.	**Whether** to win or lose, is not my concern. (**Subject**) She will **show** no interest **whether you win or lose**. (**Complement** of the verb "**Show**".)

◊ **Relative Clauses**

■ **Relative Pronouns** ("Who" , "Whom" , "Whose" , "Which" , "What" , "That")

■ **Used for people**

That's the **man who / that** stole the money.	**Subject** of the verb of the relative clause **cannot** be omitted.
The **man** (**whom / who / that**) **you** saw last night was my uncle.	(**Object** of the verb of the relative clause **can** be omitted.)
That's the girl **whose** brother is a singer.	**Possession** can **not** be omitted.

■ **Used for things**

I read a **book which / that** was written by Victoria Hislop.	**Subject** of the verb of the relative clause **cannot** be omitted.
The **cat** (**which / that**) **you** saw lying on the sofa is my favorite one.	(**Object** of the verb of the relative clause **can** be omitted.)
That's the coat the sleeves **of which** are made of velvet. That's the coat **whose** sleeves are made of velvet.	**Possession** can **not** be omitted.

◊ **NOTE**:

■ "**Whom**" , "**Which**" , "**Whose**": can be used in **expressions** of **quantity** with "**Of**" : **Some of** , **Many of** , **Most of** , **Half of** , **Neither of** , **Part of** , **Several of** , with numbers: **One** , **Two** , **Three** , **four** , etc , with the expressions: **The first** , **The second** , , **The third** , etc and also with **superlatives**.

There are three winners, **the first of whom** is my cousin.
He sold three houses, **one of** which belonged to his grandfather.
She received a lot of postcards **most of which** were from her friends.

■ In **formal** uses "**Noun + of which**" can **sometimes replace** "**Whose + noun**"

Our new hybrid car is a sophisticated project the **purpose of which** / **whose purpose** is to minimize CO_2 emissions.

■ **Relative Adverbs** ("When" , "Where" , "Why")

TIME	"WHEN"		
		We use "**when**" after words referring to **time** or words such as "**Day**" , "**Period**" , "**Time**".	**1992** was the **year when** I moved to Wales.
		"**Which**" (**Relative pronoun - more** formal.)	It was the last **semester during which** I was studying many hours a day.
PLACE	"WHERE"	"**That**" (**Relative pronoun - less** formal.)	I can remember the **day that** I met him.
		We use "**Where**" after words referring to **location** or **words** such as: "**Case**" , "**Con-**" **dition**" , "**Example**" , "**Experiment**" , "**Instance**" , "**Point**" , "**Process**" , "**Situation**" "**System**".	That's the **hotel where** we spent our honeymoon. He invented a **system where** cars could be parked easily.

	More formally, we can use "**Preposition & Which**".	He invented a **system in which** cars could be parked easily.
REASON	"**WHY**"	
	We use "**Why**" when we refer the **reason** for something.	I don't understand **why** he told me lies. You must know **the reason why** he didn't invite me.

◊ **NOTE**:

■ We use the **adverb** "**Whereby**" (or a **Preposition** + **Which**) in formal contexts to mean "**By which way** or **method**".

The computer is the facility **whereby / by which** humans exchange their knowledge.

■ We use "**Whose+noun**" to talk about something "**is belonging to**" or "**is associated with**": a "**Person**", "**Town**", "**Country**" or "**Organization**".

Athens is the capital of Greece **whose prosperity** contributes to the national economy of the country.
Russia is the largest country in the world **whose power** no other country can ignore.

■ **Prepositions in relative clauses**

The preposition usually comes **before** relative pronoun in **formal** styles.

The house **in which** she lives is in the suburbs.

After preposition we usually use "**Whom**" rather than "**Who**" in **formal** styles.

Penny, **with whom** John fell in love, was a well-known young lady.
Penny, **whom** John fell in love, was well-known young lady.

In **less formal** style a preposition **comes later** in the clause.

Penny, **who** John fell in love **with**, was a well-known young lady.

◊ **NOTE**:

■ We can **use a preposition**, usually "**From**", with "**Where**" and "**When**".

We stayed in Pella **from where** Alexander the Great started his expedition.

■ A **defining relative clause**: Gives **necessary** information and it is essential to the meaning of the **main clause**. It is **not** put between commas.

Merchants **who sell their products illegally** should be punished.

■ A **Non-defining relative clause**: Gives **extra** information and it is **not** essential to the meaning of the main clause. **It is put** between commas.

Her mother, **who is a kind woman**, has helped her a lot.

■ A number of **common prepositional phrases** are used in **non defining** relative clauses with "**Which**". These are: "**In which case**", "**At / By which time**", "**As a result of which**".

The tax evasion, **as a result of which the country lost billions**, should be punished.

- In both **defining** and **non-defining** relative clauses we can often use "Who", "That" or "Which" with <u>collective nouns</u> referring to **groups of people** (<u>government</u>, <u>company</u>, <u>orchestra</u>, etc)

The <u>company</u> **who / which / that** invented the first portable computer is Hewlett Packard.

◊ **NOTE**:

- **Adjective phrases**

Adjective phrases can be used **after nouns** with a meaning similar to a **relative clause**.
The <u>adjective</u> is followed by "**To infinitive**" or "**preposition**".

It is easy to contact with a **student** <u>re</u><u>ady to help you</u>. (...**who is ready to**...)
It was a **test** <u>difficult for almost every</u> <u>student</u>. (...,**which was difficult for**...)

An <u>adjective</u> can also **be followed** by an <u>adverb</u>.

Electric **cars**, <u>completely</u> noiseless, are used in special cases.
(...,**which are** <u>completely</u> noiseless,..)

The adjectives: <u>Affected</u>, <u>Available</u>, <u>Present</u> can be used **alone after a noun** with a meaning similar to a **relative clause**.

We will sell all the **toys** <u>available</u>.
We will sell all the **toys** <u>which are available</u>.

- **Prepositional phrases**

We can give **additional information** about <u>things</u> or <u>persons</u> using a <u>prepositional phrase</u> **with** or **without** the use of a **relative pronoun** before the <u>prepositional phrase</u>.

The <u>houses</u> <u>around this park</u> are the most expensive properties in the city.
The <u>houses</u> **which are** <u>around this park</u> are the most expensive properties in the city.

◊ <u>**Participle Clauses**</u>

- **In general**

The **implied subject** of a **participle clause** is usually **the same** as **the subject of the main clause**.

Studying hard, **Paul** managed to pass the exams.
(**Paul** was studing hard, and **Paul** managed to pass the exams.)

We **avoid** a **participle clause** when the <u>subjects</u> are **different**.

Talking loudly, **I** was kept away from the interview. (**The more accurate form is**: **People** were talking loudly, so **I** was kept away from the interview.)

◊ **NOTE**:

In **formal** English a **participle clause** can sometimes have <u>its</u> <u>own subject</u>, which is often a <u>pronoun</u> or a <u>noun phrase</u>.

Students in Greece, **some working** after school, study for at least six hours a day. (...**some of which** are working...)

When we use "**Not**" in a **participle clause** it usually comes **before** the **participle**.

Not having any money, I decided to stay at home.

Present participle (-ing) clauses

We can use a **present participle clause** to talk about **something that takes place** at the **same time as**, or **just before** an action in the **main clause**.	Open**ing** up my bag, I discovered an old DVD. (He discovered the old DVD **at the same time** he opened his bag.)
A **present participle clause** can be used to give us a <u>background information</u>.	<u>Spending</u> his life in high mountains, John is able to work under low temperatures.
A **present participle clause** can also be used **after** a "<u>quoted speech</u>" to say **what was happening** or **what someone else was doing** while <u>someone</u> **was doing something**.	"<u>Look out this car!</u>", <u>said Emmy</u>, **running** out of the yard.
Present participle clauses can also be used to talk about a <u>REASON</u> or <u>RESULT</u>.	<u>Leaving</u> London early in the morning, I had no time to call Jane. (**Reason**)
We can use a <u>present</u> participle clause after a number of **conjunctions** and **prepositions** including: "**After**", "**Before**", "**By**", "**In**", "**On**", "**Since**", "**When**", "**While**", "**With**", "**Without**", "**Unless**", "**Until**".	**Before stopping** my car, I asked Tom where is the next gas station. **Before I stopped** my car, I asked Tom where is the next gas station. (**Less Formally**)

Past participle (-ed) clauses

We use a **past participle clause** to talk about <u>REASONS</u> and <u>CONDITIONS</u>.	**Made** from silk, it is as expensive as a velvet one. (**REASON**: Because **it is made from silk**, it is as expensive as..) **Abandoned** by his friends he felt desperate. (CONDITION: **Because he was abandoned** by his friends he felt desperate.)
Past participles combined with "**Be**" & "**Have**" can form their **passive** and **perfect** forms.	**Having** finish**ed** his homework, he went out for a walk. (**Perfect form**)
We can use either "**Having + ed**" or a "**Present participle**" with a **similar meaning** to describe <u>consecutive events</u>.	**Having** reach**ed** / **Reaching** to the top, I could shoot with my camera almost everything. (**CONDITION / Consecutive event**)
"**Having + ed**" emphasizes that **the action** in the **participle clause is complete** <u>before the action in the main clause begins</u>.	**Having** finish**ed** my work, I heard the young boys asking for help. (He **had** finished his work **before** the young boys asked from him to help them.)

Passive forms of past participles.

	Being accept**ed** to Harvard University **was** the greatest day of my life. (**Because I was accepted** to Harvard University was the greatest day of my life.)

We can also use "With + subject + ing", or informally "What with" to introduce a reason for something in the main clause.

We can also use "**With** + <u>subject</u> + **ing**", or informally "**What with**" to **introduce** <u>a reason</u> for **something** in the **main clause**.	With <u>Santorini</u> being such an expensive place, <u>**I was shocked that I have found this cheap hotel room**</u>. **What with** <u>his</u> early leaving, <u>**I didn't manage to ask him about the new project**</u>.

◊ **NOTE**:

■ In formal contexts we can use a past participle after: "**Although**" , "**As**" , "**If**" , "**Once**" , "**When**" , "**While**" , "**Unless**" , "**Untill**".

> **Although lived** in poverty, he gave money to charity funds.

■ **Participle clauses correspond to defining relative clauses.**

"ing" clauses correspond to **defining relative clauses** with an **active** verb.

> The students wait**ing** for their funding from the government were disappointed. (The students **who were waiting**...)

"ed" clauses correspond to **defining relative clauses** with a **passive** verb.

> The main problem is the noise **produced** by the cars.
> (...the noise **that is produced**...)

◊ **Reduced Clauses**

We can sometimes use a "**reduced**" **clause** beginning with a **conjunction** or **adjective** but **with no verb**. Reduced clauses are usually **formal**.

> **While** on vacation, he works for two hours a day. (While he **is** on vacation...)
> **Small** in size , the new electric car is the new invention that everyone admires. (Although **it is** small in size the new...)

■ **Reduced clauses** correspond to **relative clauses**.

Verbs which **are not** normally used in **continuous form** may be used in "**Reduced relative -ing clause**". Other **verbs** except the verb "**Contain**" are: "**Belong to**" , "**Comprise**" , "**Consist of**" , "**Constitute**" , "**Equal**" , "**Own**" , "**Possess**" , "**Resemble**" , "**Result from**" , "**Surround**".

> I can't eat a cake contain**ing** cinnamon and chestnuts.
> (I can't eat a cake **which contains** cinnamon and chestnuts.)

We **can't** use an "**ing reduced form**" when we are talking about a **completed action**.

> The two boys **who won** the local competition came to my house.
> **NOT**
> The two boys **winning** the local competition came to my house.
> (A **completed action**. The two boys **won** the local competition.)

◊ **NOTE**:

■ We **can't** use an "**-ing reduced form**" when the **first verb** in the relative clause is **modal verb**.

> The instructions **that must** be followed by everyone will be given to you...
> **NOT**: The instructions **that must** follow**ing** by everyone will be given to you...

■ **Reduced relative clauses** can also used instead of **non-defining** relative clauses.

> This car, **small in size**, costs a lot of money.
> This car, **although it is small in size**, costs a lot of money.

◊ **NOTE**:

■ In <u>written</u> English particularly we can use a **reduce relative clause** beginning with:

"**Being + ed**" : To **emphasize** that the **situation is continuing** or **will happen** in **the future**.	**Being** unemploy**ed**, I think that he will leave the city as soon as possible.
"**Being + <u>adjective</u>**" : We normally use the **progressive form** of **verb** "**Be**" with an **<u>adjective</u>** when we are talking about **actions** and **behavior**.	**Being** <u>unfair</u>, I think that no one will support this competition. (**Action**)

■ We can use "**Being**" in **participle clause** to express **REASON** or **CAUSE** as an alternative to "**Because**" / "**Since**" / "**As**" adverbial clause.

> **Being** like **his father**, he is passionate about milk and cheese. (**Reason**)
> (**As he is** like **his father**, he is passionate about milk and cheese.)

◊ <u>**To-infinitive Clauses**</u>

We can use a **clause beginning with** "**to-infinitive**" to talk about: **CONDITION** , **PURPOSE** , or **RESULT**.

> **To enjoy** your holidays isn't necessary to spend a fortune. (**CONDITION**)
>
> **To avoid** the traffic jam we turned left to an alley. (**PURPOSE**)
>
> **To succeed** in the exams we studied many hours a day. (**RESULT**)

◊ **NOTE**:

We often use a <u>**to-infinitive**</u> clause <u>**instead of a relative clause**</u> after:

■ <u>**A superlative**</u> **+ noun**

> He is <u>**the strongest**</u> **boy** <u>**to win**</u> any of his opponents.

■ **The first / The second / The one** , **etc**

> She was **the first** <u>**to congratulate**</u> him.

■ **The only / The next / The last / Another / One + noun**

> **The only** lesson <u>**to study**</u> is **history**.

■ "**To-infinitive clauses**" can sometimes **replace relative clauses** with <u>**modal verbs**</u>.

> We have a lot of good friends **to contribute** us.
> (We have a lot of good friends **that can contribute** us.)

■ We often use a "**to-infinitive clause**" in the **active** or **passive form**.

> **The last** place **to visit** was this.
> **This** was **the last** place **to be visited**.

■ We use "**To be + ed**" form to talk about **future events**.

> The master chef prepares the lunch **to be** reward**ed**.
> (The master chef prepares the lunch **which will be** reward**ed**.)

◊ **Adverbial Clauses**

An **Adverbial clause** is a type of **subordinate** clause, linked to the main clause; It adds **extra information** to the **main clause** about things such as: "**TIME**" , "**REASON**" , "**PURPOSE**" , etc . Most adverbial clauses begin with a **conjunction** and can come **before** or **after** the **main clause**.

We use <u>only one</u> conjunction to connect an **adverbial** clause with the **main** clause.	<u>NOT</u>: **Because** I am studying all day, **so** I don't have time for sport activities.

■ **Clauses of time**

■ **Clauses of time** are introduced by:

After	**Just as**	
As	**Once**	
As long as	**Since**	
As soon as	**The moment that**	He bought a villa **as soon as** he got the money.
Before	**Until / Till**	
By the time	**When**	
Every time	**Whenever**	
Immediately	**While**	

■ **When** the **verb** of the **main clause** is in the <u>present</u> or <u>future</u> form , the **verb** of the **time clause** is in a <u>present form</u> too.

("**When**" , "**Before**" , "**Until**" , etc) + <u>Present</u> Tense. We **don't** use "**Will**" in a clause with a time conjunction ("**When**" , "**Before**" , "**Until**" , **etc**) to talk about a **future action**.	I **will** give it to you **when** you <u>tell</u> me why you want it. (<u>NOT</u>: **When** you <u>will tell</u> me...)
We **don't** use "**Will**" in the **time clause** to talk about an **action** that **it will be completed** <u>before another action</u> in the **main clause**.	**When I have** finished my job, <u>I will call you up to go out with me.</u> NOT: **When I** <u>will</u> **have** finished my job, <u>I will call you up to go out with me.</u>

■ **When** the verb of the **main clause** is in the <u>past form</u> , the verb of the **time clause** is in the <u>past form</u> too.

She <u>**had**</u> finish<u>**ed**</u> reading **before** they <u>came</u> home.

■ When the **time clause** <u>precedes</u> the main clause, **a** comma is used.
When the **time clause** <u>follows</u> the main clause **no** comma is used.

◊ **NOTE**:

■ We can use "**As**" , "**When**" , "**While**" to talk about **something that** happens <u>when something else takes place</u>.

I turned on my GPS device **as / when / while** <u>I was driving my new car</u>.

■ We use "**When**" <u>not</u> "**As**" <u>and not</u> "**While**" at the **beginning** of an **adverbial clause** which:

Refers to a <u>point of time</u>.	I remember John was studying history **when** <u>I met him at the library</u>.
<u>Describes</u> the <u>circumstances</u> in which the **event** in the **main clause** happens.	<u>When the temperature rises</u> the heat causes a lot of problems.

Refers to a **past period** of our lives.	**When I was younger** I used to eat a lot of sweets.
Refers to **things** that we are **sure to happen**.	Don't worry! I'll be back **when I finish sh-opping**.
Talks about **every time** something happens.	**When I drink a lot of wine**, I feel like a d-izzy chicken.
Uses "**When**" as a **question word** ("**When**" + will / would)	**When will** he come**?**

- "**If**" (Is used for things **may** happen.) — Wait for me **if** I'm late.

- **We prefer "As"** to say that **when one thing changes** , another thing changes **at the same time**. — **As** I work hard, **I feel more and more exhausted**. (**At the same time**)

- We use "**As**" or "**When**" to **highlight the moment** that something happens. — **When / As I passed the bridge**, I saw him standing behind that big tree.

- ### Clauses of reason

- **Clauses of reason** are introduced by:

As Because Because of Due to For The reason The reason for / why	On the grounds that Since	**As** he was young, he made a lot of mis-takes.
Because	It usually answers to a "**Why-question**". As a **conjunction**, used at the **beginning** of a clause,**before** a **subject** and **verb**.	**Why** did you lie to him? **Because** I was afraid of being punished. I'm happy **because I** met you.
Because of	(+) **noun** / **noun** phrase (+) **pronoun** (+) **ing form** (+) **the fact that**	She was late **because of** the **storm**. I'm happy **because of you**. It failed **because of** bad plann**ing**. **Because of the fact that** it had been snowing for days, all roads were closed.
Due to	(+) **the fact that**	**Due to the fact that** it is raining we can-not go hiking.

◊ **NOTE:**

Formal alternatives to "**Because**" are: "**As**" , "**Since**" and "**For**".	I helped her to pass the exams **because / as / since** we were friends for years.
Informal alternatives to "**Because**" are: "**Seeing that**" and "**Seeing as**".	He always goes out every night **seeing that / seeing as** his parents are rich.
"**For**" Always comes **after** a comma in written speech or a pause in oral speech.	I didn't tell him anything, **for** I don't trust him.

◊ **NOTE:**

In **formal contexts** we can also use clauses beginning with : "**Inasmuch as**", which is also written "**In as much as**", and "**In that**" which clarify **what has been said** by <u>adding detail</u>.	I think John's project is the best **in as much as / in that** <u>it combines functionality with low price</u>.

◊ **NOTE: The difference** between "**DUE TO**" and "**BECAUSE OF**"

A **predicate adjective** modifies the **subject** of the sentence. It is **connected to** the **subject** by a **linking verb**. In the sentence.	The **wall** <u>is</u> purple. The **subject** is "**wall**" , the **predicate adjective** is "**purple**" and the **linking verb** is "**is**".
"**Due**" is a **predicate adjective** + the **preposition** "**to**". It means "**the result of**" or "**resulting from**". It modifies <u>nouns</u>.	Their <u>defeat</u> **was due to** rain that started during the game.("**Defeat**"=subject / noun) **NOT**: Their <u>defeat</u> **was because of** the rain that started during the game.
"**Because of**" is a **conjunction** that means "**as a result of**". It modifies <u>verbs</u>.	They <u>were defeated</u> **because of** the rain that started during the game.

◊ <u>**Clauses of result**</u>

■ **Clauses of result** are introduced by:

As a consequence As a result Consequently	So Such Therefore	The sea is **so** cold **that** they can't swim.
Such	a(n) + (<u>adjective</u>) + **singular countable noun**	It was **such a** <u>nice</u> **dress** that she bought it.
Such	(+) (<u>adjective</u>) + **uncountable / plural noun**	It was **such** <u>delicious</u> **food**. She wore **such** <u>awful</u> clothe**s**.
Such	(+) <u>a lot of</u> + **noun**	There were **such** <u>a lot of</u> **people** on the bus that there were no seats left.
So	(+) **adjective / adverb**	He speaks **so** quick**ly** that hardly anyone can understand him.

So + <u>much</u> So + <u>many</u> So + <u>little</u> So + <u>few</u>	(+) **noun**	She won **so** <u>much</u> **money** in the lottery that she bought a mansion.
So + <u>adjective</u>	(+) **a / an + noun**	It was **so** <u>delicious</u> **a cake** that we ate it all.
As a result **Consequently** **So** **Therefore**	(+) <u>clause</u>	He didn't have a visa and **as a result** <u>**he couldn't enter into the country**</u>.

◊　**Clauses of purpose**

■　**Purpose** is expressed with:

In order to **So as to** **To**	(+) <u>infinitive</u>	She's studying **so as to** <u>qualify</u> as a lawer. (**formal**) I'll do the work early **to** <u>go</u> to the game on time. (**informal**)
So that + <u>can</u>	(**Present reference**)	She **studies** hard **so that** she <u>can</u> upgrade her score.
So that + <u>will</u>	(**Future reference**)	She **will** work hard **so that** she <u>will</u> have better career prospects.
So that + <u>could</u> **So that** + <u>would</u>	(**Past reference**)	He **gave** me directions **so that** I <u>could</u> find his house easily.
With aim of... **With a view to**...	(+) **ing**	He upgraded his knowledge **with the aim of** apply**ing** for the managerial post.
For	(+) **noun / ing**	This is a knife **for cutting** bread.

■　The <u>negative purpose</u> is normally expressed with:

In order not to **So as not to**	(+) **infinitive**	She studied hard **so as not to fail** the test. (<u>**NOT**</u> : She studied hard **not to** fail the test.)
So that + <u>can't</u> **So that** + <u>won't</u>	(**Present reference**) (**Future reference**)	**Tie up** the dog **so that** it <u>won't</u> get out of the yard.
So that + <u>couldn't</u> **So that** + <u>wouldn't</u>	(**Past reference**)	She locked up the door **so that** the burglars <u>couldn't</u> get in.
For fear	(+) **might / should**	He didn't say where he was going **for fear** he **might** be followed.
For fear of	(+) **sth / doing sth**	He gave them all this money **for fear of being shot**.

Lest	(+) **might / should**	They stayed sleepless all night **lest** robbers **should** come.
Avoid	(+) **ing** form	He took a taxi to work to **avoid being** late.
Prevent	(+) **noun / pronoun** + (from) + ing form	She put on her raincoat to **prevent herself** (from) be**ing** soaked.

◊ **NOTE**:

- **Clauses of Purpose** follow the **rule** of the **sequence of tenses**.

  She's **going to** buy a dictionary **so that** she **will** improve her vocabulary.
  They **tied** him up **so that** he **wouldn't** escape.

- In **contrastive sentences** we can use "**Not + to-infinitive**" / "**But + to-infinitive**"

  He trains every day **not to be** in a good shape **but to loose** weight.

◊ **Clauses of concession**

- **Clauses of concession** are introduced by:

Although Even though Though	(+) **clause**	**Although** it was expensive she bought it.
Despite In spite of	(+) **noun**	**Despite** his **wealth** he never lends money.
Despite In spite of	(+) **ing** form	**Despite** his **being** rich he never lends money.
Despite In spite of	(+) **that clause**	**In spite of** the fact that he is rich he never lends money.
But However	(+) **clause**	He is smart; **however** he is lazy.
Nevertheless On the other hand Whereas While Yet	(+) **clause**	She swam fast, **yet** she finished third.
However No matter how	(+) **adj** / **adv** + subject + (may) + **verb**	**However** clever you (may) **are**, you won't solve this puzzle. **However** fast you (may) **run**, you won't catch the train.
Whatever No matter what	(+) **clause**	**Whatever** you do you won't succeed.
Wherever No matter where	(+) **clause**	I'll find it **no matter where** you hide it.

Whoever No matter who	(+) **clause**	I don't believe it , **no matter who <u>says</u> <u>that</u>**.
<u>Adj / adv</u> + "THOUGH" + <u>**subject**</u> + <u>verb</u> / (may + bare inf.)		<u>**Fast**</u> **though** <u>**he**</u> <u>drives</u>, he may have one hour delay.
<u>Adj / adv</u> + "AS" + <u>**subject**</u> + <u>verb</u> / (may + bare inf.)		<u>**Exhausted**</u> **as** <u>**she**</u> <u>is</u> , she may go to the party for only a little time.

◊ **NOTE**:

We can use "**While**" or "**Whereas**" to say that there is a **contrast** with something **in the main clause**.	Some people believe that schools are responsible for the behavior of their children , **whereas / while** others argue that discipline is in their parents' responsibility.
We can use "**While**" with a meaning similar to "**Although**".	**Although / While** she doesn't eat so much , she is still corpulent.
We can use "**Whilst**" as **more formal** alternative to "**While**".	**Whilst / While** he was a good worker, he was not a very good manager.

◊ **NOTE**:

- **The comma is used** when the **clause of concession** either **precedes** or **follows** the **main clause**.

- We can use "**Though**" at the **end of the clause**.	She says she'll reward me for my efforts; I don't think she will, **though**.

◊ **Clauses of manner**

- **Clauses of manner** are introduced by:

<u>**As if**</u> / <u>**As thought**</u> **after** the **verbs**:

Act	**Look**	
Appear	**Seem**	
Be	**Smell**	It **smells** <u>**as if**</u> they are frying chicken.
Behave	**Sound**	
Feel	**Taste**	

And also after the **expressions**:

As	Do **as** you like.
How	
(In) the same way	
(In) the same way as	
(In) the way	
(In) the way that	
The way in which	

- "**Were**" can be used instead of "**Was**" in **formal** English. **In all persons** the clauses are introduced with **as if**" / "**As though**".

She behaves **as if** she **were** the queen.

- The tense forms can be used **after "As if" / "As though"** irrespective of whether the **ideas** are **true** or **untrue**.

As if As though	(+) **any tense form** (Expressing **similarity** - how someone or something **seems**).	She sounds **as if** she **is** Italian. (**She may be Italian. "Similarity"**)
As if As though	(+) **any tense form** (Expressing **probability** - the extent to which something is likely to happen).	She looked **as if** she **were** tired. (**She may have been tired. "Probability"**)
As if As though	(+) **Past Simple / Past Continuous** (Unreal in the Present)	She treats me **as if** she **were** my mother. (**But she isn't**.)
As if As though	(+) **Past Perfect** (Unreal in the Past)	She talked about Marilyn Monroe **as if** they **had been** close friends. (**But they hadn't been**.)

◊ **Exclamations**

- Are used to express: **Anger**, **Fear**, **Shock**, **Surprise**, etc. They always take an **exclamation mark** (!) Some exclamations are: **Oh dear!**, **Ah!**, **Oh!**, **Good gracious!**, etc.

What	(+) a(n) + (adjective) + singular countable noun.	What a nice day!
What	(+) (adjective) + plural noun	What nice manners!
What	(+) (adjective) + uncountable noun	What awful weather!
How	(+) adjective	How clever he is!
	(+) adverb	How slowly he speaks!
You	(+) (adjective) + noun	You (filthy) liar!
Such	(+) (a / an) + (adjective) + noun	It is such an old car!
So	(+) adjective / adverb	He's so nice boy!
Adverb or Adverbial particle	(+) subject + verb of movement	Off he went!
Here	(+) subject + verb	Here you are!
There	(+) subject + verb	There she goes! (BUT: There goes Mary!) (When the subject is noun, it follows the verb.)
Interrogative - negative question at the beginning of the sentence.		Isn't it awful!

12 ADJECTIVES / ADVERBS / COMPARISONS

■ <u>Adjectives</u>

◊ **Adjectives** describe **nouns** and are the **same** in **singular** and **plural**.

| They are **close** friends. |

◊ **NOTE: After the verbs**:

Appear	Seem
Be	Smell
Become	Sound
Feel	Stay
Get	Taste
Look	

We use **adjectives** not adverbs.

◊ **Most** common adjectives (**long** , **late** , **etc**) do **not** have particular ending. However there are certain common **endings** for **adjectives** which are formed from **nouns** and **verbs**.

able	Fashion**able**		ical	Mechan**ical**
al	Magic**al**		ious	Rebell**ious**
ant	Hesit**ant**		ish	Styl**ish**
ar	Spectacul**ar**		ist	Rac**ist**
ary	Disciplin**ary**		ive	Select**ive**
ate	Consider**ate**		less	Fault**less**
ial	Artific**ial**		like	Woman-**like**
ent	Persist**ent**		ly	Death**ly**
esque	Pictur**esque**		ory	Sens**ory**
ful	Success**ful**		ous	Humor**ous**
ian	Iran**ian**		some	Brother**some**
ible	Terr**ible**		y	Sand**y**
ic	Melod**ic**			

◊ The most common **prefixes** used with **adjectives** are:

a	**A**sexual		mal	**Mal**adjusted
ab	**Ab**normal		non	**Non**-existent
anti	**Anti**social		over	**Over**weight
dis	**Dis**interested		pre	**Pre**arrange
hyper	**Hyper**active		pro	**Pro**-war
il	**Il**legible		sub	**Sub**-zero
im	**Im**moral		super	**Super**human
in	**In**active		un	**Un**available
ir	**Ir**responsible		under	**Under**staffed

◊ **Position of Adjectives**

Many adjectives can be used either **before** the **noun** they describe, or **after** the **noun** and a **linking verb** which **connects** the **subject** with a **word** or **phrase**, that **describes** the **subject**.

■ Many **participle adjectives** can be used **after noun**.	Many people find **spiders** frighten**ing**.
	Julie was so exhaust**ed** after her exam s. She spent the next three days sleep-ing.
■ **Adjectives** used **after indefinite pronouns**. (**Something , Any-thing , Nothing , etc**)	There was **nothing strange** in this old house.
■ Some **participle** adjectives: (**Affected , Alleged , Required , Suggested , Stolen**) , **-ible Adjectives / -able Adjectives** (Avail**able** , Applic**able** , Poss**ible**) can be used **either before** or **immediately after noun**.	This the last **component** requir**ed**. I accept every poss**ible solution**. I accept every **solution** poss**ible**.

■ The **Adjectives**: "**Concerned**" , "**Involved**" , "**Opposite**" , "**Present**" , "**Proper**" , "**Responsible**" ha-ve **different meanings** when they are used in **different positions**.

Concerned people should consult their doctors. (**Worried , anx-ious**) The police will croos-examine all the **persons concerned**. (**Involved / Implicated**)	The **present crisis** will not be solved quic-kly. (**Existing crisis** in **certain time**.) The **members present** voted against the resolution. (**Existing** in **certain place**.)
Martha's **involved story**. (**Confused story**) The story is for all the **children involved**.(**All who participated**)	Answers are given on the **opposite page**. (The **back side**.)
...to give a **proper report**. (A **real / right report**) ...to read the **report proper**. (The **main part** of the **report**.)	I could see smoke coming from the wind-ows of the **house** directly **opposite**. (The **other one** far from this **side**.)
Responsible parents do not leave their babies alone. (**Reliable / Conscious**) They will find the **man responsible** for the damage.(The **agent** or **cause** of something.)	

■ Many **-ible / -able** adjectives can **only** be used **immediately after a noun** when **the noun follows** a word such: (**First , Last , , Next , Only , Superlative Adjectives**) or **EXTRA INFORMA-TION** is given **AFTER** the **noun**.	This was **the last** model suscept**ible** to high temperature. It was **the most** successful edition print-**able**. Penny is a **girl** suscept**ible** to cold. (**Information about Penny**)

◊ **Gradable / Non Gradable Adjectives**

Gradable adjectives are adjectives like "**Cold**" "**Hot**" and "**Frightened**". You can be **very cold** or a **bit cold**. **Gradable adjectives** show that **something** can have **different degrees**. **Non-gradable adjectives** are adjectives like "**Married**" or "**Wooden**".You **can't** be **very married** or a **bit** married. **Non-gradable** adjectives **do not** have **different degrees**.

Adjectives like "**Terrifying**", "**Freezing**", "**Amazing**" are also **non-gradable** adjectives.They **already CONTAIN THE IDEA** of "**VERY**" in their definitions. "**Freezing**" means "**Very cold**" , **etc**.

◊ **Patterns after Adjectives**

When an **adjective** comes **after a linking verb**, we can use a **number** of **patterns after** the **adjective** including "**to-infinitive**" , "**-ing form**" or "**that clause**".	It **was irresponsible to leave** the kids alone. I **felt** overweight eat**ing** all this food. He **was sure that he needed our help**.

◊ **Compound Adjectives** are formed with:

■ **Present participles**		A long-play**ing** record. A free pay**ing** student.
■ **Past participles**		Undercook**ed** meat. A roll**ed** up carpet.
■ **Cardinal numbers**	(+) <u>nouns</u>	A **three - year** <u>contract</u>.
■ <u>Prefixes</u> & <u>suffixes</u>		A <u>modern</u>-day costume. An **open**-<u>ended</u> discussion.
■ **Badly** **Ill** **Poorly** **Well**	(+) <u>past participle</u>	A **badly**-<u>furnished</u> room. An ill-<u>advised</u> boy. A **poorly** <u>kept</u> garden. A **well**-<u>timed</u> joke.

◊ **NOTE: Present** and **Past Participles** can be used as **adjectives**.

The lecture was bor**ing**.   We were exhaust**ed**.

◊ <u>Certain adjectives</u> are used with "**The**" as <u>nouns</u> to talk about <u>groups of people</u> in general.
These are:

The elderly	**The** disabled	**The** hungry
The middle-aged	**The** living	**The** strong
The old	**The** sick	**The** weak
The young	**The** poor	**The** unemployed
The blind	**The** rich	
The deaf	**The** homeless	

Young students are full of curiosity.	It refers to young students. ("**Young**" as **adjective**.)
The young are full of curiosity.	"**Young**" In general ("**The young**" as **noun**.)
The young people **in our town** are planning the concert.	It refers to a **specific** group of young people (**in our town**). ("**The young**" as **adjective**)

◊ **When** there are **two or more adjectives** , they **normally** go in the following order:

Opinion Adjective	**Beautiful**
Size / Age	**Big / Old**
Shape / Color	**Round / Brown**
Origin / Material	**Italian / Oak**
Used for or **be about**	**Dining , breakfast , etc**
Noun	**Table**

◊ **NOTE: The adjectives "Afraid" , "Alike" , "Alone" , "Ashamed" , "Asleep" , "Content" , "Ill" , "Glad"**

Are **never** followed **by a noun**.   The **baby** is **asleep**.
(**NOT**: The **asleep** <u>baby</u>.)

◊　**NOTE: Nouns as Adjectives**

As you know, a noun is a **person**, **place** or **thing**, and an <u>adjective</u> is a word that **describes** a noun.

Clever teacher.
Small office.
Black horse.

Sometimes we use a noun to **describe** another noun. In this case, the <u>first noun</u> "acts as" an **adjective**.

History teacher.
Ticket office.
Race horse.

◊　**NOTE**: The "**noun** as **adjective**" is in **singular form**. For example:

Boat race	**Boat** races	(<u>NOT</u>: Boats race / Boats races)
Toothbrush	**Tooth**brushes	(**NOT**: Teethbrush / Teethbrushes)
Shoe-lace	**Shoe**-laces	(<u>NOT</u>: Shoes-lace / Shoes-laces)

Exceptions: When we use the **nouns**: "<u>**Clothes**</u>", "<u>**Sports**</u>", "<u>**Customs**</u>", "<u>**Accounts**</u>", "<u>**Arms**</u>", we use them in **plural form**.

Clothe**s** shop / Clothe**s** shops
(**NOT**: **Clothe** shop / **Clothe** shops)
Sport**s** club / Sport**s** clubs
(**NOT**: **Sport** club / **Sport** clubs)
Customs duty / Customs duties
Account**s** department / Account**s** departments
Arm**s** production / Arm**s** production**s**

◊　**NOTE: Nouns of** : **MATERIAL** , **PURPOSE** , **SUBSTANCE** can be used as **adjectives**.

A **cotton** skirt.
A **shopping** bag.
A **glass** surface.

Material
Purpose
Substance

◊　**Certain adjectives** which derive from **nouns** of **material**, **purpose**, **substance** are used **metaphorically**.

Silky hair.
Stony expression.

Hair like **silk**.
Expression like **stone** (without a smile).

■　<u>**Adverbs**</u>

An adverb can describe: <u>a verb</u> , <u>an adjective</u> , <u>an other adverb</u> , <u>a phrase</u> , <u>or a clause</u> and **answers to questions** such as :

"**How**"	Adverbs of **manner**	**Slowly**
"**When**"	Adverbs of **time**	**Yesterday**
"**Where**"	Adverbs of **place**	**Next door**
"**How often**"	Adverbs of **frequency**	**Usually**
"**To what extent**"	Adverbs of **degree**	**Extremely**

◊　**Sentence adverbs:**

A **sentence adverb** is an **adverb** that **modifies** the <u>whole sentence</u>.

Thankfully, <u>he didn't discover my mistake</u>.

◊　**Relative adverbs (Where , Why , When).**

A **relative adverb** marks the <u>relative clause</u>.

The street <u>**where** you live</u>.

◊ **Formation of Adverbs from Adjectives**

Adjectives	(+) **ly**	Quick ---> Quick**ly**
Adjectives ending in :	**Consonant** + **y** (Drop **y** & add **ily**)	Slee**py** ---> Slee**pily**
Adjectives ending in :	**ic** (Add **-ally**)	Trag**ic** ---> Trag**ically**
Adjectives ending in :	**le** (Drop **le** & add **ly**)	Irritab**le** --->Irritab**ly**
Adjectives ending in :	**e** (Add **ly**)	False ---> Fals**ely**
		BUT: Whole --> Who**lly**, True-->Tru**ly**

◊ **Adjectives** ending in "**ly**"

Elder**ly**		
Father**ly**	Form their **adverb** with:	
Friend**ly**		
Live**ly**	**in a(n)** ...**way**	**in a** lively **way**.
Lone**ly**		
Mother**ly**	**in a(n)** ...**manner**	**In a** motherly **manner**.
Sil**ly**		
Ug**ly**		

◊ **Compound Adverbs** are **Adverbs** that are constructed **from two words**:

For example: <u>Some</u>**where**, <u>Every</u>**where**, <u>Now</u>**here**, <u>There</u>**fore**, <u>Where</u>**upon**, <u>Here</u>by , etc.

◊ **Adverbs** and **Adjectives** which have the **same** form.

Best	Extra	Monthly
Better	Far	Past
Big	Fast	Quick(**ly**)
Cheap(**ly**)	Fine(**ly**)	Quiet(**ly**)
Clean(**ly**)	Free	Right
Clear(**ly**)	Further	Slow(**ly**)
Close(**ly**)	Hard	Straight
Cold	High	Sure
Daily	Hourly	Thick
Dead	Inside	Thin(**ly**)
Dear(**ly**)	Kindly	Tight
Deep	Last	Weekly
Direct	Late	Well
Dirty	Long	Wide
Early	Loud(**ly**)	Wrong
Easy	Low	Yearly

Ann was our **last** guest.
He drives a **slow** car.

She came in **last**.
He drives **slow**(ly).

◊ **Adverbs** with **two forms** and **differences** in meaning.

Close	Near / shut
Closely	Carefully
Deep	A long way down
Deeply	Profoundly
Direct	By the shortest route
Directly	Immediately
Easy	Gently and slowly
Easily	Without difficulty , undoubtedly

Fair	Right
Fairly	Adequately / enough
Free	Without cost
Freely	Willingly , of one's own free will / not under the control of another
Full	Entire , total
Fully	Completely
Hard	With effort / difficult
Hardly	Scarcely
High	At / to a high level
Highly	Very much
Just	Soon / hardly
Justly	Justifiably / rightly
Last	After all others
Lastly	Finally
Late	Not early
Lately	Recently
Near	Close
Nearly	Almost
Pretty	Fairly
Prettily	In a pretty way / fine
Short	Brief / little / meager
Shortly	Unexpectedly / soon / quickly
Sure	Convinced
Surely	Definitely
Wide	Broad
Widely	To a large extend
Wrong	Not right
Wrongly	Unjustly

◊ **Position of Adverbs**

Front position	At the **beginning** of the sentence.	**Lastly** I **found** my lost book.
Mid position	Normally **before** the <u>main</u> verb or **after** the <u>auxiliary</u>.	At university I **usually** <u>see</u> him alone. He <u>will</u> **always** be rich.
End position	At the **end** of the sentence.	Run **fast**!

■ Adverbs of Manner ("Easily" , "Beautifully" , "Happily" , "Quickly" , "Really" , "Softly" , "Well" , etc) can go in **any position**. We place them in **front position** to **give emphasis**.

She **climbed up** the stairs **quickly**. **Quickly** she **climbed up** the stairs. (**emphasis**)

■ When there is <u>more than one adverb</u> in the sentence, their usual order is: "**Adverb** of <u>manner</u> - <u>place</u> - **adverb of** <u>time</u>".

She was studying <u>hard</u> in her room <u>yesterday</u>.

■ When there is a **verb of movement** then the order is: "**Place** - adverb of <u>manner</u> - adverb of <u>time</u>".

She **goes** to **school** <u>hastily</u> <u>sometimes</u>.

■ Adverbs of Time & Frequency consisting **more than one word**: "**As a rule**" , "**From time to time**" , "**Every so often**" are usually put either in **FRONT** or **END** position but <u>not</u> in **MID** position.

He goes to the park on his bike **every so often**. **Every so often** he goes to the park on his bike.

Adverbs of Frequency go **before** the <u>auxiliary</u> in **short** answers.

"**Does** he help you to clean the house?" Yes he **always** <u>does</u>.

- **Adverbs of Definite time** ("**Now**" , "**Then**" , "**Today**" , "**Tomorrow**" , "**Yesterday**" , "**Last June**" , etc)
and of **Definite Frequency** ("**Annually**" , "**Daily**" , "**Monthly**" , "**Weekly**" , "**Yearly**", "**Every day**" , etc)

Adverbs of **Definite Frequency**, like all **adverbs** of **Definite time** typically go in **END position**.	All the students must come here **now**! Most companies pay their taxes **yearly**.
Sometimes, usually for **reasons** of **emphasis** or **style**, <u>some</u> **adverbs** of **Definite Frequency may go** at the **FRONT**.	**Every day**, more than one thousand people die on our roads.

- **Adverbs of Indefinite Frequency**: ("**Already**" , "**Always**" , "**Ever**" , "**Hardly ever**" , "**Never**" , "**Often**" "**Rarely**" , "**Regularly**" , "**Seldom**" , "**Sometimes**" , "**Still**" , "**Usually**" , "**Yet**" , etc) are <u>generally</u> put in the **MID position**. They are put:

After the <u>auxiliary</u> verb.	He <u>**will**</u> **always** come first.
After the verb "<u>**Be**</u>".	You <u>**are**</u> **always** late.
Before the <u>main</u> verb.	He **usually** <u>comes</u> late.

- **Adverbs of Place**:

Adverbs of **place** indicate **where** something happens. **Generally** put in **end position**.

Aboard	**Far**	**Outdoors**
Anywhere	**Here**	**Outside**
Away	**In**	**Over**
Back	**Indoors**	**Somewhere**
Backwards	**Inside**	**There**
Behind	**Near**	**Towards**
Below	**Nearby**	**Under**
Down	**Off**	**Up**
Downstairs	**On**	**Upstairs**
East , **West** , etc	**Out**	**Where**

These **adverbs** are put **behind** the <u>**direct object**</u> of the **verb**.	He left his <u>**notes**</u> **somewhere**. I didn't see <u>**him**</u> **here**.

- **Adverbs of Degree**: "**Almost**" , "**Completely**" , "**Enough**" , "**Extremely**" , "**Even**" , "**Fairly**" , "**Hardly**" , "**Just**" , "**Nearly**" , "**Only**" , "**Pretty**" , "**Quite**" , "**Scarcely**" , "**Too**" , "**Very**" , etc

Adverbs of Degree tell us about the **intensity** or **degree** of **an action**, of **an adjective** or of **another adverb**. **Adverbs of degree** are usually placed **before** the <u>**adjective**</u>, <u>**adverb**</u>, or the <u>**verb**</u> they modify.	The water was **extremely** <u>hot</u>.

◊ **NOTE**: "**Too**" and "**Enough**"

"**Too**" and "**Enough**" indicate degree. They are used usually with **adjectives** or **adverbs**.

"**Too**" **precedes** the <u>**adjectives**</u> and the <u>**adverbs**</u>.	He is **too** <u>old</u> to ride this wild horse. It is **too** <u>late</u> for the kids to go out.
"**Too**" is often is **followed** by "**to**" + **infinitive**.	The coffee was **too** <u>hot</u> to drink.
"**Too**" can be **followed** by "**for someone / for something**".	The dress was **too** <u>small</u> for her.
"**Enough**" follows the <u>**adjectives**</u> and the <u>**adverbs**</u>.	Tony was <u>tall</u> **enough** to play on the basketball team. I got here <u>**early**</u> **enough**.

"Enough" is often is **followed** by **"to" + infinitive**.	She's not <u>**old** enough to get married</u>.
"Enough" can be **followed** by **"for someone / for something"**.	The jacket was <u>**big** enough for me</u>.
"Enough" can also be used with <u>**nouns**</u>. In such cases, **"Enough"** usually **precedes** the <u>**noun**</u>.	I have **enough <u>money</u>** for the purchase of this CD player.

◊   **NOTE: The adverbs of degree: "Absolutely" , "Completely" , "Constantly" , "Continually" , "Entirely" , "Greatly" , "Perfectly" , "Regularly".**

Are **usually** put in **MID** or **END** position , but **NOT** in **FRONT** position.	It is a **completely** new smart phone.

◊   **NOTE: Adverbial Phrases** can **modify: Adjectives , Adverbs , Verbs , Determiners , Other**

■   **Adverbial phrase** with <u>**verb**</u>

We use **adverbial phrases** to **modify verbs**.	Children <u>**grow up** really quickly</u>. I <u>**exercise** very regularly</u> and I <u>**eat** quite healthily</u>.

■   **Adverbial phrase** with "<u>**Be**</u>"

We use **adverbial phrases** with **"Be"**.This is especially typical of <u>**adverbs of place**</u>.	I **am <u>upstairs</u>**. I'll only be a minute. A: Have you seen my gloves? B: They **are <u>right there</u>**, on the table.

■   **Adverbial phrases** with <u>**Adjectives**</u> & <u>**Adverbs**</u>

We use **adverbial phrases** with **adjectives** and **adverbs**.	I found it <u>**extremely difficult** to talk to her</u>. He drives <u>**really carefully**</u>.

■   **Adverbial phrases** with **Determiners**

We use **adverbial phrases** with <u>**determiners**</u> , especially words like: "<u>**All**</u>", "<u>**Some**</u>", "<u>**Half**</u>", "<u>**Many**</u>" , "<u>**Few**</u>" (**quantifiers**).	<u>**Some** of my friends</u> found the test extremely **difficult**. <u>**Few** candidates</u> passed the exams easi**ly**.

■   **Adverbial phrases** with **other phrases**

We use **adverbial phrases** with <u>noun phrases</u>, **pronouns** and <u>**prepositional**</u> phrases.	That's **quite** <u>a tree</u>. (e.g. it's very big.) There was **hardly <u>anyone</u>** at the concert. We climbed **right <u>over</u>** <u>the top of the hill and got down again</u>.

◊   **NOTE:**

■   We **avoid** putting an <u>**adverb**</u> between a **main verb** and a <u>direct object</u> , or **before** an **"ing form"** or **right after** the **"infinitive"**.

I can **play** <u>tennis</u> **quite well**.
 NOT:
 I can **play <u>quite</u> well** <u>tennis</u>.

I would like **to go back <u>again</u>**.
 NOT:
 I would like **to go <u>again</u> back**.

I trained play**ing <u>perfectly</u>**.
 NOT:
 I trained <u>**perfectly**</u> play**ing**.

◊ The use of the **adverb** of **manner** "Really"
The use of the **adverbs** of **indefinite frequency**: "Already" , "Still" , "Yet"
The use of the **adverbs** of **degree**: "Even" , "Fairly" , "Only" , "Pretty" , "Quite" , "Rather"

◊ The **adverb** of **manner** "Really"

The meaning of "**Really**" can change according to **its position** in a sentence. **Immediately before** an <u>adjective</u> it means "**Very**". **In other positions** it can mean "**Actually**" or "**In fact**".	They are looking **really** <u>exhausted</u>. (**Very exhausted**) She didn't want to come with us. But I **really** had persuaded her to come.

◊ The **indefinite frequency adverbs** "Already" , "Still" , "Yet"

"**Already**" can go **either** in the **MID** or in the **END** position.	They have **already** been to London. **Or** They have been to London **already**.
"**Still**" is usually put in the **MID** position.	I am **still** thinking about the plan.
"**Yet**" is usually put in **END** position in **negations** & **questions** or with **expressions of uncertainty**. To avoid mistakes,do <u>not</u> use "**Yet**" in **affirmative** statements.	Has she not call you **yet**? (**Question , uncertainty**)

◊ The **adverbs** of **degree**: "Even" , "Fairly" , "Only" , "Pretty" , "Quite" , "Rather"

▪ "**Even**" and "**Only**" are usually put in the **mid** position, but **if** they refer to the <u>subject</u> they usually put **before** it.	He can **even** run fast. **Even** a <u>child</u> can solve this problem. **Only** my <u>father</u> can solve this problem.

▪ "**Rather**" is used:	
<u>Unfavorable</u> **comments**.	He is **rather** <u>mean</u> with money.
Favorable comments meaning "**to an unusual degree**".	The lecture was **rather** informative. (It was **more** informative **than we expected**.)
With **comparative degree**.	It is **rather** sunn**ier** today than yesterday.
The **usual position** for "**Rather**" is **between** "**A**" / "**An**" and an <u>adjective</u>.	He was **a rather** <u>stupid</u> man.
Less often, but with **similar meaning**, "**rather**" is used **before** "**A**" / "**An**" and an <u>adjective</u>.	He was **rather a** <u>stupid</u> man.
With a **SINGULAR** <u>noun</u> or "**A LOT OF**" , "**Rather**" must be come **BEFORE** "**A**" / "**An**".	There is **rather a** <u>surplus</u> of food. <u>**NOT**</u> There is **a rather** <u>surplus</u> of food. There is **rather** <u>a lot of</u> water.

▪ "**Quite**"("**Fairly**" to some degree) is used in <u>**favorable comments**</u>.	She is **quite** good at painting.
"**Quite**" is used **BEFORE** "**A**" / "**An**" and an <u>adjective</u> where it means "**Moderately**".	She is **quite a** <u>good</u> dancer. (**Moderately**)
Less often "**Quite**" is used **BETWEEN** "**A**" / "**An**" and an <u>adjective</u> where it means "**Completely**".	He is **a quite** <u>good</u> student. (**Completely**)

- ■ "Quite" meaning "Completely" is used with **some** Adverbs , Verbs and Adjectives such as:

		I **quite** <u>enjoyed</u> the film.
Alone	**Horrible**	
Amazing	**Impossible**	
Brilliant	**Perfect**	
Certain	**Ridiculous**	
Dead	**Right**	
Dreadful	**Sure**	
Different	**Useless** , etc	I'm **quite** <u>sure</u> that he stole the money.
Exhausted		
Extraordinary		

- ■ "**Fairly**" and "**Pretty**" are synonymous with "**Quite**" and "**Rather**". They can be used **after** "<u>A</u>".

He is <u>a</u> **fairly** / <u>a</u> **pretty** well behaved person.

- **Comparisons of Adjectives and Adverbs**

◊ **REGULAR Comparative and Superlative form of Adjectives and Adverbs.**

- **Adjectives** of <u>one</u> syllable add **(e)r** , **(e)st** to form their **comparative** and **superlative** forms.

Positive	Comparative	Superlative
Short	Short**er** (than)	**The** short**est** (of / in)
Simple	Simpl**er** (than)	**The** simpl**est** (of / in)
Big	Big**ger** (than)	**The** big**gest** (of / in)

- **Adjectives** of <u>two or more</u> syllables take **"More" / "The most"**

Positive	Comparative	Superlative
Modern	**More** modern (**than**)	**The most** modern (**of / in**)
Intelligent	**More** intelligent (**than**)	**The most** intelligent (**of / in**)

- **Adjectives** of <u>two</u> syllables ending in : "<u>ly</u>" , "<u>y</u>" , drop "y" and add -ier , -iest

Positive	Comparative	Superlative
Ho<u>ly</u>	Hol**ier** (**than**)	**The** hol**iest** (**of / in**)
Funn**y**	Funn**ier** (**than**)	**The** funn**iest** (**of / in**)

- **Adjectives** ending in : "<u>w</u>" also add **er** , **est**

Positive	Comparative	Superlative
Narro<u>w</u>	Narro<u>w</u>**er** (**than**)	**The** narro<u>w</u>**est** (**of / in**)

- We usually put **"More" / "Most"** before <u>three or more</u> syllable **adjectives**. | **The most** <u>expensive</u> of our cars is the Rolls-Royce.

◊ **NOTE**:

- We normally use **"Than"** with <u>comparative</u> form. | Tom is short**er than** Tony.

- We normally use **"The ...of" / "The ...in"** , **"The...on"** with the **superlative form**. **"In"** and **"On"** refer to <u>places</u> and <u>groups</u>. | She is **the** smart**est** of all.
One of **the most** dangerous rivers **on** <u>earth</u>.
The fast**est** swimmers **in** <u>our class</u>.

- For **emphasis** we can put an **"Of-phrase"** at the **beginning** of the sentence. | <u>**Of the boys from school**</u> John is **the most** intelligent.

- Sometimes In <u>in</u>formal contexts we **leave out "The"** after a <u>linking</u> **verb** , when a **superlative** is at the **end** of the sentence. | Which one **is** (**the**) heaviest?

- When **"Most + adjective"** is used **without "The"** , **"Most"** means something like **"Very"**. | The topic that she chose was **most** **difficult**.

- **Certain adjectives** form their **comparative** and **superlative** forms <u>either</u> with **"er" / "est"** <u>or</u> with **"More" / "Most"**. These are:

Clever	Pleasant	
Common	Polite	
Cruel	Quiet	Quiet , quieter , the quietest
Friendly	Shallow	or
Gentle	Simple	Quiet , more quiet , the most quiet.
Narrow	Stupid	

However, we can drop "y" and add "-ier" / "-iest" to: "Unhappy" , "Unhealthy" ,"Unlikely" , "Unlucky" , "Unsteady" , "Untidy".	Now she feels unhappier. or Now she feels more unhappy.

■ **Adverbs** of <u>one</u> syllable add (e)r , (e)st to form their **comparative** and **superlative** forms.

Positive	Comparative	Superlative
Fast	Faster	The fastest

■ **Adverbs** of <u>two</u> syllables and **Adverbs** that are formed from <u>Adjectives + ly</u> add "More" / "The most" to form their **comparative** and **superlative** degrees.

Positive	Comparative	Superlative
Often	More often	The most often
Patient<u>ly</u>	More patient<u>ly</u>	The most patient<u>ly</u>

◊ **IRREGULAR Comparative** and **Superlative forms** of **Adjectives** and **Adverbs**.

Positive	Comparative	Superlative
Good / Well	Better	Best
Bad / Badly	Worse	Worst
Much	More	Most
Many / a lot of	More	Most
Little	Less	Least
Far	Farther / Further	Farthest / Furthest

◊ **NOTE:**

■ "**Well**" is the <u>adverb</u> of "**Good**" .

> She is a **good** dancer.
> She dances **well**.

■ Further / Farther   (+) (<u>adjective</u>)

> His house is **further / farther** <u>away</u> **than** John's.

■ Very   (+) <u>positive</u> degree

> I'm **very** <u>happy</u> with my new job.

■ A bit
Even   (+) <u>comparative</u> degree
Far
Much

> It's **much** <u>worse</u> than last year.
> The weather is **even** <u>less</u> bearable to-day.

■ Any
(Used in negations   (+) <u>comparative</u> degree
and questions.)

> Can you write **any** quick<u>er</u> please?

◊ **Types of Comparisons**

■ **As**...(positive degree)...**as**

For hair **as <u>soft</u> as** silk try this new shampoo.

Not as / so...(positive degree)...**as**

The service is**n't as / so <u>good</u> as** it used to be.

Such a(n)...**as / so**

It is not **such a** long way **as** we thought.

■ **Before** the **first** "**As**" we can use **words** and **phrases** such: "**As about**" , "**Almost**" , "**Just**" , "**Just about**" , "**Nearly**".

She **almost as** subborn **as** her brother.

■ **Informally** before the **first** "**As**" we can use **words** and **phrases** such: "**Not anything like**" , "**Nothing like**" , "**Nowhere near**" , "**Not nearly**".

The land is **nowhere near as** fertile **as** in this region.

■ We use "**as many... as**" , "**as much... as**" to say that a <u>quantity</u> or <u>amount</u> is **larger than expected**.

There weren't **as many people** there **as** I expected.
Jonh did **as much <u>work</u> as** Mary.

■ We use "**as few...as**" , "**as little... as**" to say that a <u>quantity</u> or <u>amount</u> is **smaller than expected**.

There are **as few <u>houses in this village</u> as** in the previous one.
Jim has **as little <u>food</u> as** Sam.

■ We also use "**as much as**" , "**as many as**" with a <u>noun phrase</u> <u>or clause</u> , or with the words "<u>**Ever**</u>" , "<u>**Possible**</u>" and "<u>**Usual**</u>".

He drinks **as many as <u>three bottles of</u> <u>milk a day</u>**.
We want to visit John **as much as <u>pos-</u> <u>sible</u>**.

■ We can put "**a** + <u>singular noun</u>" between an **adjective** and a second "**as**".

I want **as cheap <u>a coat</u> as** possible.

■ In **negative** in**formal** forms we can use "**Not as**" or **less commonly** "**Not so**".

Mary is **not as** patient **as** Jane.

■ We <u>**DON'T**</u> use: "**Not <u>as</u>** + adjective + <u>a / an</u> + <u>noun</u>".
<u>**BUT**</u>: In **negative forms** we use:"**Not such a / an** + adjective + <u>noun</u>".

<u>NOT</u>: This is **not <u>as</u> good <u>a</u> <u>manner</u>**.

<u>BUT</u>: This is **not such <u>a</u> good <u>manner</u>**.

■ "**As** + <u>clause</u>". We can use a clause **after** "**As**" to **compare two situations**.

Maybe we will visit Ann, **as <u>we did last</u> <u>Christmas</u>**.

■ **Twice**
Three , etc **times** | **as**...(positive degree)...**as**
Half

She earns **twice as <u>much</u> as** me.

She is **half as <u>heavy</u> as** her sister.

◊ **NOTE:**

■ In **writing** as well as in **formal speaking** "**As**" can act like a **relative pronoun**.

The competition will last one hour, **as it** was agreed during our last conference. (...**which** was agreed...)

■ In **formal forms** we can **sometimes invert** the <u>subject</u> and the **verb after** "**As**".

We bought three dvds, **as did your <u>bro-</u> <u>ther</u>**.
or
We bought three dvds, **as your <u>bro-</u> <u>ther</u> did**. (...**as** your <u>brother</u> **did**.)

◊ **NOTE: Comparisons with:**

The same as		The Ford Focus costs **the same as** the VW Golf.
Look , Sound Smell , Taste	(+) <u>like</u>	She **looks** <u>like</u> her sister.
Less **The least**	... (<u>positive degree</u>)...**than** ... (<u>positive degree</u>)...**of / in**	I have **less** <u>free time</u> **than** Cathy but Laura has **the least** <u>free time</u> **of** all.
More of a	... (<u>positive degree</u>)...**than**	She is **more of a** <u>friend</u> **than** a classmate.
The comparative..., **, the comparative...**		**The less** you sleep , **the more** tired you feel.
Comparative + and + comparative		The weather is getting **hotter and hotter**.
Prefer + ing ...+ to + ing ...		She **prefer** liv**ing** for the moment **to** th**ing** about the future.
Prefer + <u>noun</u> + to + <u>noun</u>		Most people **prefer** <u>summer</u> **to** <u>winter</u>.
Prefer + to infinitive rather than + infinitive without to / noun		I prefer **to live** in a small house **rather than live** in a apartment / **rather than** in an apartment.
Would prefer +to inf. rather than + infinitive without to		I **would prefer to book** our tickets now **rather than wait** for the last minute.
Would rather + infinitive without "To" than infinitive without "To"		He **would rather go** alone **than go** with Edward.
Would sooner+infinitive without "To" than infinitive without "To"		He **would sooner go** alone **than go** with Edward.
<u>Clause</u> + **"whereas"** / **"while"** + <u>clause</u>		<u>Mary enjoys adventure</u> while / whereas <u>her sister prefers peace and quiet</u>.

◊ **NOTE: Comparisons** with **"So..."** , **"Too..."** , **"Enough..."**

■ **So + adjective + <u>that - clause</u>**	It seems **so expensive** <u>that a lot of people won't buy it</u>.
■ **So + adjective + <u>as</u> + <u>to-infinitive</u>** (**More formal** with the **same** meaning as the previous one.)	Global warming is becoming **so extreme** <u>as</u> **to threaten** the existence of life in the future.

- **Too + adjective + <u>to-infinitive</u>**

  She is **too young <u>to drive</u>** a car.

- **Adjective + enough + <u>to-infinitive</u>**

  He is not **intelligent enough <u>to solve</u>** this problem.

- In **formal forms** we can use "**Sufficiently**" <u>before adjectives</u> to express a meaning similar to "**Enough**".

  She is not **sufficiently <u>familiar</u>** with my parents.
  She is not <u>**familiar**</u> **enough** with my...

◇ **NOTE**:

"**Like**": Is a **preposition**, which means that it can be used <u>before</u> a <u>**noun**</u> or <u>**pronoun**</u>. It should <u>**not**</u> be used **before a <u>whole claus</u>**-e containing a <u>verb</u>.

He works **like** a <u>**mule**</u>.
She looks just **like** <u>**her**</u> mother.
<u>**NOT**</u>: She looks **like** <u>she **is** a princess</u>.
<u>**BUT**</u>: She looks **like** a princess.

"**As**": Is a **conjunction**, and it can be used **before <u>a clause</u>** containing a <u>**subject**</u> and a **verb**.

As <u>I</u> **told** you, the car was parked behind that tree.

◇ "**Like**" is used:

- **For similarities**

  He works **like** a **mule**.

- **With**:

Nouns Pronouns ing form	to **express similarity**	**Frogs legs** are supposed to taste **like** **chicken**. Is that your mum? You look **like her**. It's looks **like** old wash**ing** machine.

- **After**:

Feel Look Smell Sound	**(+) noun**	She **looks like** her **mother**. It **smells like** burnt **toast**.

◇ "**As**" is used:

- **To say what** somebody or something **really is** (jobs or roles).

  He works **as** a dentist.
  (**He is a dentist**.)

- **In certain expressions**:

As usual As...as As much Such as The same as	As you know As you suggested As we agree As ours / yours...	She was late **as usual**.

- **After**:

Accept Be known Class Describe	Refer Regard Use	He **regarded as** an expert in computers.

■ **In clauses** of **manner** to mean "**in the way that**".	We must right the essay **as <u>they have shown us</u>**.
■ "**As**"can also be used in the same way as "**Because**".	They stayed at home , **as** it was raining all day.

◊ **NOTE**: **Adverbial particles**

Words like "**Down**" , "**In**", "**Out**", "**Up**", etc , are **not** always **prepositions**. Read the sentences:	He was driving **down the street**. Please <u>**sit down**</u>. He climbed **up the stairs**. <u>**She is not up**</u> yet. He is **in the room**. You can <u>**come in**</u>.

In the expressions "<u>**sit down**</u>", "<u>**she is not up**</u>" and "<u>**come in**</u>" the words "**down**", "**up**" and "**in**" have **no objects**. They are **adverbs** and <u>**not**</u> **prepositions**.
Small adverbs like these are often called **adverb particles** or **adverbial particles**. Examples are: "**Across**" , "**About**" , "**Above**" , "**Before**" , "**Behind**" , "**Below**" , "**Down**" , "**In**" , "**Off**" , "**On**" , "**Out**", "**Up**" , etc

13 NOUNS / ARTICLES

■ **NOUNS**

◊ **The nouns are**:

Abstract or **Mass nouns**	Invasion , visit , knowledge , etc
Concrete (something **physical** which someone can: **Taste** , **smell** , **hear** or **see**.)	Water , air , perfume , sound , etc
Proper (express the **actual name** of the **person**, **place**, **thing** or **idea**.)	John , Athens , London , etc
Collective (express **total things**)	Audience , family , government , etc
Common	Book , sofa , car , etc

◊ The **nouns** form their **plural** number adding:

	Singular	Plural
■ **"S"** to the common nouns.	Book	Books
■ **"S"** to the noun ending in: **Vowel** + **"o"** **Double "o"** **Abbreviations** **Musical instruments** **Proper nouns**	 Video Taboo Photo (instead of photograph) Cello East river , Kate	 Videos Taboos Photos Cellos East rivers , Kates
■ **"S"** to the noun ending in: **Vowel** + **"y"**	Boy Play	Boys Plays
■ **"es"** to nouns ending in:**"s"** , **"ss"** , **"x"** , **"ch"** **"sh"** , <u>**consonant** + **"o"**</u>	Bus Class Fox Church Rash Pota<u>to</u>	Buses Classes Foxes Churches Rashes Pota<u>toes</u>
■ **Some** nouns ending in **"o"** can take either **"s"** or **"es"**. **These are:**	Buffalo Mosquito Volcano Zero Tornado	Buffalos / Buffaloes Mosquitos / Mosquitoes Volcanos / Volcanoes Zeros / Zeroes Tornados / Tornadoes
■ **"ies"** to nouns ending in <u>**consonant** + **"y"**</u>	Bo<u>dy</u> Par<u>ty</u>	Bo<u>dies</u> Par<u>ties</u>
■ **"ves"** .To **some** nouns ending in **f / fe**.	Scarf **BUT** Chief Roof Cliff Safe	Scarves Chiefs Roofs Cliffs Safes
■ Some nouns of Greek or Latin origin form their plural adding Greek or Latin **suffixes**.	Basis Crisis Terminus Criterion Medium	Bases Crises Termini Criteria Media

◊ **COMPOUND NOUNS**

■ **Common compound noun patterns**

Noun + noun	**Fish tank**
Adjective + noun	**Full moon**
ing form + noun	**Waiting room**
Noun + ing form	**Energy-saving**

■ The **first** noun in a **compound** noun **usually** has a **singular form**, **even if it has plural meaning**.

The <u>decision</u>-making committe**s** (<u>**NOT**</u>: The **decisions**-making committe**s**)

■ **Compound Nouns**: Can form their **plural** number with the ending "**s**" or with ending "**es**":

	Singular	Plural
To the **second** noun if the compound consists of **two nouns**.	Corkscrew	Corkscrew**s**
To the **first** noun if the compound consists of **two** nouns connected a **preposition**.	Doctor **of** philosophy	Doctor**s** **of** philosophy
To the **noun** if the compound consists of an **adjective** and a **noun**.	**Steering** wheel	**Steering** wheel**s**
At the **end** of the compound if this is **not made up** of **any nouns**.	Runaway	Runaway**s**
The plural of **hyphenated** or **spaced** compound **nouns** are formed by **pluralizing** the **chief element** of the compound.	**Father**-in-law **Father** figure	**Fathers**-in-law **Fathers** figure
When a **hyphenated** compound **does not have a noun** as one of its elements, **we pluralize** the **final element**.	Know-it-**all**	Know-it-**alls**
The **plural** of compounds ending in "**ful**" is formed adding an "**S**".	Cup**ful**	Cup**fuls**
When the **first** element of a compound is a **possessive** we simply **pluralize** the **final** element.	Collector'**s** item	Collector's item**s**

◊ **NOTE:**

■ We can use "**NOUN + OF + NOUN 'S**" to talk about **something** that **someone owns** or "**NOUN + OF + POSSESSIVE PRONOUN**" to talk about **about a relationship**.

The new **car of** John'**s**. (John **owns** this new car.)
A **friend of** mine. (relationship)

■ We can also use a "**NOUN + OF + NOUN without 'S**" when we talk about a **relationship between people**.

She is the **wife of** my brother. (**Relationship between people**)

◊ **Irregular Plurals**

Singular	Plural
Aircraft	**Aircraft**
Child	Children
Deer	**Deer**
Fish	**Fish**
Foot	Feet
Goose	Geese
Headquarters	**Headquarters**
Hovercraft	**Hovercraft**
Louse	Lice
Man	Men
Means	**Means**
Mouse	Mice
Ox	Oxen
Salmon	**Salmon**
Sheep	**Sheep**
Spacecraft	**Spacecraft**
Species	**Species**
Tooth	Teeth
Trout	**Trout**
Woman	Women

◊ **Countable / Uncountable nouns**

■ Nouns can be **countable** , those can be counted , or **uncountable**.

1 box , **2 boxes**.
Bread , **wood** , ect.

■ **Uncountable** nouns take a **singular** verb and are **not** used with "**a**" / "**an**".

Luggage **is** obtained from the luggage reclaim area.

BUT: "a relief" , "a pity" , "a shame" , "a wonder" , "a knowledge of sth" , "a help".

■
Some
Any
No
Much

can be used with **uncountable** nouns.

Can I have **some** **bread** please?

- **Uncountable nouns are:**

Abstract or **Mass nouns (Fluid , solids , gases , particles)**	Beer, gold , air , oil , knowledge , etc
Subjects of study	History , maths , accountancy
Games	Football , basketball , billiards , darts
Languages	Spanish , French , Japanese ,etc
Diseases	Flu , tuberculosis , chickenpox , etc
Natural phenomena	Darkness , fog , gravity , snow , hail
Collective nouns	Baggage , cutlery , furniture , money rubbish , stationery , etc

Some nouns

Accommodation , advice , anger , applause , assistance , behavior , belongings , business , camping cash , chaos , clothing , conduct , countryside , courage , education , employment , equipment , evidence , furniture , health , homework , information , intelligence , leisure , knowledge , luck , luggage , machinery , money , music , parking , pollution , progress , research , seaside , scenery , shopping , sightseeing , traffic , transport , trouble , truth , wealth , work , etc.

◊ **NOTE**:

■ **Some** nouns are used **uncountably** when we are talking about **the thing in general**.	Social **knowledge** is everything. (knowledge **in general** / "Knowledge" uncountable noun).
■ Some nouns are used **countably** when we are talking about **particular examples** of **things** or **ideas**.	**This new solar car** has been **a success**. (Success of **something specific** / "Success" as **countable** noun).

◊ **NOTE**:

■ **With expressions** of DURATION , DINSTANCE , MONEY we use a **singular** verb **after** the **noun**.	Two month**s** **was** too long time for her , to be in a hospital. (**Duration**) Three mile**s** remain**s** until the end of the tunnel. (**Distance**) I think fifty Euro**s** **is** too much to afford for this gadget. (**Money**)
■ When **names** and **titles** ending in "**-S**" **refer to a single unit** we use a **singular** verb **after** them.	The <u>Bahamas</u> **has** developed a new energy program. ("**Bahamas**"= **a group of islands**.)
■ After "**PERCENT (%)**" referring to a **singular** or **uncountable** noun we use **singular** **verb**. If it refers to a **plural noun** we use **plural** verb.	**50%** of the **company**'s income come**s** from exports. **90% of the students** in Africa **are** poor.

- Many **uncountable** nouns can be made **countable**.

A bar	of chocolate
A bit	of chalk
A box / sheet	of paper
A can	of coke
A carton	of milk , etc
A clap / peal	of thunder
A flash / bolt	of lightning
A glass	of water / beer / wine
A jar	of jam
A kilo	of meat
A packet	of tea
A piece	of paper / cake / information / advice / furniture , etc
A pint	of beer
A pot	of yoghurt
A pound	of meat
A rasher	of bacon
A slice	of bread
A tube	of toothpaste
An ice cube	

◊ **Plural nouns**:

- **Objects** consisting of **two parts**:

Garments	Trousers , pajamas , etc
Instruments	Binoculars , compasses , etc
Tools	Scissors , pliers , etc

- We use a **plural verb** with the **plural nouns** given below.

Arms	Goods	Premises
Ashes	Headquarters	Riches
Barracks	Looks	Stairs
Belongings	Outskirts	Surroundings
Clothes	Particulars	Wages , etc.
Congratulations	People	
Earnings	Police	

- The following plural nouns:

Economics	Physics
Linguistics	Politics
Mathematics	Statistics
News	

Take a <u>singular</u> verb when they refer to the **academic subject**. | I think that **mathematics** <u>is</u> the most important science.

- AFTER : "a / the majority of" , "a / the minority of" , "a number of" , "a lot of" , "a plenty of".

we use <u>plural</u> verb. | **The majority of** these cars <u>are</u> not reliable.

◊ **NOTE**: We can use **singular verb** with "**The number of**".

The number of people playing tennis **is** increasing.

◊ **Collective nouns**:   Are those that denote **a collection of persons or things** regarded **as a unit**.

Army	**Crew**	**People**
Audience	**Crowd**	**Press**
Baggage	**Cutlery**	**Public**
Class	**Enemy**	**Staff**
Clergy	**Family**	**Team** , etc
Club	**Government**	
Committee	**Group**	
Company	**Jury**	
Council	**Money**	

◊ **NOTE**: In **American** usage **a collective noun takes**:

A **singular verb** when it refers to the **collection considered as a whole**.	**The family was** united on this problem.
A **plural verb** when it refers to the **members of the group considered as individuals**.	**My family are** always fighting **among themselves**.

◊ **NOTE**: In **British** usage the **collective nouns** are **more often treated as plurals**.   **The government have** not announced a new policy.

◊ **How certain nouns** can be used in **singular** and **plural** with a **different** meaning.

Singular	Plural
Give me a **glass** of water, please?	I've been wearing **glasses** since I was ten years old.
Has she always had a short **hair**?	There are so many **hairs** in the sink.
Would you rate this on a **scale** of 1 to10?	Can you put that fish on the **scales** please?
In Japan it is not **custom** to kiss your friend.	Our bags were thoroughly searched at **customs**.
Have you got any line **paper** I could use?	He show his **papers** to the customs officer.
She is wearing a ring made of **wood**.	John loves Sunday afternoon to go for a walk in the **woods**.
I can't talk now I have a lot of **work** to do.	A lot of Dali's **works** are on display in this museum.
We had at least 200 **people** at our wedding.	The **peoples** of Europe are hoping for a change.
The **rain** is falling really heavily now.	The villagers are hoping for the **rains** to come soon.
You need **experience** for this job.	I had a lot of interesting **experiences** in Asia. (**adventures**)

We need **a compass** to find out direction.

Use your **compasses** to draw some circles.

◊ To describe **people** we add "ar" , "er" or "ee" to the <u>end</u> of verbs or "ist" , "ian" to the end of <u>nouns and verbs</u> making any necessary **spelling changes**.

Employ	Employ**ee**
Li**e**	Li**ar**
Drive	Driv**er**
Act	Act**or**
Art	Art**ist**
Music	Music**ian**

◊ **Nouns** can be formed from **verbs**.

age	Drain	Drain**age**
ence	Refer	Refer**ence**
sis	Analyze	Analy**sis**
al	Propose	Propos**al**
ion	Protect	Protect**ion**
tion	Acclimatize	Acclimatiz**ation**
ance	Hinder	Hind**rance**
ment	Content	Content**ment**
y	Injure	Injur**y**
ation	Investigate	Investig**ation**
sion	Decide	Deci**sion**

◊ **Nouns** can be formed from **adjectives**.

ance	Arrogant	Arrog**ance**
iness	Lonely	Lonel**iness**
cy	Fluent	Fluen**cy**
ity	Familiar	Familiar**ity**
ence	Patient	Pati**ence**
ment	Content	Content**ment**
ion	Desperate	Desperat**ion**
ety	Anxious	Anxi**ety**
y	Honest	Honest**y**

■ ARTICLES

◊ Indefinite article (A / An) & Definite article (The)

■ "A / An"

"A" / "An" is used with <u>singular</u> <u>countable nouns</u> (indefinite nouns) to talk about indefinite persons , things or events.	A black <u>horse</u>. There is **a** <u>man</u> standing at the door. (**Indefinite person**) I didn't have **a** <u>headache</u> for months. (**Indefinite thing**)
To describe someone / something. To mention the type of someone / something.	She is **a** <u>beautiful</u> girl. Singapore is **an** <u>independent</u> city state.
To say what person's <u>job</u> is.	He works as **a** <u>doctor</u>.
"A" / "An" can also be used meaning "per":	He goes to the gym twice **a** (**per**) week.
With money Fractions Weight / measure Whole numbers Price / weight Frequency / time Distance / fuel Distance / speed	A (one) **pound** A (one) **quarter** A (one) **meter** A (one) **thousand** 2€ **a kilo** Two **times a** day 60 **miles a** gallon 60 **km an** hour
"A" / "An" can also be used with "illnesses".	A fever , a cold , a toothache

◊ NOTE:

We can use "**Some**" in the **affirmative** with **plural** <u>countable</u> nouns or <u>uncountable</u> nouns.	There are **some** <u>children</u> at the bus stop. Give me **some** <u>milk</u> please.
We can use "**Any**" in <u>questions</u> and <u>negations</u>.	Are there **any cups** in the cupboard<u>?</u> There is<u>n't</u> **any sugar** left.

■ "The"

"**The**" is used with <u>singular</u> and <u>plural</u> nouns , <u>countable</u> or <u>uncountable</u> ones.

To talk about something <u>specific</u>.	Can I try on **the** <u>blue dress</u> please? (Which dress? The blue one. **Specific**)
When the **noun** is mentioned for a <u>second</u> time.	There is a <u>rat</u> in the kitchen. I killed **the** <u>rat</u> with my boot.
When the **following phrase** or **clause** identifies a <u>particular person</u> or <u>object</u>.	I live in **the** <u>small house</u> with a blue door. ("**Small house**" = object)
When we **talk about things** that are unique.	**The** Universe / **The** Earth , etc
We use "**The**" or <u>no</u> **article** to give a <u>person's title</u> or his / her **unique position**.	He is **the** <u>chairman</u> of a medical company. (**Unique position**)

or
He is **chairman** of a medical company.

◊ **NOTE**:

■ **Plural** , **abstract** and **uncountable** nouns do **not** need **an article** if they are used to **talk about things in general**.

Knowledge is good for everyone.
("**Knowledge**" in general.)

■ To **limit plural** , **abstract** and **uncountable** nouns a **define article** is required.

The knowledge of the English language is important for everyone.

■ "**A**" / "**An**" or "**The**" are used before a **singular** countable nouns when we refer to **a GROUP** of **people** , **animals** or **things**.

A / The **dolphin** lives in the sea.
(We mean **all dolphins**.)

■ "**A / An**" or "**The**" are **never** used **before** a **noun** in the **plural** when they refer to **a GROUP** of **people** , **animals** or **things**.

Dolphin**s** **are** intelligent animal**s**.
(**NOT**: The dolphin**s** **are** intelligent animal**s**.)

■ "**THE**": **Is used before**:

■ **Nouns** which are **unique**.		The Earth , The Acropolis , etc
■ **Names of**:	Cinemas	The Palace , etc
	Hotels	The Hilton , etc
	Theatres	The Rex , etc
	Museums	The British Museum , etc
	Newspapers / Magazines	The New York Times , etc
	Ships	The Santa Maria , etc
	Institutions	The Security Council , etc
	Galleries	The Fox Gallery , etc
■ **Musical instruments & dances**	The ciello , The Salsa , etc	
■ **Names of**:	Families	The Parkers
	Nationalities ending in "sh" , "ch" , or "ese"	The English , The Dutch , The Japanese , etc
■ Other **Plural** Nationalities that are used **with - without "The"**.		(**The**) North Americans , (**The**) Austrians
■ **Titles**		The Patriarch , The King , etc BUT: "The" is omitted before **proper names**: **King Carlos**
■ **Adjectives** used as **nouns** to talk about **groups** of **people**.		The **young** , The **unemployed** , The **homeless** , The **blind** , etc
■ **The words**:	Beach	
	Cinema	
	City	
	Coast	
	Countryside	
	Library	She went to **the library** to return some books.
	River	
	Sky	

		Station Shop Theatre Village Weather , world , etc	
■	The words:	"Morning" , "Afternoon" , "Evening" , "Night" , "Weekend(s)"	I'll be at home late **in the evening**. **BUT**: **At** night , **At** noon , **At** midnight , **By** day , **By** night , **At** 4 o' clock.
■	Historical references events		**The** Russian Revolution **The** Renaissance , **The** Cold War **BUT**: World War II
■	The words:	"Only" , "Last" , "First" used as **adjectives**.	He was **the first** person to arrive.
■	With seasons	"The" is <u>optional</u> with **seasons**. But we always use "**The**" when it is under- stood **which particular season** is.	(The) summer. I am going to Greece in **the summer**. (He / She means **next summer**.)

■ **"THE" : Is omitted before:**

■	Proper nouns		I'll saw **Tom** yesterday.
■	Names of:	Activities Colors Days Drinks Games Holidays Months Sports	I like **fishing**. He likes **blue**. He plays **basketball**.
■	Meals & languages (**Not** followed by the word "language".)	They like **stew potatoes**. We speak **French**.	**BUT**: The <u>latin</u> language is hardly used now.
■	The word "Work"	"**Work**" (= **place** of work) **never** takes "**The**"	She is at **work**.
■	Names of cities Names of streets Names of squares Names of bridges Names of parks Names of stations Names of countries Mountains Lakes Islands Continents	London , etc Carnaby street , etc Trafalgar square , etc Tower bridge , etc Central park , etc Euston station , etc England , etc Olympus , etc Lake Victoria , etc Sicily , etc Asia , etc	**BUT**: **The** Hague ,**The** Vatican City **BUT**: **The** Oxford street , **The** E65 **BUT**: **The** Bridge of sighs , **The** Forth bridge **BUT**: **The** Argentine ,**The** Netherlands , **The** Sudan ,**The** USA
■	Possessive adjectives		That isn't <u>**your**</u> pen.
■	Two - word names:	Whose **first** word name is a **person** or a **place**.	**Eleftherios Venizelos** airport. **BUT**: **The White House**. (Because the first world "**White**" is not the name of a **person** or a **place**.)

■ Names of:	Pubs , restaurants , shops , banks , hotels .	Which have the **same name** of the fo-under and end in: "-**S**" or "-'**S**". **Lloyds** Bank , **Richard's** Bar. **BUT**: **The** Hot Ice Pub.
■ The words:	"Bed" , "Church" , "College" , "Court" , "Hospital" , "Prison" , "School" , "University".	When they are **connected** with the **subject** with a **cause** or **relation**. **John** went **to hospital**. (He was hospitalised **because he was sick**.) **BUT**: His mother went **to the hospital** to see him last week. (She was**n't sick**, but **she went there as a visitor** and afterwards she left.)
■ The words:	"Home" , "Father" , "Mother" when we talk about **our home / parents**.	**Father** is at home.
■ The words:	Flu / **The** flu , Measles / **The** measles , Mumps / **The** mumps	**BUT**: She's got malaria.
■ Means of transportation.	By bus , By car , By plane , By train	She travelled **by bus**. **NOT**: She travelled **by the bus**. **BUT**: She caught **the** 5 o'clock bus.

◊   **NOTE:**

■ When "**Most**" is used as a **determiner** followed by a **noun** does **not** take "**The**".		**Most people** like swimming. **BUT**: Of all European countries , Greece has **the most** ancient monuments.

■ A couple of A few A good number of A great number of	A large number of Both Many Several (of)	are followed by a **countable** noun.
■ A good deal of A great deal of A large amount of A large quantity of	A little A small amount of A small quantity of Much / Too much	are followed by an **uncountable** noun.
■ A lot of Hardly any Lots of	No Plenty of Some	are followed by a **countable** or **uncountable** noun.

14 DETERMINERS / PRONOUNS

■ **The determiners are:**

Demonstratives	"This" / "These" , "That" / "Those"
Possessive adjectives	"My" , "Your" , "His" , etc
Indefinite Pronouns	("Some" , "Any" , "Every" , "No" , "Both" , Each , "Either" , "Neither" , "Enough" , "Several" , "Most" , "All" , etc.)
Numbers	("One" , "Two" , "Three" , etc.)
Indefinite article	"A" / "An" (See chapter 13)
Definite article	"The" (See chapter 13)

◊ **The demonstratives ("This" - "These" / "That" - "Those")**

■ **"This" - "These" are used:**

For people or things **near** us.
This box is yours.

For **present / future** situations.
I'm going out with Ted **this** week.

When the speaker is **in** or **near** the **place** he is referring to.
This house was build in 1856. (The speaker is **near** or **in** the house).

To **introduce** people or to **identify** ourselves on the phone.
"Ann, **this** is Jane."

"That" - "Those" are used:

For people or things **not near** us.
That boy over there is my son.

For **past** situations.
That day **was** the worst of his life.

To refer back to something **that happened** in the **past**.
We **were** living to New York. **That's** fantastic.

When speaking on the **phone** to ask who is the other person.
"Hello this is Alan Smith. Who's **that** please?"

◊ **The possessive adjectives:**

Followed by a **noun**:

My	**Its**
Your	**Our**
His	**Your**
Her	**Their**

■ <u>**Possessive Adjectives**</u> (<u>NOT</u> Objective Personal Pronouns) precede gerunds.

Correct	Incorrect
What do you **think** about <u>**his**</u> buying such an expensive car?	What do you **think** about **him** buying such an expensive car?
He **resents** <u>**your**</u> being more popular than he is.	He **resents** **you** being more popular than he is.

- Other examples with **verbs** like "**Think**" & "**Resent**" include the **verbs** of "**Liking**" & "**Disliking**" :

  "**Appreciate**" , "**Detest**" , "**(Dis)approve of**" , "**(Dis)like**" , "**Enjoy**" , "**Hate**" , "**Love**" , "**Object to**" , etc

- Other examples with **verbs** like "**Think**" & "**Resent**" include also the **verbs** of "**Thinging**":

  "**Forget**" , "**Imagine**" , "**Remember**" , "**Think of**" , etc

◊ **Possessive Case**

- "**S**" (**For people** or **animals**)

Singular noun (The cat**'s** claws , the boy**'s** hat)	(+ '**s**)
Regular plural noun (The tourists**'** passport.)	(+ **'**)
Irregular plural noun **not** ending in "**S**" (The **men's** room , the **children's** playroom.)	(+ '**s**)
Compound noun (His mother-in-law**'s** car.)	(+ '**s**)
After the **last** of **two** or **more** names to show **common possession**. (Ann and Sally**'s** flat.) They share the same flat. (Ann**'s** and Sally**'s** flat.) Each one has got a flat.	(+ '**s**)
After one **name** and a **possessive adjective** to show <u>**common possession**</u>. **Bill's** and **my** car had to be towed last night.	(+ '**s**)

◊ **NOTE**:

Generally, the "apostrophe with **s**" ('**s**) is simply added **to the end** of the <u>compound structure</u>:	<u>My mother-in-**law's**</u> car. <u>A friend of **mine's**</u> team.

- "**Of**" (**For things**)

"**Of**"	(+) <u>thing</u> (+) **abstract noun**	The door **of** the <u>house</u>. The beauty **of** the <u>view</u>.
"**Of**" When there is a **deter miner** (<u>This</u> , <u>Any</u> , <u>A</u> , <u>One</u> , etc) **before** the **noun**.	(+) **possessive case**	Look at <u>**this**</u> **painting of** Picasso**'s**. **or** <u>One</u> **of** Picasso**'s paintings**.

"Of"	(+) Possessive pronouns (+) Personal pronouns	A dress **of hers**. He is one **of them**.
"Of" "Of" / "'S" To talk about **places** or **organizations**.	(+) people (**in longer phrases**)	He is the brother of one **of my friends**. The attractions **of London**. **or** **London's** attractions.

■ <u>Possessive case</u> precedes gerunds.

<table>
<tr><th>Correct</th><th>Incorrect</th></tr>
<tr><td>They objected to the youngest girl'<u>s</u> being given the command position.</td><td>They objected to the youngest girl being given the command position.</td></tr>
</table>

◊ **NOTE**:

■ We can **use** a **possessive case only** to talk about a **person** or a **group of people**. We can **not** use it when we talk about **animals** or **things**.

They objected to **the stolen pets** being **sold out** in bazaars.
NOT:
They objected to **the stolen pets'** being **sold out** in bazaars.

■ We **don't use possessive case** if the **object** is **complex** (**more than one objects**).

I really enjoyed **John and his wife** show**ing** me around.
NOT:
I really enjoyed **John and his wife's** show**ing** me around.

■ **Most of the time** in <u>conversation</u> between <u>native</u> **English speakers** the <u>possessive adjective</u> is **not** used **before gerunds**.

Do you mind **me** ask**ing**?
or
We really appreciate **you** giv**ing** us information.
NOT: We really appreciate <u>**your**</u> giv**ing** us information.

■ We use "The" <u>instead of</u> **possessive adjectives** with <u>**parts of**</u> <u>**the body**</u> <u>after prepositions</u>.

She slapped the boy <u>on</u> the <u>**face**</u>. (**NOT**: <u>On</u> **his** face.)

■ <u>Possessive Adjective</u> + Own

Is used to **emphasize** the fact that **something belongs** to **one person** and **no one else's**.

She's got <u>**her**</u> **own** car.
or
She's got the car **of** <u>**her**</u> **own**.

◊ **The indefinite pronouns**

■ **"All"**

It refers to **two** or **more** <u>people</u>.	**All** student<u>s</u> failed.
It is the **opposite** of "**None of**".	**All** of them failed.
It takes a **verb** in the <u>plural</u>.	**All** of them **have** a lot of money.
It has **positive** meaning and **not negative**.	**All** of them have been promoted.
"**All** + <u>that-clause</u>"(means **the only thing**). It takes a **singular verb**.	**All** <u>that he said **was** not to worry</u>.
To make <u>negative</u> sentences with "**all**" we usually use "**not all**" rather than "**all...not**".	**Not all** the car**s** are safe.
"**None of**" and "**Not all (of)**" have **different** meanings.	<u>NOT</u>: **All** the car**s** are **not** safe.
	Not all of them went to the lecture.
	(**Some** of them went.)
	None of them went to the lecture.
	(**Not one** of them went.)
We usually put "**All**" **after** the verb "**be**" and **after** <u>the first auxi-liary verb</u>.	Next month we **are all** going on holidays.
If there **is no auxiliary** we usually put "**All**" <u>**before** the verb</u>.	We **will all** help this old lady.
We usually need to put "**of**" after "**All**" when they are followed by "<u>**a pronoun**</u>" , "<u>**a determiner**</u>" , or "<u>**possessive form**</u>".	We **all** <u>went</u> out together.
	All of <u>us</u> went to the hospital to visit Ann.

■ **"Both"**

"**Both** + <u>plural</u> noun / <u>personal</u> pronoun"	Pan and Ann **are** singers.
It refers to **two** or **more** people or things.	**Both** Pam & Ann **are** singers.
It is the **opposite** of **neither / not either**.	**Both** of <u>them</u> **are** singers.
It takes a **verb** in the <u>plural</u>.	**Both** girls **are** singers.
It has **positive** meaning.	
We usually need to put "**of**" after "**Both**" when it is **followed** by "<u>**a pronoun**</u>" , "<u>**a determiner**</u>" , or "<u>**possessive form**</u>".	**Both of** <u>us</u> decided to buy this house.

■ **"Whole"**

Is used with **SINGULAR** <u>countable</u> nouns.	A <u>whole</u> house. (= **All** the house)
We always use: ("**A**" , "**The**" , "**This**" , "**My**") + <u>Whole</u> + Counta-ble noun.	
BEFORE: Day / Week / Night / Month / Summer, etc we pre-fer "**All**" rather than "**The whole**".	He studied **all day** without a break.
We can use "**All the**" / "**The whole**" <u>before</u> "**Way**" and "**Time**".	He was sleeping **all the time**.
	He was sleeping **the whole time**.

■ **"Either" / "Neither"**

"**Either**" (**Any one of two**) / "**Neither**" (**Not one and not the oth-er**).	There was a chair on **either** side of the fire-place.
Before a <u>pronoun</u> or a <u>determiner</u> we use "**either of**".	I **don't** like **either of** <u>my</u> grammar teach-er**s**.
The **noun** or **pronoun** after "**Either of**" is <u>plural</u>.	

"Either...or" is used to talk about a **choice between** two **alternatives**.

We must **either go now or stay till** the end.

"Either" after "**NOT**". After mentioning a **negative idea** or **fact**, we can add another **negative point** using "**Not...either**".

Peter is**n't** here. John is **not** here **either**.

"**Neither**": Refers to **TWO** people or things. It is used **before a singular countable** noun.

Neither girl enjoy**s** horror films.

"**Neither of**" / "**Either of** + plural noun / personal pronoun"
"**Neither of**" has **negative** meaning.
It takes a **verb** either in the **singular** or in the **plural**.

I don't like **either of them**.
Are **either of them** at home?
Neither of them is / **are** French.

"**Neither...nor**" "**Either...or...**" "**Not only...but also**"	(+) **singular** or **plural** verb depending on the **subject** which follows "**nor**", "**or**", "**but also**".

Neither Bill **nor John is** willing to help us.
Neither Bill **nor** the girl**s are** willing to help us.
Not only Sue **but also** her friend**s are** willing to help us.

■ "**None**" / "**None of**"

"**None**" refers to **more** than **two people or things**.
It is **not followed by a noun**.
It has **negative** meaning.

"Are there any **mistakes**?"
"No, **none**."

We can use "**None**" (**without following a noun**) if it is **clear from the context** what is meant.

He didn't train hard and as a result he won **none**, so far.

"**None of**"

Is used **before nouns** or **object pronouns** followed by **verb** either in **singular** or in **plural**. It is the **opposite** of "**All**".

None of three girls know(**s**) how to use it.

■ "**No**" / "**Not any (of)**" / "**Not a**"

Are used **before COUNTABLE** or **UNCOUNTABLE** nouns.
"**No**" / "**Not any**" and their compounds (**No one**, **Nothing** / **Not anyone**, **Not anybody**, **Not anything**, etc) are used in **negations**.

I know **no one** at this party.
(I don't know **anyone** at this party.)

No one Nobody Not anybody Not anyone	Indefinite Pronouns used for people.
Not anything Nothing	Indefinite pronouns used for things.
Nowhere	Adverb of place

We **don't** use "**Not a**" / "**Not any of**" in **initial position** in a clause. Instead of this we use "**No**" and "**None of**".

None of the girls play(**s**) violin.
NOT: **Not any of** the girls play(**s**) violin.

- **"Each"**

It is used with **singular** <u>countable</u> nouns.
It means "**one by one**" , **considered individually**.
We also use "**each**" as a **pronoun**.

Each <u>member</u> of the team was given a medal.
Each had to present a different solution for this problem.

"**Each**" has "**of**" constructions.

The General spoke to **each of** the soldiers.

"**Each**" can be used for <u>**TWO things**</u> or **people**.

He was carrying a **suitcase** in **each** <u>hand</u>.

- **"Every"**

It refers to a **group** of people or things and it means:
"**All**" , "**Everyone**" , "**Everything**".
We use "**Every**" when we talk about **three** or **more** <u>things</u> or <u>people</u>.
It is used **before** <u>singular countable</u> nouns.

Every <u>kid</u> <u>is</u> sensitive. (**All** the kids)

We use "**Every**" with: <u>**Almost**</u> , <u>**Nearly**</u> , <u>**Practically**</u> , <u>**Virtually**</u>
to <u>**emphasize**</u> that we are talking about <u>**a group as a whole**</u>.
When we talk about <u>**events**</u> at **regular intervals**: "<u>**Every single**</u>
<u>**day**</u>" , "<u>**Every few weeks**</u>" , "<u>**Every couple of days**</u>" , etc.

<u>**Almost**</u> **every** student should be vaccinated (**A group of student as a whole**.)
He goes climbing <u>**every few weeks**</u>.

"**Every**", and <u>**its compounds**</u> , takes a **verb** in <u>**singular**</u>.

Every worker in the factory **has** been well trained.(**Each member** of the workers.)
<u>**Everything**</u> is OK.

Everybody	Indefinite Pronoun (For people)
Everything	Indefinite Pronoun (For things)
Everywhere	Adverb of place

- **"One" / "Ones"**

Are used to **avoid** repetition of a **countable noun**.

"Which **dress** do you like?"
"This **one**."

- **"A lot of" / "Lots of"**

"**A lot of**" / "**Lots of**" + **countable** or <u>**uncountable**</u> noun.
They are normally used in **positive** sentences.

A lot of children attended the ceremony.
She's got **lots of** <u>furniture</u>.

"**A lot of**" can also be used in **questions** or **negations** in informal English.

Was there **a lot of** disagreement over the proposal**?**

- **"Many" / "Much"**

"**Many**" + **countable noun** / "**Much**" + **uncountable noun**.

They are normally used in **questions** & **negations**.

Are there **many cakes?**
There isn't **much** <u>wine</u>.

"**Many**" & "**Much**"	are often used in **positive** sentences after <u>**so**</u> , <u>**too**</u> & <u>**how**</u>.

Soon she realized <u>**how**</u> **much** money she had spent.

You should eat less; you're eating <u>**too**</u>
much.

If it is clear from the context what is meant, we can use "**Much**" and "**Many**" <u>without a following noun</u>.
We can use "**Much of**" to mean "**a large part of**".
We can use "**Many of**" to mean "**a large number of**".

He did **much** inside the class.

I was sitting in the front row for **much of** the performance.

We can use "**Many**" between "<u>The</u>" or "<u>a possessive pronoun</u>" and "<u>a plural noun</u>".

He is one of <u>**the**</u> **many** other student<u>s</u> who hate this project.
Despite **his** **many** failed effort<u>s</u> he still insists on this project.

We usually need to put "**Of**" after "**Much**" and "**Many**" when they are followed by "<u>a pronoun</u>", "<u>a determiner</u>", or "<u>possessive form</u>".

I' ve lost most of my friends, **many of** <u>whom</u> got married.
Many of John<u>'s</u> friends got married.

We usually use "**Many**" rather than "**A lot of**" or "**Lots of**" with **time expressions (<u>Days</u>, <u>Minutes</u>, <u>Months</u>, <u>Weeks</u>, <u>Years</u> , <u>Hours</u>, etc)** and "**Many + <u>numbers</u> + of**".

He spent **many** <u>**hours**</u> studying.

He spent **many** <u>**hundreds**</u> of Euros.

■   "A few" , "Few" , "Only a few" , "Very few" , "The few"

"A few"	(some , **a small number**)	
"Few"	(some, not many , **almost none**)	
"Only a few"	(**not many , not enough**)	(+) **countable** noun
"Very few"	(**not many , not enough**)	
"The few"	(**not many , not enough**)	

We can use "<u>**The few**</u>" followed by a **noun** to suggest "**Not enough**".

It is one of <u>**the few cars**</u> that have extra equipment.

In comparison we use "**fewer**" with a <u>plural</u> **noun**. The opposite of "**fewer**" is "**more**".

You should eat **fewer bananas**.
You should eat **more bananas**.

We usually need to put "**Of**" after "**Few**" when it is **followed** by "<u>a pronoun</u>", "<u>a determiner</u>", or "<u>possessive form</u>".

Few of <u>us</u> love dancing.
Few of John'<u>s</u> friends are over 25.

■   "A little" , "Little" , "Only a Little" , "Less" , "The little"

"A little"	(some , **a small amount of**)	
"Little"	(**not much , almost none**)	
"Only a little"	(**not much , almost none**)	(+) **uncountable** noun
"Less"	(**not much , almost none**)	
"The little"	(**not much , almost none**)	

We can use "<u>**The little**</u>" followed **by an uncountable noun** to suggest "**not enough**".

I spent <u>**the little**</u> **time** studying history.

In comparison we use "**less**" with **an uncountable noun**.

You should drink **less coffee**.

The opposite of "**less**" is "**more**"

You should drink **more coffee**.

We usually need to put "**Of**" after "**little**" when it is **followed** by "<u>a pronoun</u>", "<u>a determiner</u>", or "<u>possessive form</u>".

She looks **little of** <u>her</u> mother.

When we talk about: "<u>**A period of time**</u>" , "<u>**A distance**</u>" , "<u>**A sum of money**</u>" we use "**Less than**" <u>**NOT**</u> "**Fewer than**".

I intend to finish my job in **less than four hours**.

- **"Some"**

| It is used before **countable** or <u>uncountable</u> nouns. | I'll buy **some apples**. He gave me so-me <u>money</u>. |

| **"Some"** <u>and its compounds</u> (Somebody , Someone , Something , Somewhere) are normally used in **positive** sentences.
They can also be used in **questions** when we want to make: **an** <u>offer</u> , <u>a request</u> , or **when we** <u>expect</u> a <u>positive</u> answer. | There is <u>some</u>one at the door.

Would you like **some**thing to eat?
Could I have **some**thing to drink? |

Someone Somebody	Indefinite Pronouns (People)
Something	Indefinite Pronoun (Thing)
Somewhere	Adverb (Place)

Is there <u>some</u>one waiting for me?
(**I expect there is someone.**)
BUT:
Is there <u>any</u>one waiting for me?
(I'm asking **general**.)
I've left the book **some**where.

- **"Any"**

| It is used before **countable** or <u>uncountable</u> nouns. | Is there **any** <u>sugar</u>? |

| **"Any"** <u>and its compounds</u> (Anyone , Anybody , Anything , Any-where are **normally** used in **questions**. | Is there **any**one waiting for me? |

Anyone Anybody	Indefinite Pronouns (People)
Anything	Indefinite Pronoun (Thing)
Anywhere	Adverb (Place)

I can't see **any**thing weird in this place.

You can find this food **any**where.

| These compounds can be used in **positive** sentences.
They can also be used in **positive** sentences after "**If**". | You can go **anywhere** you want.

If anything is broken , I will hold you re-sponsible. |

| **"Any"** and **its compounds** are used with <u>negative words</u>: Hard-<u>ly</u> , <u>Never</u> , <u>Without</u> , <u>Seldom</u> , <u>Rarely</u> , etc. | I **never** go **anywhere** alone at night.
(**NOT**: I **never** go <u>no</u>where alone.) |

- **"Ever"**

It can be added to certain **question words** to mean "**Any**".
These words are:

	Whoever	(**any** one who)
	What(so)ever	(**any**thing that)
	Whichever	(**any** of)
	Whenever	(**any** time that)
	Wherever	(**any** place that)
	However	(In **any** way that)

You can come **whenever** you like.
(**Any** time you like.)

- **"Else"**

"Else" (Means: "**more**" , "**different**"). Is followed by a **singular verb**.

It can be used with **indefinite pronouns**: (Everyone, Nobody , etc) and **adverbs of place**: (Anywhere , Somewhere , etc)	**Nobody else** know**s** him better than her.
It can also be used with: <u>Who</u> , <u>What</u> , <u>Where</u> , <u>How</u>. "Else" forms its **possessive case** with " **'s**". "**Or else**" (means "**otherwise**")	<u>What</u> **else** can be done to prevent crime? Don't use my pen. Take someone **else's** Get an umbrella **or else** you'll get wet.

- **"Several"**

We can use "<u>Several</u>" followed by a **countable noun** to suggest "**Some**".	There are <u>**several**</u> **houses** available.
It is the opposite of "**A lot of**" , "**Many**". It takes **verb** in the **plural**.	There are **several children** who **play** basketball in the school.
We usually need to put "**Of**" after "**Several**" when it is **followed** by "<u>a pronoun</u>" , "<u>a determiner</u>" , or "<u>possessive form</u>".	**Several of us** love dancing. **Several of** John'**s** friends are over 25.

◊ **NOTE: The indefinite pronouns**

A few / A little All Any Both Many / Much Most One , Two , etc Several / Some	Are **followed** by "<u>Of</u>" and words such as: <u>This</u> , <u>That</u> , <u>These</u> , <u>Those</u> , <u>The</u> , <u>A</u>	How **much** <u>**of**</u> <u>**the**</u> money I gave you did you spend?
	Are **followed** by "**Of** " when a <u>noun</u> follows preceded by <u>possessives</u>-<u>other words</u>.	I liked the **two of** <u>**her**</u> <u>books</u>. I bought **several of** <u>**these**</u> <u>miniatures</u>.

◊ **NOTE:**

- We use **singular verb** with: ("Any of" , "None of" , "The majority of" , "A lot of" , "Plenty of" , "Some" , "Some of" , "All", "All of") + an <u>UNCOUNTABLE</u> noun.

All of the <u>money</u> **has** now been spent.   **None of** the <u>luggage</u> **is** very heavy.

- We use **singular verb** with: ("Every" , "Each") + a <u>singular</u> noun.

Every <u>success</u> **is** unique.   **Each** <u>boy</u> **has** his own character.

- We use <u>singular</u> verb with: "One of" + **plural noun / pronoun**.

One of these cars <u>is</u> 4X4   There are four vacuum cleaners in the hotel. **One of them** come<u>s</u> from China.

■ **The pronouns are:**

◊ **The subjective personal pronouns:**

Before verbs as **subjects**.

I	It
You	We
He	You
She	They

◊ **The objective personal pronouns:**

After verbs as **objects**.

Me	It
You	Us
Him	You
Her	Them

◊ **The possessive personal pronouns:**

NOT followed by a noun

Mine	----
Yours	Ours
His	Yours
Hers	Theirs

The demonstrative pronouns:

This	These
That	Those

◊ **The interrogative pronouns:**

Who	Which
Whom	What
Whose	

The relative pronouns:

Who	Which
Whom	What
Whose	

(And also: **Whoever** , **Whomever**
Whichever , **Whatever**)

◊ **The reflexive pronouns:**

Myself , **Yourself** , **Himself** , **Herself** , **Itself** , **Ourselves** , **Yourselves** , **Themselves**.

When the **subject** and the **object** of a sentence **refer to the same person** or **thing**, we use a **reflexive pronoun** rather than a **personal pronoun**.

Did **you** sleep **yourself?**

■ **Reflexive Pronouns** are used:

After certain verbs: (**Behave** , **Burn** , **Cut** , **Enjoy** , **Hurt** , **Kill** , , **Look** , etc) when the **subject** and the **object** of the **verb** are the **same**.

Did you **cut yourself?**

They can also be used **after**: (**Be** , **Feel** , **Look** , **Seem** , etc) to describe **emotions** or **states**.

She hasn't **been herself** recently. (**State**)

Reflexive pronouns can be used after **prepositions** but **not** after **prepositions of place**.

She is very pleased **with herself**.
She looked **behind** her.
(**NOT**: She looked **behind** herself.)

Certain Verbs: (**Wash** , **Shave** , **Dress** , **Undress** , **Meet** , Rest , **Relax** , **Stand up** , **Get up** , **Sit down** , **Wake up** , etc) do **not** take **reflexive pronoun**.

She **woke** up and **dressed**.

(**NOT**: She **woke** up herself and **dressed** herself.)

Reflexive Pronouns also mean **without help**.

He painted his house **himself**.
(**Without help**.)

- **"Wash" and "Dress"**
  Can be used with a **reflexive pronoun** to talk about **young children** or **animals**.

  The **little girl** is washing **herself**.

- **Verbs + Reflexive Pronouns**

  Some verbs, which commonly used with <u>**reflexive pronouns**</u>, can have **different meanings** when they are used with <u>personal pronouns</u>.

Compose <u>herself</u>.	**Calm** herself.
...when <u>she</u> **composed** it.	...when <u>she</u> **produced** it.
...and **distinguished** <u>themselves</u>.	**Did something so well** that they was admired.
...to **distinguish** <u>them</u>.	**Show the difference** between them.
Explain <u>myself</u> to somebody.	**Give reasons** for my behavior to sb.
He **explained** <u>it</u> very clearly.	He **explicated** <u>it</u> very clearly.

- <u>**Verbs**</u> **+ Reflexive Pronouns +** <u>**Preposition**</u>

  A few verbs are often used with a **reflexive pronoun** followed by a **particular preposition**:

  Acclimatize...**to** , **Avail**...**of** , **Brace**...**for** , **Busy**...**with** , **Console**...**with** , **Content**...**with** , **Distance**...**from** , **Established** ...**as** , **Familiarize**...**with** , **Impose**...**on** , **Occupy**...**with** , **Organize**...**into** , **Pride**...**on** , **Tear**...**away from**

  I can't <u>**acclimatize**</u> **myself** <u>to</u> new working conditions.

- With **verbs** followed by <u>**direct object**</u> **+ preposition +** <u>indirect object</u> we usually use a **personal pronoun** **NOT** a **reflexive pronoun**, as <u>indirect object</u>.

  John will not keep this <u>**jacket**</u> **for** <u>him</u>.
  NOT:
  John will not keep this <u>**jacket**</u> **for** <u>himself</u>.

- If we **need to make it clear** that the <u>**subject**</u> and the <u>indirect object</u> refer to the **same person** we use a **reflexive pronoun**.

  <u>**Penny**</u> will not buy a **bike** for <u>her</u>. ("**Her**" could be either Penny or someone else.)
  <u>**Penny**</u> will not buy a **bike** for <u>herself</u>. ("**Herself**" = Penny)

- **Note this idioms**:

Enjoy yourselves!	**Have a good time!**
Behave yourself!	**Be good!**
He likes being himself.	**He likes being alone.**
By myself , By yourself , etc	**On my own , on your own , etc**
Help yourself to tea.	**You're welcome to take some tea if you want.**
Do it yourself.	**Do it without being helped.**
Make yourself at home!	**Feel comfortable.**
Make yourself at heard.	**Speak loudly to be heard by others.**
Make yourself understood.	**Make your meaning clear.**

◊ **The intensive pronouns** for **emphatic structures**:

They have the **same form** as a **reflexive** pronoun but **different meaning**. They **give emphasis** to the **noun** or **the fact that** a certain person **performs an action**.

She **herself** organizes the **feast**.

◊ **NOTE: Compare** "Verbs + Reflexive Pronoun" with "Verbs + Each other / One another".

John and **Penny** blamed **themselves** when their house was robbed.
(They say it was the fault of **both of them**.)
John and **Penny** blamed **each other** / **one another** when their house was robbed.
(John said it was Penny's fault , and Penny said it was John's fault.)

◊ **NOTE**:

■ With **some verbs** we **have to** use the **preposition "With"** before **"Each other"** / **"One another"**

(Dis)agree , Argue , Coincide , Compete , Cooperate , Get along , Get on , Live , Play , Work.

Look! Those two babies **playing with each other**.

■ **After verbs**: "Embrace" , "Fight" , "Hug" , "Kiss" , "Marry" we **can omit** "Each other" , "One another".

Two friends **hugged** (each other / one another) when they met.

■ For **emphasis** we **can separate** "Each" and "Other".

When the earthquake started, they **each** helped the **other**.

■ **NOTE**: "Other" structures

The others	The rest	These books are Tom's; **the others** are mine.
Others	**Several more** apart from those **already mentioned**.	Someome believe it is unhealthy not to eat meat while **others** believe that it is much better for our health.
Each other	One another	Good friends always help **each other**.
Every other	Alternate	I go jogging **every other** day.
The other day	A few days **ago**.	I bumped into George **the other day** , he looked well.
The other one(s)	**Not** this / these but **something else**.	These shoes are too small. Can I try **the other ones** , please?
Another	**One more** apart from those already mentioned. **Another** can also be used with expressions of **distance, money , and time**.	Can you give me **another** cup of coffee please? It'll cost me **another 5$** to buy it.

15   IT & THERE

◊   "IT"

■   The **introductory** "It" as **subject** is used to talk about:

Weather	**It's freezing** today , isn't it?
Time	**It's two** o'clock.
Distance	**It's** almost **2 miles** far from here.
Describe various situations	Don't drink the milk. **It smells** terrible.
To give an opinion followed by to-infinitive	**It** will be **great to go** on holiday.
To give an opinion about a place	**It's very cold room**.

■   As an **alternative** to:

"That"	**It was** a misfortune **that** the contest w-as cancelled. (**That** the contest was cancelled **was** a misfortune.)
"Wh"	**It is** obvious **why** this project failed. (**Why** the this project failed **is** obvious.)
"ing"	**It's** awful driv**ing** in this dusty road. (Driv**ing** in this dusty road **is** awful.)
"To-infinitive"	**It will** be great **to go** on holiday. (**To go** on holiday **will** be great.)

◊   NOTE:

In <u>writing</u>, we **don't** usually use the introductory "It" as an **alter-native** to a **noun** as <u>subject</u>:	The small <u>village</u> **was** the most beau-tiful. **NOT**: **It was** the most beautiful , the small <u>vil-lage</u>.
This is **common** in **in**formal speech in order to **explain** someone's statement.	I think it will cost you a fortune , but **it is the best choice** , to buy a new <u>house</u>.

◊   "IT" as subject

■   "It + be + adjective / noun"

It is good for me.
It is three o'clock.

■   It + verb + to-infinitive clause

With verbs such: "Help" , "Hurt" , "Pay" , etc	**It** will **help to find** the solution.

■   It + verb + <u>object</u> + <u>to</u>-infinitive clause

With verbs of EMOTIONS: "Amaze" , "Annoy" , "Frighten" , "Hurt" , "Shock" , "Surprise" , "Upset" , "Worry" , etc	**It frightened <u>me</u> to** see him injured.

■ **It + verb + <u>that</u> clause**

With the verbs: "Appear" , "Come about" , "Emerge" , "Follow"
, "Look" , "Seem" , "Transpire" , "Turn out" , etc

It appears <u>that</u> they are rich.

■ **It + verb + <u>object</u> + <u>that</u> clause**

With the verbs: "Down on" , "Hit" , "Strike" , etc

It strikes <u>me</u> <u>that</u> she is poor.

◊ **NOTE: Passive formal patterns: "It + passive verb + <u>that clause</u> / <u>wh-clause</u>"**

■ **It + be + passive verb + <u>that clause</u>**

Verbs: "Agree" , "Allege" , "Announce" , "Assume" , "Believe" ,
"Calculate" , "Claim" , "Consider" , "Decide" , "Demonstrate"
, "Discover" , "Establish" , "Estimate" , "Expect" , "Feel" , "F-
ind" , "Hope" , "Intend" , "Know" , "Mention" , "Plan" , "Propo-
se" , "Recommend" , "Reveal" , "Say" , "Show" , "Suggest" ,
"Suppose" , "Think" , "Understand" , etc

It is said <u>that</u> the oil price will increase.

or less formally

They said <u>that</u> the oil price is going to increase.

■ **It + be + passive verb + <u>wh-clause</u>**

With the verbs: "Discover" , "Establish" , "Explain" , "Find" ,
"Know" , "Reveal" , "Show".

It was discovered <u>why</u> these species disappeared.

or less formally

They discovered <u>why</u> these species disappeared.

◊ **"IT" as object**

■ The introductory **"It"** as **object** is used with a **number of patterns**:

■ **Verb + It + <u>that clause</u> / <u>if clause</u> / <u>wh-clause</u>**

With verbs of EMOTIONS: "Can't bear" , "Can't stand" , "Hate"
, "Like" , "Love" , "Resent" , etc

I **can't stand it** <u>if you give up your job.</u>

I **hated it** <u>when</u> I saw that it was fake.

■ **Verb + It + <u>adjective</u> + <u>that clause</u> / <u>wh-clause</u> / <u>to-infinitive clause</u>**

Verbs: "Believe" , "Consider" , "Feel" , "Find" , "Make" , "Think"
, etc

He found it <u>weird</u> <u>that</u> she didn't pay the bill.

■ **Verb + It + <u>as</u> + <u>adjective</u> + <u>that clause</u> / <u>if-clause</u> / <u>when clause</u>**

Verbs: "Accept" , "Regard" , "See" , "Take" , "View" , etc

I see it <u>as</u> <u>obligatory</u> <u>that</u> they should join the club.

■ **"Would appreciate" + It + <u>if clause</u>**

I **would appreciate it** <u>if you sent me fur-ther details about the project.</u>

■ **"Leave" / "Owe" + It + <u>to-somebody</u> + <u>to-infinitive</u>**

I think we should **leave it <u>to Jane</u> to decide** whether to go or not.

◊ **"THERE"**

We can use "There" with a <u>definite noun</u> when we treat **information** as **already familiar** to the **listener** or **reader**.

I won't buy this house. **There is** <u>the building</u> beside this one which is derelict. (The **listener knows** about building beside the house.)

■ We also use **"There"** as a **dummy subject** with the verb **"be"** followed by a **noun phrase**:

To **introduce** a **new topic**.
With **numbers** or **quantities**.
To say **where** is **someone / something**.
With an **indefinite pronoun** or expressions of **quantity** and the **to-infinitive**.
With an **indefinite pronoun** or expressions of **quantity** and an "**-ing**" verb.
If we want to show the <u>subject</u> of the **to-infinitive** we use "**for**".

There is a **meeting** this evening.
There was **a lot of people** last night.
There are some things **under the table**.
There is **nothing** good **to watch** on television.
There is **someone** wait**ing** to see you.

There is a lot of work **for <u>you</u> to do**.

◊ **NOTE: "There + be"**

"There + be" is used to <u>introduce new information</u> **for first time**, saying that **someone** or **something exists**.

There are <u>some letters</u> for you on your desk.

Because we use **"There"** to **introduce** <u>topics</u> the noun after **"There + be"** often has an **indefinite meaning** so we **often** use: "<u>**A / An**</u>", "<u>**Any + noun**</u>", "<u>**Anyone + noun**</u>", "<u>**Some(thing)**</u>", "<u>**No(body)**</u>"

There is <u>a difficult problem</u> for all of us.
NOT:
There is <u>the difficult problem</u> for all of us.

■ **"There + be"** is often **followed** by:

<u>Noun</u> + <u>that clause</u> / <u>wh-clause</u> / <u>ing</u> / <u>to-infinitive</u> clause.

There is a chance <u>that</u> we should not <u>ignore</u>.

There are questions <u>why</u> they gave <u>up school</u>.

■ **There + be + Bound / Certain / (Un)likely / Supposed / Sure + to be.**

There is bound <u>to be</u> a great success.
There is certain <u>to be</u> wrong again.
There is supposed <u>to be</u> a new parking place.

■ **"There + auxiliary / modal verb + be"**

There will be a seat for everyone.
There must be a restaurant with traditional food.

■ **"There + seem / appear + <u>to be</u>"**

There seems <u>to be</u> a good place for jogging.
There appears <u>to be</u> an easy way.

■ **"There + be + <u>passive reporting verb</u> + <u>to be</u>"**

With the verbs: "**Estimate**", "**Expect**", "**Find**", "**Reckon**", "**Report**", "**Say**", "**Think**".

There is <u>estimated</u> <u>to be</u> an excellent investment.

■ "**Verb + there + <u>to be</u>**"

I couldn't **imagine there <u>to be</u>** so many people who can help me.

◊ **NOTE:**

■ "**There + Arise / Emerge / Exist / Follow / Remain / Take place**".

During WWII **there existed** military c-amps.

◊ **NOTE:**

If the **noun** after "**There**" is <u>singular</u> or <u>uncountable</u> the verb is <u>singular</u>.	**There <u>is</u>** a <u>**student**</u> who stud<u>ies</u> Fren-ch.
If the **noun** is <u>plural</u>, the **verb** is usually <u>plural</u> (Although "**Ther-e's**" is often use <u>in</u>formal speech.)	**There <u>are</u>** many student<u>s</u> who **study** history. **There'<u>s</u>** many student<u>s</u> who **study** his-tory. (**Informal**)
If a **noun** phrase **after** "**There**" consists of two or more **nouns** in a list we use a <u>singular</u> verb if the **first** noun is <u>singular</u> , and a <u>plural</u> verb if the **first** noun is <u>plural</u>.	**There <u>is</u>** a <u>**car**</u> and two bicycle<u>s</u> near the station. **There <u>are</u>** pencil<u>s</u> and a **notepad** in my bag.

◊ **Expressions** with "**It's no**" and "**There's no**"

It's no accident that	There's no alternative but to
It's no bad thing to	There's no chance of / no hope of + ing
It's no coincidence that	There's no choice but to
It's no doubt the case that	There's no denying that
It's no doubt true that	There's no doubt / no chance that
It's no good + ing	There's no harm in + ing
It's no longer necessary to	There's no need to
It's no secret that	There's no point in + ing
It's no surprise that	There's no question of + ing
It's no use + ing	There's no reason to

16   QUESTIONS & SHORT ANSWERS / SO+AUXILIARY+SUBJECT / BUT

◊   **QUESTIONS**

■   **Yes / No questions**

To form "**Yes**" / "**No**" questions we put the verb <u>**to be**</u> , the <u>**auxiliary**</u> verb or the <u>**modal**</u> verb **before** the **subject**.	He <u>**is**</u> watching T.V **<u>Is</u> he** watching T.V.?
With other verbs we form "**Yes**" / "**No**" questions with "**Do**"/ "**Does**" (**Present simple**) or "**Did**" (**Past Simple**).	He likes pizza. **<u>Does</u> he** like pizza?

■   **"Wh" / "How" questions**

Begin with a **question word**:

(**Who** , **What** , **Where** , **Why** , **When** , **Whose** , **Which** & **How**) We put the <u>**auxiliary**</u> or <u>**modal**</u> verb **before** the **subject**.	**How** old <u>**is**</u> he? **What** kind of work <u>**do**</u> **you** do? **When** <u>**will**</u> **you** come back again? **Why** <u>**must**</u> **they** go? **Why** <u>**are**</u> **you** so angry?
When there is a <u>**preposition**</u> , it usually goes at the **end** of the question.	**Who was he** accused <u>**by**</u>? (**More usual**)
In **formal** English it can be put **before** the <u>**question**</u> word.	<u>**By**</u> **whom was he** accused? (**Formal English**)
Questions are used to ask for **information** or **permission**.	**How** far <u>**is**</u> the **station**? (**Information**) **May I** go out? (**Permission**)

They also used to make:	**Suggestions** **Requests** **Offers** **Invitations**	**Shall we** play tennis? **Could you** help me with the dishes? **Would you** like some more coffee? **Would you** like to come to the beach with me?

◊   **NOTE: Subject / Object questions**

■ When "**Which**" , "**What**" , "**Who**" , "**Whose**" or "**Why**" refers to the <u>**subject**</u> of the sentence, the **question word** comes **before** the **verb without** the use of the auxiliary "**Do**".	**Which** <u>**train**</u> arrived first? The 6.15 from London or the 7.30 from Oxford? **Who** <u>**won**</u> the contest? George won the contest. **John** hit William. **Who** (**John**) hit William? (**NOT**: Who did hit William?) **Why** <u>**people**</u> hate him?
■ When the **question word** is the <u>**object**</u> of the sentence, we **have** to use the auxiliary "**Do**".	<u>**Which**</u> **car do** you like more? The blue one. John hit **William**. <u>**Whom**</u> (**William**) **did** John hit?

■ **We normally** use the following **question words** to ask about:

People	Things / Animals	Place
Who	What	Where
Whose (possession)	Which (of)	
Which (of)		
What		

Time	Quantity	Manner / Reason
How long / How often	How much	How / Why
What time	How many	
When		

■ "Which": Is used when there is a **limited choice**.

It can also be used with the <u>comparative</u> and the <u>superlative</u> **degree**.

Which is your favorite movie star **Meryl Streep** or **Demi Moore**?
Which is <u>more</u> comfortable , a bicycle or a motorcycle?
Which is <u>the quickest</u> rout to Athens?

■ "What": Is used when there is a **unlimited choice**.

It can also be used in the following patterns:

What do / does...look like?
What is ... **like**?
What for?
What color?
What size?
What kind?
What short?
What time?

What kind of <u>music</u> **do** you like?

What does Ann **look like**?
What is your new teacher **like**?

What color are his eyes**?**

■ "What" and "Which" are sometimes both possible.

Which / What fruit **does** he like eating?

■ "How come": Is used to ask about the **reason** for something.

How come <u>you are</u> so late?
<u>NOT</u> :
How come <u>are you</u> so late?

■ "How about": Is used to make **suggestions** or to **offer** something. It is also used when asking for **information** or an **opinion** on something.

How about a cup of tea?
(Suggestion)
How about your job?
(Information)

■ **Negative Questions**

They are formed with "**Not**" but there is a **difference** in **word order**.

Auxiliary + <u>n't</u> + <u>subject</u> + verb (**short form**)
Auxiliary + <u>subject</u> + <u>not</u> + verb (**full form**)

Has<u>n't</u> <u>she</u> called you yet?
Has <u>she</u> not called you yet?

Negative questions are used to express:

Surprise	**Didn't you** know that she was my Mum?
Annoyance or sarcasm	**Can't you** be more patient?
A wish to persuade someone	**Won't you** tell me who is she?
Expectation of a "Yes" - answer	**Don't you** know that she was promoted?

◊ **Question tags**

The **question tags** are **short questions** added to the **end of the statement** to ask for **confirmation of** or **agreement with** the **statement**. They are formed with the **auxiliary** verb and the appropriate **personal pronoun**. They take the **same auxiliary verb as in statement**, if there is one, **otherwise** they take "**Do**" / "**Does**".

A **positive** statement is followed by **negative** question tag.	She speaks French, **doesn't** she? He **is** rich, **isn't** he?
A **negative** statement is followed by a **positive** question tag.	He **didn't** like it, **did** he? She **isn't** poor, **is** she?

■

Statement	Question tag	
"I am"	"Aren't I ?"	I **am** older than you , **aren't I?**
"I used to"	"didn't I?"	He **used to** go to school with you , **didn't he?**
Imperative	Will you? / Won't you? / Can you ? / Could you?	**Phone** me later, **will you? / won't you / can you? / could you?**
"Don't" (Negative imperative)	"Will you?"	**Don't** come round so late again , **will you?**
"Let's"	"Shall we?"	**Let's** go home now , **shall we?**
"Let <u>me</u> / <u>him</u> / <u>her</u>"	"Will <u>you</u> / Won't <u>you</u> ?"	**Let <u>her</u>** decide for herself , **will <u>you</u>? / won't <u>you</u>?**
"I have" / "I had" (Possess)	"Haven't I ?" / "Hadn't I ?"	She **has got** her own office , **hasn't she?**
"I have" / "I had" (Idiomatic)	"Don't I ?" / "Didn't I ?"	We **had** a great time , **didn't we?**
"There is / There are"	"Isn't there / Aren't there ?"	**There is** a book for me , **isn't there?**
"This is / That is"	"Isn't it ?"	**That's** your car over there , **isn't it?**

The **question tags** can be said with a **rising intonation** when we are <u>not</u> **sure** and **we expect** an answer or with a **failing intonation** when **we are sure** and **don't really expect** an answer.

They are going to New York , <u>**aren't they**</u>? (**We are not sure**.)	He caused the accident , **didn't he?** (**We are sure**.)

■ **Question tags** can also be **Affirmative - Affirmative**.

If said with a **rising intonation**, we ask for **more information**.	She is seeing John , **Is she?** (**Ask for information**.)
If said with a **failing intonation**, we express **negative feelings** such as **disappointment** or **disapproval**. We **don't expect an answer**.	I'll be **punished** , **will I ?** (**Negative feeling / disappointment.** **We do not expect something else**.)

◊ **Echo tags**

The **echo tags** are **response** to **affirmative** or **negative** sentences. They are used in everyday speech to **ask for more information** or to show **anger** , **concern** , **confirmation** , **interest** , **surprise** , etc.

Affirmative:	He quit his job. **He did** , did<u>n't</u> he? (**Confirmation**)
Negative:	He has**n't** called. **He hasn't** , **has she?** (**Confirmation**)

◊ **SHORT ANSWERS**

The **short answers** are used to **avoid repetition** of the **question asked before**.

The **positive** short answers are formed with: "Yes + <u>personal pronoun</u> + auxiliary verb". ("**Do**" , "**Did**" , "**Can**" , "**Have**" , "**Had**" , "**Will**")	"**Can** she do it?" **Yes**, <u>she</u> can.
The **negative** short answers are formed with: "No + <u>personal pronoun</u> + negative auxiliary verb. ("**Don't**" , "**Didn't**" , "**Can't**" , "**Haven't**" , "**Hadn't**" , "**Won't**")	"**Did** he mention anything?" **No**, <u>he</u> didn't.

◊ **NOTE:**

■ **"One" / "Ones"**

We use **"One" / "Ones"** to talk about a <u>specific</u> item.	Do you want to buy **a new car**. I can suggest you **one**.
After **"The"**, **unless** it is **followed** by an **adjective**.	Is this your car? No **the** other **one** is mine.
After a <u>possessive adjective</u>. We prefer a **possessive pronoun** or a **phrase with an** <u>adjective</u>.	You can take <u>my</u> <u>new</u> one. You can take **mine**. (**Rather than**: You can take **my one** / **informal** speech , **without adjective**).

■ **NOTE: We do NOT usually use "One" , "Ones"**

To **replace** an <u>uncountable</u> noun instead of **"One" / "Ones"** we use **"Some"**.	Don't worry! I will not leave all the <u>luggage</u> here. I may leave **some**. (**NOT**: leave **one**)

■ **NOTE : We can either include or leave out "One" / "Ones"**

After: **"Which"** , **"Whichever"** , **"Superlatives"**.	I can't decide whether to buy a big or a small camera. You can buy **whichever (one)** you want. I will buy this new laptop. It is **the best** / **the best one**.
After: **"Neither"** , **"Either"** , **"Another"** , **"Each"** (**But not** after **"Every"**).	There are ten books left. **Each (one)** costs ten Euros.

After: "The first / second / last" , "The other" , "This" , "That" , "These" , "Those".	I had visited two places. **The first** (one) was the best.
"These one" and **"Those one"** are only used in **in**formal speech.	Which shoes did she like? She liked **those ones**. (**In**formal) She liked **those**. (**Better**)
After: **color** adjectives.	I have to give back this jacket and buy the **blue** (**one**).

◊ **"SO + AUXILIARY + SUBJECT"**

■ **"So + auxiliary + subject"** , **"Neither / Nor"**

■ **In general**

We use "So"and "Neither / Nor" to indicate <u>similarity</u> between or among **people** or **things**.	I have a **red Ferrari. So** has **Jane**. The **green car** is ugly. **So** is the **yellow one**. The **girls** are wearing blue. **So** is **Kate**. **Mike** isn't very smart. **Neither / Nor** is **Joe**.
■ If we use the <u>present simple</u> or <u>past simple</u> tense forms of most **verbs** in the **first sentence**, we follow **"So"** or **"Neither / "Nor"** by the <u>appropriate form</u> of <u>"DO"</u>.	Max <u>swims</u> everyday.**So** <u>do</u> the other boys. Steve **esca**p<u>ed</u> from prison. **So** <u>did</u> Mark. Mike <u>doesn't</u> play soccer. **Neither / Nor** <u>does</u> John. You <u>didn't</u> eat the last piece of cake, and **neither / nor** <u>did</u> I.
■ If we use a <u>MODAL</u> in the first sentence , we use the <u>Affirmative Form</u> of the **same modal verb** after **"So"** or **"Neither / Nor."**	Joe <u>can</u> swim. **So** <u>can</u> Mary. Sam **wo**n't go. **Neither / Nor** <u>will</u> Max. Mary <u>should</u> study more. **So** <u>should</u> Joe. Jim **couldn**'t lift the box. **Neither / Nor** <u>could</u> Jack.
■ If we use a **perfect** expression (<u>Have + past participle</u>) in the **first sentence**, we follow **"So"** or **"Neither / Nor"** by the appropriate form of "<u>Have</u>" or "<u>Modal + Have</u>".	Bill <u>has eaten</u> too much.**So** <u>has</u> Tom. John **has**n't finished his meal. **Neither / Nor** <u>has</u> Jane. Bill <u>may have eaten</u> too much. **So** <u>may have</u> Mary.

◊ **NOTE**:

We **can** use **"So"** instead of a **clause** <u>after</u> certain **verbs** to do with **OPINION**: **"Be afraid"** , **"Appear"** , **"Assume"** , **"Believe"**, **"Expect"** , **"Guess"** , **"Hope"** , **"Imagine"** , **"Presume"** , **"Say"**, **"Seem"** , **"Suppose"** , **"Suspect"** , **"Tell"** , **"Think"**.	He will pass the exams. He **expects so**. (Instead of: He **expects to pass**...) Do you believe she will win the race? I **imagine so**. (Instead of: I **imagine that she will win**...)
<u>Some verbs</u> are commonly used **before "Not"** or in **"Not...so"** in **short negative replies**.	Jim: I think Tom won't buy this watch if it isn't waterproof. John: I <u>suppose</u> not. / I **do not** <u>suppose</u> so.
Before "Not" we can use: verbs to do with **OPINION**: **"Be afraid"** , **"Assume"** , **"Guess"** , **"Hope"** , **"Presume"** , **"Suspect"** , etc	Did you remember to buy a ticket? **I am afraid not**.

With **verbs** to do with **OPINION**: "Believe" , "Expect" , "Imagine" , "Think" we **prefer** "Not...so" in **informal contexts**.	Do you **believe** she will win the race? I **don't believe so**. (Informal)

◊ **NOTE**

We can use "So + <u>pronoun</u> + auxiliary verb" in a **short answer** to say that **we can see** that **something** is **true now that it has been told**, particularly if it **surprises** (<u>!</u>) us.	Look! I saw many used cars on this w- eb site. I think there is something good for you John. **So** <u>it</u> **does!** (John answered. He did <u>not</u> **know** about the cars before.) Look! I saw many used cars on this w- eb site. I think there is something good for you John. **Yes,** <u>it</u> **does**. I know Paul, Peter told me yesterday. (**NOT**: **So** <u>it</u> **does!** John knew about it. Peter had told him about.)
We **can** also use "So" implying: "<u>I knew before you told me</u>" , in **short answers** with **verbs** such as: "**Appear**" , "**Believe**" , "**Gather**" , "**Hear**" , "**Say**" , "**Seem**" , "**Tell**" , "**Understand**".	The competition has lasted two hours. **So** I have **heard**. (**Short answer**)
We can also use "So + auxiliary verb + <u>subject</u>" to say that a se- cond person does or will do the **same thing** as the **person already mentioned**.	I **will** see Ann tomorrow. **So will** <u>I</u>
In **the negative** we use: "**Neither**" , "**Nor**" or "**Not**...either".	John is **not** a trained player. **Neither** <u>is</u> **Paul** / **Nor** <u>is</u> **Paul** / **Paul** <u>is</u> **not either**. or **Paul is not** a trained player **either**.

■ **NOTE**: "Do so"

We can use "**Do so**" to **replace** a **verb**, and the **word** or **phrase** that **follows it** so as to complete the meaning.	He asked me whether Paul and Mary didn't **sell their old house**. I told him that they had no intention to **do so**. ("to **do so**" = to **sell their old house**.)
We can use "**Do so**" where the **verb** describes **an action**, but we **avoid** it with **verbs** that **describe** <u>states</u> and <u>habitual actions</u>.	I will **go jogging** on Sunday and I think I will meet many friends while **doing so**. (**Action**.) Many students don't like <u>studying</u> on **weekends**. But I **do**. (**State**) **NOT**: "But I **do so**"
"**Do so**" is mainly used in **formal** contexts. **Less formally** we can use: "**Do it**" or "**Do that**".	We postponed our visit to Jane. We **did that** because she was sick. **or** We postponed our visit to Jane.We **did so** because she was sick. (**Formally**)
We use "**Do**" rather than "**Do so**" in **in**formal English, especially af- ter **modal verbs** or **perfect tenses**. In these cases we can **often leave out** "So" or "Do so".	Do you like drinking tea? You **should**! / you **should do**!) (**NOT**: Do so) **Could** you **have bought** this car? Yes, I **could** have!

◊ **NOTE: "To"**

■ We can use **"To"** to replace a **clause** beginning with a "**to-infinitive**" and the **word** or **phrase** that **follows it** when it is clear what we are talking about.

I would like **to study** history. I hope **to** next semester. (**To study history next semester**.)

■ We **can** use **"To"** or **leave it out**:

After verbs such as: **"Agree"** , **"Ask"** , **"Begin"** , **"Promise"** , **"Start"**.	I have to study hard before the final exams. I have **started** (**to**) already.
After most **nouns** such us: **"Chance"** , **"Idea"** , **"Opportunity"** , **"Promise"** , **"Suggestion"**.	I will buy a vintage car. I' ve never had the **opportunity** (**to**) before.
After "Want" and **"Would like"** in "**if-clauses**" and "**wh-clauses**".	You should visit her first. You can go **wh**enever you **would like** (**to**).

■ We **don't** use **"To"** after **"Like"**.

You can go whenever you **like**. ("**NOT**: ...whenever you **like to**.")

◊ **NOTE:**

■ We **can not** leave out **"To"**

After verbs: **"Advise"** , **"Afford"** , **"Be able"** , **"Choose"** , **"Deserve"** , **"Expect"** , **"Hate"** , **"Hope"** , **"Intend"** , **"Love"** , **"Mean"** , **"Need"** , **"Prefer"** , which **MUST HAVE a complement**.	You may see **the manager** if you **need to**. ("**The manager**" = complement) (**NOT**: You may see if you **need to**.)

■ We **can** use **"To"** after "**negations**".

You don't need to work overtime if you don't want **to**.

◊ **NOTE:**

When **"Have"** / **"Have got "** is the **main verb** in the **first clause** or **sentence** we can use either **"Have (got)"** or **"Do"** to avoid repetition in the **following clause** or **sentence**.	**Have** you **got** a pencil? I am sure you **have** / I am sure you **do**.
When **"Have"** is **followed** by a **noun** to **describe** an **action**: (**Have a lunch** / a **shower** / a **good time** , etc) we usually use **"Do"**.	I would like to **have a lunch** with Mary. I hope she **does**.
When we use the verb **"Be"** in the **previous sentence** or **clause** , the "**to-infinitive**" of **"Be"** is repeated **in the next**.	It **is** not an expensive car. It doesn't have **to be**.

■ **"BUT"**

But + noun + **affirmative auxiliary verb** (Positive contrast to **negative statement**.)	Jim has **never** been to a pop concert , **but** John **has**.
But + personal pronoun + **affirmative auxiliary verb** (Positive contrast to **negative statement**.)	Jim has **never** been to a pop concert , **but** they **have**.
But + noun + **negative auxiliary verb** (Negative contrast to **positive statement**)	John **looks** happy , **but** Jane **doesn't**.
But + personal pronoun + **negative auxiliary verb** (Negative contrast to **positive statement**)	John **has done** his homework , **but** she **hasn't**.

◊   **NOTE:**

Asking for permission / Making requests	Giving or Refusing permission / Answering requests
Can I close the window? I'm freezing.	Yes, you **can**. Yes **of course** you **can**.
Could I close the window? I'm freezing.	Yes, you **may**. Yes **of course** you **may**.
May / Might I use your computer?	No you **may** not. I'**d rather** you did**n't**.

■ **Making suggestions / invitations**

Will you join me to the dinner? **Would you** join me to the dinner? **Would you like to** join me to the dinner?	I'**d** like. I'**d** love to. Yes, **all right**. I'm afraid I can'**t**.

■ **Making offers**

Shall I help you? **Can I** help you? **Would you like me to** help you?	**Yes**, please. **No**, thank you. **No** thanks.

17   NOMINALIZATION

◊ Sometimes we can use a **noun** or **noun phrase** for an **idea usually expressed** by a **verb**. This process is referred to as **nominalization**, which is actually the **noun form** of a **verb**.

> This information enables us **to formulate** a precise conclusion.
> This information enables **the formulation** of a precise conclusion.

■ An **adverb** that modifies a **verb** becomes **adjective**.

> Children saw that the sports center of their school **had damaged tragically**.
>
> Children saw a **tragic damage** in the sports center of their school.

◊ **NOTE**: We use **nominalization** for a number of reasons:

■ To **avoid** mentioning the **agent** , **a person** or **thing** that **performs an action**.

> Two years ago the crime **was investigated by the police** for first time.
>
> Two years ago the **investigation** of the crime began for first time.
> (**No agent** is mentioned.)

■ To express **two clauses** as **one clause**.

> The ancient weapons **were discovered** few kilometers far from this place. The local press **announced** the event.
>
> The **discovery** of the ancient weapons few kilometers far from this place **were announced by** the local press.

■ Sometimes we use nominalization with: **"Do"** , **"Give"** , **"Have"** , **"Take"** , **"Make"**.

> The students **reacted rapidly**.
>
> The students **had a rapid reaction**.

◊ **NOTE: Common in**formal alternatives include:

Do + the cooking / the gardening / the ironing / the shopping / the washing-up , etc

Give + a call / an explanation / a hug / a kiss / a look / a shout / a sigh / a warning / a welcome , etc

Have + a chat / a drink / a fall / a feeling / a guess / an influence / a hook / a respect / a rest / a shower / a sleep / a talk , etc

Take + action / aim / a (deep) breath / a decision / a (quick) glance / a look / shelter / a shower / a walk , etc

Make + an agreement / an announcement / an arrangement / an assumption / a comment / a contact / a decision / a discovery / a progress / a recommendation / a start / a use (of) , etc

18 COMPLEX PREPOSITIONS & PREPOSITIONS AFTER VERBS

◊ **Generally**

Prepositions can be either **one** word.
or
Two or **more** words.

We are concerned **about** him.

As far as I am concerned.

◊ **Complex prepositions**

■ **Common "Two - word" prepositions**

Ending "Of"	Ending "For"	Ending "From"
Ahead of	As for	Apart from
As of (from)	But for	As from
Because of	Except for	Away from
Devoid of	Save for	
Instead of		
Irrespective of		
Out of		
Outside of		
Regardless of		
Upwards of		

Ending "To"	Ending "With"	Others
According to	Along with	All over
As to	Together with	As against
Close to		As regards
Due to		Depending on
Near to		In between
Next to		Rather than
Owing to		Such as
Prior to		
Relative to		
Subsequent to		
Thanks to		
Up to		

■ **Common "three - word" and "four - word" prepositions**

Ending "Of"

As a result of	In danger of	In the case of
At risk of	In favor of	In the event of
By means of	In front of	In view of
By virtue of	In light of	On account of
By way of	In liue of	On behalf of
For luck of	In need of	On grounds of
For the sake of	In place of	On the part of
For want of	In respect of	On the strength of
In aid of	In search of	On top of
In case of	In spite of	With the exception of
In charge of	In terms of	

Ending "As"	Ending "For"	Ending "From"
As far as	In exchange for	As distinct from
As well as	In return for	With effect from

Ending "To"	Ending "With"
As opposed to	At a variance with
By reference to	In accordance with
In addition to	In comparison with
In contrast to	In compliance with
In reference to	In conformity with
In regard to	In contact with
In relation to	In live with
With reference to	In touch with
With regard to	
With respect to	

◊ **Verb + preposition**

■ **Verb + object + prepositional phrase**

Associate...with	Implicate...in
Condemn...as	Insure...against
Confuse...with	Interest...in
Deprive...of	Isolate...from
Discuss...with	Protect...against
Dismiss...as	Protect...from
Exchange...for	Reschedule...for
Explain...to	Rob...of
Feed...on	Schedule...for
Force...on	Translate...into
Grab...by	

I will try to **discuss the problem** with George and Sally.

With **few** verbs we can **change their preposition** if we change the **word order**.

Blame for / on	Supply with / for / to
Entrust with / to	Trust with / to
Issue with / to	
Present with / to	

They **presented me** with a **watch** when I retired.
or
They **presented** a **watch** to **me** when I retired.

■ **Verb + preposition + object + preposition + object**

Agree with...about / over...
Apologize to...for...
Appeal to...for...
Apply to...for...
Argue with...about / over...
Boast to...about...
Collaborate with...on...
Compete with...for...
Complain to...about...
Contend with...for...
Count on...for...
Depend on...for...
Quarrel with...about / over...
React to...with...
Refer to...as...
Rely on...for...
Respond to...with...

They **apologized to John for the mistake**.

She **rely on her father for the loan**.

■ **Verb + preposition + ing**

Admit to	Inquire about	She **apologize for** not tell**ing** the truth.
Apologize for	Insist on	
Benefit from	Persist in	
Concentrate on	React by	
Confess to	Refrain from	
Disapprove of	Rush into	
Dream of	Start by	
End by	Succeed in	
Go ahead with	Vote for	
Help with	Worry about	

■ **Verb + <u>object</u> + preposition + ing**

Accuse...of	Prevent...from	He **blame** <u>her</u> **for** damag**ing** his bike.
Advise...against	Prosecute...for	
Blame...for	Suspect...of	
Congratulate...on	Talk...into	
Discourage...from	Thank...for	
Praise for...	Trick...into	

■ **Verb + preposition + <u>subject</u> + ing**

Approve of	Know about	My job **relies on** <u>my</u> offer**ing** high qua-lity service.
Arise from	Laugh about	
Come from	Laugh at	
Count on	Lead to	
Depend on	Protest at	
Disapprove of	Rely on	
End in	Result in	
End with	Speak of	
Finish with	Start with	
Follow from	Think about	
Insist on	Worry about	

◊ **Phrasal verbs: World order**

Some phrasal verbs can be used <u>transitively</u> or <u>intransitively</u>.	They **covered up** <u>John's</u> mistakes. **Transitive** ("**John**" is the **object**.)
	Cover up again. **Intransitive** (**No object**)

■ **Phrasal verbs** can be used **transitively or intransitively <u>with the same meaning</u>. Examples**:

Answer back	Take over	I will **cover up** <u>John's</u> mistakes. (**Transitive = conceal**)
Call back	Tidy away	
Clear away	Wash up	
Cover up		I don't like to **cover up**.
Help out		(**Intransitive = conceal**)

■ **Phrasal verbs** can be used **transitively or intransitively <u>with different meaning</u>. Examples**:

Break in	Turn in	I've always **looked up** John for his deter-mination. (**Transitive = admire**)
Cut out	Wind up	
Hold out		

Look out	Our job is **looking up**.
Look up	(**Intransitive = improve**)
Pick up	
Split up	

- **With most phrasal verbs**, the **object** can go **before** or **after** <u>the particle</u>. **Examples**:

Bring about	Mess up	They want to **leave** their town **out**.
Check over	Shoot down	
Clean up	Sort out	They want to **leave out** their town.
Drink up	Throw away	
Gather up	Try out	
Get down	Use up	
Leave out	Wake up	
Make up		

| We **usually** put the <u>object</u> **after the particle**. | I must **take down** <u>the recipe</u>. I am going to cook for the dinner.
Rather than:
I must **take** <u>the recipe</u>. I am going to cook for the dinner **down**. |

| We **always** put the <u>object</u> **before the particle** if the **object is** a <u>pronoun</u>. | I will not be able to **sort** <u>them</u> **out**.
NOT:
I will not be able to **sort out** <u>them</u>. |

| If the <u>object</u> consists of **two** or **more** items **connected with** "And", we can put the **particle before** or **after** them if **one** or **both** of the items are <u>pronouns</u>. | When I visit London I will **look** <u>John</u> **and** <u>his</u> mother **up**.
Or
When I visit London I will **look up** <u>John</u> **and** <u>his</u> mother. |

- **With most phrasal verbs**, the <u>object</u> must go **after** the **particle**. **Examples**:

Account for	Look around	When I **bump into** <u>George</u>, I'll take some friends with me.
Act on	Look out over	
Approve of	Make up for	
Bump into	Provide for	
Call on	Result from	
Check into	Run into	
Do away with	Send away for	
Flick through	Stick at	
Get away with	Take after	
Grow out	Take against	
Look after		

- **With a few phrasal verbs** the <u>object</u> must go **between the verb** and the **particle**. **Examples**:

Hear out	Shut up	He doesn't like to **order** <u>them</u> **about**.
Order about	Stand up	
Pull to	Tell apart	
Push to		

- **A few three**-word phrasal verbs have <u>two objects</u> one **after** the **verb** and other **after** the **particle**. **Examples**:

Help...on with...	Take...out of...	I will **help** <u>you</u> **off with** <u>your jacket</u>.
Help...off with...	Take...out on...	("**Help off with**" : **A three-world phrasal verb**.)
Set...off against...	Take...up on...	("<u>you</u>" , "<u>your jacket</u>": The **objects**.)
Talk...out of...		

19 PREPOSITIONS AFTER NOUNS AND ADJECTIVES

◊ **Noun + preposition (Related to verbs and adjectives)**

Many **nouns** are **followed by** the same **prepositions** as their related **verbs** or **adjectives**.

To accuse of / accusation of To agree with - about - on / agreement with - about - on To amaze about / amazement about To be anxious about / anxiety about To be bored with / boredom with To contribute to / contribution to To depart from / departure from etc.	They **accused** him **of** stealing the car. The **accusation of** fraud charges them.

■ **Nouns usually** followed by **different prepositions** from their **related adjective**.

To be ashamed of To be fond of To be proud of	Feel shame about / at Have fondness for Take pride in	We are **proud of** the inauguration of our new headquarters. We **take pride in** the inauguration of our new headquarters.

■ **Nouns** which **take a preposition** while their **related verb** does **not**.

Admiration for / To admire Answer to / To answer Attack on / To attack Ban on / To ban Damage to / To damage Decrease of - in - by / To decrease Delay in / To delay Demand for / To demand Discussion about / To discuss A fear of / To fear Ignorance of / To ignore Improvement in - on / To improve Influence on / To influence Interview with / To interview Lack of / To lack Proof of / To prove Question about / To question Reduction in / To reduce Solution to / To solve Support for / To support	His **admiration for** Michael Jordan led him to become a professional player. He used **to admire** Michael Jordan more than any other NBA player.

◊ **Noun + preposition + ing**

Approval for Change from Focus on Interest in Opposition to	Protest about Sign in , etc	The **scientists focus on** recycling the useless products.

◊ **Noun + preposition + noun**

Damage to Decrease in Demand for Factor behind Increase in , etc	There is a **demand for** the **acquirem- ent** of new equipment. **Rather than** There is a **demand for** acqui**ring** the new equipment.

◊ **Noun + of + ing** or **Noun + to-infinitive** with **similar meaning**.

Some nouns can be **followed** by **either** "**Of + ing**" or "**To-infinit- ive**" with **similar meaning** (usually **after** "**The**") Aim Option Idea Plan Opportunity	**The opportunity of** buying new shar- es is an advantage for us. **Or** **The opportunity to buy** new shares is an advantage for us.

◊ **Noun + of + ing** and **Noun + to-infinitive** with a **difference in meaning**.

Chance	There is no **chance of** winn**ing**. (**Likelihood**) This is my last **chance to win**. (**Opportunity**)
Way	Our **way of** think**ing** is not the same wi- th your way. (**Manner**) This is the only **way to go**. (**Road**)

◊ **Noun + of + noun** and **Noun** at the **end** of **the sentence** with a **difference in meaning**.

Sense	This project has a unique **sense of cr- eativity**. (**Feeling**) A **word** with many **senses**. (**Meanings**)

◊ **Noun + of + ing BUT NOT with** infinitive.

Cost of Difficultly of Effect of Fear of Likelihood of Possibility of	Probability of Problem of Prospect of Risk of Sign of	There no **sign of** committ**ing** suicide.

◊ **Noun + to-infinitive BUT NOT with ing**

Ability to Attempt to Concern to Decision to Desire to Determination to Failure to Inability to	Permission to Proposal to Reason to Refusal to Reluctance to (Un)willingness to Wish to	He has the **ability to negotiate** with his clients.

◊ **With**: **Noun + in** and **Noun + of** we use:

		The **increase in mass production** will bring us extra profit. (When we talk about **what is increasing** (**mass production**)).
Cut in	Cut of	
Decline in	Decline of	
Decrease in	Decrease of	
Downturn in	Downturn of	
Drop in	Drop of	
Fall in	Fall of	
Gain in	Gain of	There is an **increase of 20%** of the mass production.
Growth in	Growth of	(When we talk about **the amount of** an
Increase in	Increase of	**increase** (**20%**)).
Jump in	Jump of	
Leap in	Leap of	
Rise in	Rise of	

◊ **Adjectives + preposition**: Expressing **FEELINGS** or **OPINIONS**.

Many **adjectives** which refer to **feelings** or **opinions** are **followed** by **particular prepositions**.

Amazed at / by	Intolerant of	
Ashamed of	Jealous of	
Bored with	Keen on	
Confident of	Nervous about / of	She was **nervous about** the exams.
Content with	Proud of	
Crazy about	Satisfied with	
Critical of	Scared of	
Enthusiastic about	Shocked at / by	
Envious of	Surprised at / by	
Fed up with	Tired of	
Impressed by / with	Upset about	
Indifferent to	Wary of	
Interested in	Worried about	

◊ **Adjectives + preposition** which are related **to somebody** or **with something**.

Afraid for somebody	**Disappointed with someone**
Afraid of something	**Disappointed at - about something**
Angry - Annoyed - Furious with someone	**Glad for someone**
Angry - Annoyed - Furious about something	**Glad of something**
Answerable to someone	**Pleased for someone**
Answerable for something	**Pleased at - with - about something**
Anxious about someone	**Right for someone**
Anxious for something	**Right about something**
Bad , Good for someone	**Sorry for someone**
Bad , Good at something	**Sorry about something**
Concerned about someone	**Wrong of someone**
Concerned with - for something	**Wrong about something**

20   MORE ABOUT PREPOSITIONS

◊   **"AT"**

■ "At" is used with **an exact point of time**, for example with **hours** and **moments**. It is also used with the **names of feasts**.

At **3 o'clock**
At **this moment** , at **noon** , at **bedtime**
At **Christmas** , **etc**

■ "At" is also used to show the **exact point** of: **Houses** , **small villages** , **stations** , **streets** , **etc**

It can be used as a **preposition** of **direction towards**.

She waited for half an hour **at the corner** of the **street**. ("**the corner**" = **exact point** of the **street**).
Throw a stone **at** a fierce dog.

◊   **"IN"**

■ "In" is generally used with **Future Tense** to show **the period within which** the action **will happen**.

In **summer**
In **1990** / In **the 1990s**

■ It is **also used** with **seasons, years,** and **parts of the day** , **centuries** , **months** , **long periods of time**.

In **summer** , in **2000** , in **the morning**
In **May** , in **the 21st century**
In **the future** , in **the Ice Age**.

■ "In" has the idea <u>within a larger area</u> and is consequently used with **bigger towns** , **valleys** , **countries**.

I was standing <u>in</u> **the street** when the storm broke. ("In **the Street**": **Within a larger area**). In **Larisa** , in **the valley of Tempe** , in **Greece** , **etc**

■ "In" is also used with everything (clothes , jewellery , etc) **actually worn on the body**.

A girl **in a red dress**.
A woman **in gold earrings**.

◊   **"ON"**

■ "On" is used with **more general points of time** than "**At**" , usually with **days** and **dates**.

On **Wednesday**
On **Friday morning**
On his **birthday**

On **New Year's Eve**
On **Christmas day**
On **March 14 1985**

◊   **NOTE:**

We do **not** use "**At**" , "**In**" , "**On**" with "**Last**", "**Next**" , "**Every**" , "**This**".

I went to London **last** June.
(**NOT:** I went to London **in last** June.)

◊   **"BY"**

■ "**By**" is used to show the **latest time at which** an action **will be finished**. Therefore , it is used with the **Future Tense**.

He **will** probably arrive **by 6 o'clock**.

◊   **"SINCE"**

■ "Since" is used when we refer to a **previous point** of **time**. It is **normally** used with **perfect tenses**.

I **have** lived in this house **since 2005**.

◊ **"FOR"**

■ "For" is used with **periods of time** to show **how long an action lasts**. It is **frequently** used with **Perfect Tense** in the **spoken English** , but it is also found with the other tenses.

I **have** lived in this house **for** three ye- ars.

■ It is also used for **direction** only when the **verb** indicates **beginning of a movement**.

He **left for** home.
They **set off for** London.

◊ **"FROM"**

■ "From" is used with a <u>starting point</u> of any action in the **past** or in the **future** and is **usually** found with "To" , "Until" or "Till".

He liv**ed** in London **from** <u>2005</u> **until** last year.
I **shall** be at home **from** <u>6p.m.</u> **until** 9p.m. (**The time of speaking** could be at 5:30p.m.)

◊ **NOTE**:

"Since" and "For" can also be used in a similar way to "As" and "Because" **to give the reason** for an **action** or a **situation**. How- ever, there are **important differences** between them.

Since John had already eaten, I made a sandwich for me. (He **knows** that John had already eaten. The **reason** is **alrea- dy well-known**."**Since**" like "**As**")

"For" suggests that the **reason** is **given** as an **afterthought**. It is **never** placed at the **beginning** of the **sentence** and is more cha- racteristic of **written**, **rather than** of **spoken English**:

I decided to stop the work I was doing , **for** it was very late and I wanted to go to bed. ("**For**" like "**Because**")

◊ **"AGAINST"**

■ "Against" has the meaning of the **direction opposite to** some- thing or in **contact with** something.

They row **against** the stream.
He leaned **against** the tree.

◊ **"TO" / "TOWARDS"**

■ "Towards" has the **sense of direction** , while "**To**" **generally that** of **destination**.

She stood up and walked **towards** him. (**In that direction**)

She went **to** the city. (The city was her **destination**.)

◊ **"UNDER" / "UNDERNEATH" / "BENEATH"**

"Under" , "Underneath" and **"Beneath"** have **the same meaning** but:

"Under" is the ordinary **preposition of position**.

The toys are **under** the table.

"Underneath" is also used as an **adverb**.

I found nothing **underneath**.

"Beneath" is more often used **figuratively**.

His actions are **beneath** contempt.

◊ **"OVER" vs "ABOVE"**

"Over" means **vertically above**.	We hung your calendar **over** the fire-place.
"Above" means **higher than**.	They saw the snowy mountains towering **above** them.

◊ **"BELOW" vs "UNDER"**

"**Under**" means **vertically below**.	The key was found **under** the sofa.
"Below" means **lower than**.	We could see the valley **bellow** us.

◊ **"BETWEEN" vs "AMONG"**

■ "**Between**" is used with:

Two persons or **things**.	He stood **between** his **son** and his **wife**.
Any two of a **larger number**.	He walked across the garden **between the flower beds**.
The speaker **and a group**.	Ladies and Gentlemen! **Between our selves** , I have...

■ "**Among**" is used with <u>more than two</u> **persons** or **things**. | Life **among** the Eskimo**s**.

◊ **"OF" vs "OFF" vs "OUT OF"**

"**Of**" is used only in **fixed expressions** with the **sense of "From"**. It is also used with **permanent qualities** of **character** and **ages**.	Die **of**... , Made **of**... , Ask **of**... (**With the sense of "From"**) A man **of** fifty three. (**Age**) A man **of** violent temper. (**Permanent quality** of **character**.)

■ "**Off**" has the meaning **from the place of** and also **down from**.

Take the book **off** the table. (**From the surface of the table**.)	He fell **off** his horse. (**Down from the horse**.)

■ "**Out of**" means **from the interior** and it has "**into**" as **an opposite**.

He took his handkerchief **out of** his pocket.	She took the parcels **out of** the car and carried them **into** the house.

◊ **"WITH"**

"**With**" is used with anything **which is carried** , **physical features** , **peculiarities**.	A lady **with** a **black bag**. A bird **with big wings**. A boy **with strange habits**.
Is also used with <u>qualities</u> of **character**.	A man **with** <u>common sense</u>. (**Quality of character**.)

◊ List of prepositional phrases

■ List of prepositional phrases beginning with "AT"

At / by one's side
At / for a fraction of
At / from the outset
At / in the end
At / on sight
At / on the double
At a / one time
At a disadvantage
At a discount
At a distance
At a glance
At a guess
At a high speed
At a loose end
At a loss
At a low ebb
At a moment's notice
At a price
At a rate of
At a speed of
At a standstill
At all costs
At all events
At an advantage
At any cost
At any rate
At breakfast
At ease with
At face value
At fault
At full strength
At hand
At heart
At home with
At issue
At large
At the risk of

At least
At length
At liberty
At most
At night
At noon
At odds with sb over sth
At once
At one's best
At one's discretion
At one's disposal
At one's leisure
At one's request
At peace / war with
At play
At present
At random
At sea
At the / in front of
At the age of
At the beginning
At the expense of
At the foot of
At the hands of
At the height of
At the latest
At the mercy of
At the peak of
At the same time
At the thought of
At the time of
At the top of
At this juncture
At times
At war with
At work

■ List of prepositional phrases beginning with "BY"

By / air / see / land
By / under the name of
By / with luck
By accident
By all accounts
By all means
By any chance
By any standard
By appointment
By birth
By check
By coincidence
By courtesy of
By definition
By degrees
By design
By dint of

By law
By marriage
By means of
By mistake
By my watch
By nature
By no means
By oneself
By order of
By process of
By profession
By reason of
By request
By rights
By sight
By surprise
By the side of

By far

By virtue of

By force

By way of

By hand

■ List of prepositional phrases beginning with "FOR" / "FROM"

For / in a good cause

For life

For / to the benefit (of)

For love

For a change

For my / your , etc

For a good reason

For real

For certain / sure

For the good of

For fear of

For the sake of

For good

For want of

For granted

From experience

For hire

From memory

For lack of

■ List of prepositional phrases beginning with "IN"

In (no) time

In / at the forefront of

In / out of focus

In / out of one's element

In / out of prison

In / out of season

In / out of stock

In / out of touch (with)

In / out of use

In / with difficulty

In / within sight of

In a deep sleep

In a flash

In a heap

In a hurry

In a mess

In a pile

In a sense

In a temper

In abeyance

In abundance

In accordance with

In action

In addition to

In advance

In agony

In agreement with

In aid of

In all likelihood

In an instant

In an uproar

In answer to

In anticipation of

In arrears

In awe of

In blossom

In brief

In bulk

In cash

In character

In charge of

In code

In collaboration with
In combination with
In comfort
In command of
In common
In comparison with
In compensation for
In conclusion
In confidence
In confinement
In confusion
In conjunction with
In connection with
In consequence of
In contact with
In contrast with / to
In control of
In convoy
In custody
In danger
In debt
In decline
In defense of
In detail
In disgrace
In disguise
In disorder
In dispute
In distress
In doubt
In due course
In duplicate
In earnest
In effect
In error
In essence
In excess of
In exchange for
In existence
In fact
In fairness to
In favor of
In fear of
In flames
In flower
In full
In future
In gear
In general
In good / bad condition
In good faith
In hand
In harmony (with)
In haste
In hiding
In high spirits
In honor of
In horror (of)
In ink / pencil
In isolation
In its infancy

In jeopardy
In keeping with sth
In labor
In league with
In length
In light of
In line with
In long run
In love with
In memory of
In mid-air
In mind
In moderation
In mourning (for)
In name
In office
In one's absence / presence
In one's spare time
In operation
In opposition to
In origin
In other words
In pain
In parliament
In particular
In person
In pieces
In place of
In possession of
In poverty
In practice
In preference to
In preparation for
In principle
In private
In progress
In proportion to / with
In public
In pursuit of
In quantity
In question
In reality
In recognition of
In relation to
In reply to
In reserve
In residence
In respect of
In response to
In retrospect
In return
In revenge for
In reverse
In ruins
In safety
In sb's interest
In sb's opinion
In search of
In secret
In self-defense
In settlement of

In short
In silence
In small change
In store for
In succession
In support of
In suspense
In sympathy with
In tears
In terms of
In terror
In the absence of
In the aftermath
In the balance
In the case of
In the course of
In the distance
In the event of
In the extreme
In the eyes of
In the flesh
In the form of
In the habit of
In the interests of
In the lead
In the making
In the meantime
In the midst of
In the mood of
In the name of
In the night
In the open
In the process of
In the right
In the seclusion of
In the shade
In the space of
In the time for
In the times of
In the wake of
In the way of
In the wrong
In theory
In town
In trouble
In tune with
In turmoil
In turn
In two minds
In twos / threes / tens
In uniform
In unison
In vain
In view of
In vogue
In words

■ **List of prepositional phrases beginning with "ON"**

On (the) watch (for)
On / behind schedule
On / off the record
On / off the road
On / under oath
On / under pain of
On / of the air
On / off balance
On / a diet
On a journey / trip / cruise
On a large / small scale
On a pension
On a regular basis
On a spree
On account of
On an expedition
On an island
On approval
On average
On bail
On behalf of
On board
On business
On condition that
On credit
On demand
On display
On edge
On end
On file
On fire
On foot
On good terms
On guard
On hand
On horseback
On impulse
On leave
On loan
On no account
On occasion
On one's (own) terms
On one's own

On one's own initiative
On order
On paper
On parade
On patrol
On principle
On purpose
On reflection
On remand
On sale
On second thoughts
On show
On strike
On suspicion of
On the agenda
On the assumption that
On the brink of
On the dot
On the edge of
On the eve of
On the grounds of
On the horizon
On the hour
On the increase
On the job
On the move
On the off chance
On the outskirts
On the part of
On the phone
On the point
On the run
On the strength of sth
On the tip of my tongue
On the top of that
On the understanding that
On the verge of
On the way to
On time
On tiptoe
On trial
On vacation

■ **List of prepositional phrases beginning with "OUT"**

Out of / in fashion
Out of / in print
Out of / in step
Out of breath
Out of context
Out of control
Out of curiosity / jealousy
Out of date
Out of doors
Out of hand
Out of ideas
Out of one's mind

Out of order
Out of pity
Out of place
Out of practice
Out of reach
Out of respect for
Out of sight
Out of spite
Out of the ordinary
Out of the question
Out of work

- **List of prepositional phrases beginning with "TO"**

To / on the contrary
To accompaniment of
To an extent
To date
To excess
To one's astonishment
To one's credit
To one's dismay

To one's face
To the / this day
To the best of
To the detriment of
To the exclusion of
To the full
To the satisfaction of

- **List of prepositional phrases beginning with "UNDER"**

Under / in the circumstances
Under age
Under arrest
Under consideration
Under construction
Under cover of
Under discussion
Under lock and key
Under misapprehension
Under one's protection
Under orders

Under pressure
Under regulations
Under repair
Under strain
Under stress
Under suspicion
Under the command of
Under the impression that
Under the influence (of)
Under treatment

- **List of prepositional phrases beginning with "WITH" / "WITHIN" / "WITHOUT"**

With / in reference to
With / without success
With a view to
With an eye to
With compliments of
With regard to
With regret
With respect to
With the aid of
With the exception of
With the help of
With the intention of
Within / Without earshot
Within / without reason
Within limits
Within one's budget

Within one's power
Within one's rights
Within reach (of)
Within a doubt
Within walking / striking distance
Without a break
Without a hitch
Without delay
Without exception
Without fail
Without foundation
Without precedent
Without question
Without respite
Without warning

◊ **Preposition combinations**

- Verb - **preposition combinations**

Agree **on**
Agree **with**
Approve **of** + ing
Arrive **at** / **in**
Complain **about**
Consent **to**

Comment **on**
Consist **of**
Depend **on**
Laugh **at**
Object **to**
Succeed **in**

Compare sb / sth... **with** / **to**
Excuse...**for**
Prefer...**to**
Remind...**of**
Thank...**for**

■ Adjective - **preposition combinations** with verb "Be"

Be afraid **of**	Be in favor **of**
Be accustomed **to**	Be interested **in**
Be aware **of**	Be opposed **to**
Be bored **with**	Be satisfied **with**
Be certain **of**	Be surprised **at / by**
Be disappointed **with**	Be tired **of**
Be familiar **with**	Be worried **about**
Be happy **with**	

■ **Prepositions** in fixed phrases

According **to**	**In** contrast **to / with**
Along **with**	**In** deference **to**
As well **as**	**In** hopes **of**
Because **of**	**In** lieu **of**
By means **of**	**In** pursuit **of**
By way **of**	**In** search **of**
In addition **to**	**In** spite **of**
In case **of**	**In** the face **of**
In consideration **of**	**In** terms **of**

◊ **The use of preposition collocations**

A connection	**BETWEEN two** things	NOT **among / by / with two** things
A decline / decrease	**IN** sth	NOT **of** sth
An increase	**IN** sth	NOT **of** sth
To agree , to disagree	**ON** sth	NOT **for** sth
To approve , to disapprove	**OF** sb / sth	NOT **for** sb / sth
To accuse sb	**OF** sth	NOT **for** sth
To addicted	**TO** sth	NOT **with / on / in** sth
To adjust	**TO** sth	NOT **with / in** sth
To affect	**Sb / Sth**	NOT **on** sb / sth
To apply	**TO sb / sth for sth**	NOT **in** sb / sth
To argue	**ABOUT** sth	NOT **for** sth
To arrive	**AT** a conclusion	NOT **in** a conclusion
To be a hazard	**TO** sb / sth	NOT **for** sb / sth
To be accustomed	**TO** sth	NOT **with** sth
To be aware	**OF** sth	NOT **about** sth
To be capable	**OF** sth	NOT **for** sth
To be concerned	**WITH / ABOUT** sth	NOT **for** sth
To be eligible	**FOR** sth	NOT **in / to** sth
To be equal	**TO** sth	NOT **as / with** sth
To be essential	**TO / FOR** sth	NOT **about** sth
To be exempt	**FROM** sth (not to have to do sth)	NOT **for** sth
To be faced	**WITH** sth	NOT **by** sth
To be familiar	**TO** sb (to be known by sb)	NOT **with** sb
To be familiar	**WITH** sb / sth (to know sb / sth)	NOT **to** sb / sth
To be harmful , to be harmless	**TO** sb / sth	NOT **for** sb / sth
To be ignorant	**OF** sth	NOT **about / for** sth
To be inferior	**TO** sb / sth	NOT **from - than** sb / sth
To be liable	**FOR** sth (responsible for sth)	NOT **about / to** sth
To be liable	**TO** sth (likely to suffer from sth)	NOT **for / about** sth
To be married	**TO** sb	NOT **with** sb
To be necessary	**FOR / TO** sth	NOT **in** sth
To be interested	**IN** sb / sth	NOT **about** sb / sth
To be opposed	**TO** sth	NOT **against** sth
To be opposite	**Something**	NOT **from / over** sth
To be (un)popular	**WITH** sb ((dis)liked by sb)	NOT **for** sb

To be related	**TO** sb / sth	NOT **with** sb / sth
To be relevant	**TO** sb / sth	NOT **with** sb / sth
To be satisfied	**WITH** sth	NOT **by** / **for** sth
To be sensitive	**TO** sth	NOT **with** / **for** / **by** sth
To be similar	**TO** sth	NOT **as** sth
To be suitable	**FOR** sth	NOT **to** / **in** sth
To be superior	**TO** sb / sth	NOT **from** or **than** sb / sth
To be valued	**OF** sb (appreciated by somebody)	NOT to be valued **at** sb
To be valued	**AT** sth (a price of something)	NOT to be valued **of** sth
To benefit	**FROM** sth	NOT **with** / **on** sth
To blame sb / sth	**FOR** sth	NOT **about** sth
To comment	**ON** sth	NOT **about** / **for** sth
To comply	**WITH** sth	NOT **by** sth
To concentrate	**ON** sth	NOT **about** / **over** sth
To connect sth	**WITH** sth else	NOT **in** / **on** sth else
To contribute	**TO** sth	NOT **in** sth
To decrease sth	**BY** a certain amount	NOT **with** a certain amount
To depend	**ON** sb / sth	NOT **in** or **by** sb / sth
To differ / be different	**FROM** sb / sth	NOT **than** / **to** sb /sth
To disconnect sth	**FROM** sth else	NOT **of** / **with** / **to** sth else
To distinguish	**BETWEEN** two things / people	NOT **among** / **from** two things or…
To emerge	**FROM** sth	NOT **by** sth
To excuse sb	**FOR** sth (to forgive sb for sth)	NOT **from** sth
To excuse sb	**FROM** sth (to exempt someone from sth)	NOT **for** sth
To experiment	**ON** sth (animals , etc)	NOT **in** / **with** sth
To experiment	**WITH** sth (methods / substances)	NOT **in** / **on** sth
To graduate	**FROM** sth (a university , college)	NOT **in** / **by** sth
To graduate	**IN** sth (a subject / science)	NOT **from** sth
To have / give reason	**FOR** sth	NOT **about** sth
To have a lack	**OF** sth	NOT **for** sth
To have an advantage	**OVER** sb / sth	NOT **to** / **from** sth
To have an intention	**OF** doing sth	NOT **for** doing sth
To have respect	**FOR** sb / sth	NOT **of** sb / sth
To increase sth	**BY** a certain amount	NOT **with** a certain amount
To invest	**IN** sth	NOT sth **on** sth
To know	**OF** / **ABOUT** sth	NOT **for** sth
To lecture	**ON** a topic (give a lecture)	NOT **about** a topic
To lecture sb	**ABOUT** sth (warn , reprimand)	NOT **on** sth
To notify sb	**OF** sth	NOT **for** sth
To object	**TO** sb / sth	NOT **against** sb / sth
To offer justification	**FOR** sth	NOT **about** sth
To place a ban	**ON** sth	NOT **for** / **about** sth
To prefer sb / sth	**TO** sb / sth else	NOT **from** sb / sth else
To put emphasis	**ON** sth	NOT **to** sth
To quit	**Something**	NOT **from** sth
To refer	**TO** sth	NOT **at** / **in** sth
To rely	**ON** sb / sth	NOT **in** - **by** sb / sth
To result	**FROM** sth (to arise from sth)	NOT **of** sth
To result	**IN** sth (end up)	NOT **to** sth
To submit sth	**TO** sb	NOT **for** sb
To suffer	**FROM** / **WITH** sth	NOT **by** sth
To take notice	**OF** sth	NOT **for** / **about** sth
To threaten sb	**WITH** sth	NOT sb **to do** sth
To undergo / prescribe treatment	**FOR** sth	NOT **of** / **about** sth
To wish	**FOR** sth	NOT wish **sth**

21   EXPRESSIONS WITH "GET"

◊   **Get + Adjective** or <u>**Adverb**</u>

(**Become**: What the **adjective** or <u>**adverb**</u> expresses).

Get old. **Get ready**. **Get <u>well</u>**.

◊   **Get + Past participle**

(**Become**: What the **past participle** expresses, mainly **unwelcome**.)

Get drunk.

◊   **"Get"** with the meaning **of understand sb / sth**.

I don't **get** you.
I didn't **get** his name.

◊   **Get + Object**

Get + Object
With the **meaning of**: "**Take**" , "**Find**" , "**Catch**" , "**Spend**" , "**Earn**".

Get a telegram. (**Take a telegram**.)
Where did you **get** the **coat**? (...**find**...)
Get me a **chair**! (**Catch**)
Get an illness. (**Spend**)
How does he **get his** living? (**Earn**)

Get + (Object) + Preposition or <u>**Adverb**</u>
(An **effort** or a **movement** from **one point** to **another**.)

Get about.
Get across.
Get (them) out / on / up.
Get (it) <u>away</u>.

Get + (Object) + Present participle
(**Start sth**)

Get going!
Can you **get** this **old car** going again?

Get + Object + <u>Adjective</u> or **Past participle**
With the **meaning of**: "**Do**" , "**Cause**" something.

Get the **children <u>ready</u>**.
Get the **lunch** cooked.
He **got** his **car** crashed in an accident.

◊   **Get + to-infinitive**

Get + to-infinitive
(**End up**)

They soon **got to be** friends.
When you **get to know** him better , you will like him.

Get + object + to-infinitive
(**Persuade / Tell** someone to do sth , **Manage** sth)

You will never **get him to talk**.
(**Persuade**)
I can't **get** the **mixer to work**.
(**Manage**)

◊   **Have / Had got**

Have got / Had got
(**Own / Have sth**)

I**'ve got** a new car.

Have got <u>to</u> / Had got <u>to</u>
(**Must** , **Have / Had to**)

We**'ve got <u>to</u>** visit her.

22 PUNCTUATION

◊ **In general**

Punctuation in the English language helps the reader to understand a sentence through visual means other than just the letters of the alphabet. The use of punctuation marks the structure and organize the text.

◊ **The usage of the punctuation marks**

■ **The period or full stop or point** (.)

The period (.) is used when we want to mark the end of a sentence.	The house in which she lives is in the suburbs**.**
It is use to indicate an abbreviation.	Mr. and Mrs. Hamilton will arrive at 6a.m.
We can use a series of three dots (**...**) when we want to indicate an **intentional omission** of one or more words.	You **ought to have been** more careful...

■ **The comma** (,)

The comma (,) is used to disambiguate the meaning of sentences, by providing boundaries between **clauses** or **phrases**.	There are three winners , the first of whom is my cousin.
It is used with a **series** of **verbs** , **nouns** and **adjectives**.	Today Tom will **train , swim , relax** in new hotel's facilities. (**Series** of **verbs**)
	For the recipe it is necessary to add **salt , cinnamon , pepper** and water. (**Series** of **nouns**)
	This lounge is **old , dirty** and dark. (**Series** of **adjectives**)
It is used to separate **clauses** or **phrases**.	Her mother, **who is a kind woman**, has helped her a lot. "it**'s** quite warm", **she** said.
We usually **put** a **comma after** a **sentence connector** at the **beginning** or at the **end** of a sentence.	John had planned to visit us today. **However,** he changed his mind due to the rainy weather. There are a lot of activities for every member. Track sports, **for instance**.
The comma is also used to **separate numbers**.	December **23 , 2016**
In **question tags** , **echo tags** and **short answers**.	Give me a hand , **will you?** He quit his job. He did , **didn't he?** "Can she do it?" Yes , **she can.**
If the direct speech is at the **beginning** of the sentence, we put the comma **before** the **final quotation mark**.	"Let's go out for a walk ," he said.

If the <u>direct speech</u> is at the **end** of the sentence, we put the comma **before** the **first quotation mark**.	He said ,"<u>Shall I take you home</u>?"

■ **The exclamation mark (!)**

The exclamation mark (!) is used to express an **exclamation** , **admiration** , **surprise** or **anger** in a usually short sentence.	What a nice day! How clever he is! "Wow"! She said when she saw the huge cake. You take your hands off me!

■ **The question mark (?)**

The question mark (**?**) is used to mark all the direct questions.	How old is John**?**

■ **The colon (:)**

The colon (:) is used to **introduce** a **list**.	We will need to buy some things for the journey such as: **clothes** , **gloves** , **boots** , **scarves** and a **map**.

■ **The semicolon (;)**

The semicolon (;) is used to separate two **independent** but **related clauses**.	He wants to stop the process; she wants to continue it till the end.

■ **The quotation marks (" ")**

The quotation marks (" ") are commonly used to **highlight** someone else's words.	"I will buy this house," she said.
Are also used in bibliographic references.	"From Earth to the Moon", by Jules Verne.

■ **The apostrophe (')**

The apostrophe (') is a punctuation mark that is mainly use to indicate the grammatical **possession** as well as the **contraction** of two words.	The boy's toy. She hasn't come yet.

■ **The hyphen and the dash (-) & (--)**

The hyphen (-) is used to **join two** or **more words together**.	State-of-the-art.
It is used to show that a **word** has been **divided into two parts** at the **end** of one line and the **beginning** of the next.	They apologized to John for their mistakes.
The dash (--) is used **in pairs** to **mark off information** that is **not essential** to the meaning of the rest of the sentence.	Her mother - who is a kind woman - has helped her a lot.

■ **Parentheses and brackets ( ) & [ ]**

The parentheses **()** ,also called round brackets, are used to **mark off information** that is **not essential** to the meaning of the rest of the sentence.	His brother (who works as a lawyer) lives in New York since 2015.
The brackets **[ ]** are used when we want **to add further explanation** to the meaning of a sentence.	He [the president of the company] will announce the new investment project.

23 GERUND OR INFINITIVE (Revision) - LIST OF IRREGULAR VERBS

◊ **Verbs followed by gerund**   **Verbs followed by infinitive**

A

Acknowledge   Avoid   **Afford**
Admit   Agree
Advise   Aim
Advocate   Appear
Allow   Arrange
Anticipate   Ask
Appreciate   Attempt

B

Begin   **Beg**
Begrudge   Be determined

C

Can't bear   Catch   **Care**
Can't help   Cease   Choose
Can't resist   Complete   Claim
Can't see   Consider   Condescend
Can't stand , etc   Continue   Consent

D

Defend   Discuss   **Dare** (also without to)
Delay   Dislike   Decide
Deny   Don't mind   Demand
Despise   Dread   Deserve
Discover

E

Encourage   Escape   **Endeavour**
Enjoy   Excuse   Expect

F

Face   Finish   **Fail**
Fancy   Forget

G

Go (physical activi- Grudge   **Guarantee**
ties: swimming , etc)

H

Hate   **Happen**
                                                                Have
                                                                Help (also without to)
                                                                Hesitate
                                                                Hope

I

Imagine
Involve

K

Keep

L

Leave off   Love   **Learn**
Like   Long

M

Mention   Miss   **Manage**
Mind   Mean

N

Necessitate   **Need** (also without to)
                                                                Neglect

O

Observe   **Offer**
Overhear   Ought

P

Permit	Prohibit	**Plan**
Postpone	Propose	Prepare
Practice	Put off	Proceed
Prefer		Promise

Q

Quit

R

Recall	Report	**Refuse**
Recollect	Require	Resolve
Recommend	Resent	
Regret	Resist	
Relish	Resume	
Remember	Risk	

S

Spend (time , money)	Suggest	**Seem**
Start		Stop
Stop		Swear

T

Tolerate	**Tend**
Try	Threaten
	Trouble

U

Understand	**Undertake**
Urge	Used

V

Volunteer
Vow

W

Waste (time , money)	**Want**
Worth	Wish
	Would hate / love / like / prefer

Y

Yearn

◊ **List of irregular verbs**

Verb	Past	Past Participle
Abide	Abode / Abided	Abode / Abided
Arise	Arose	Arisen
Awake	Awoke	Awaked / Awoke
Be	Was	Been
Bear	Bore	Borne / Born
Beat	Beat	Beaten
Befall	Befell	Befallen
Beget	Begot	Begotten
Begin	Began	Begun
Behold	Beheld	Beheld
Bend	Bent	Bent
Bereave	Bereaved / Bereft	Bereaved / Bereft
Beseech	Besought	Besought
Beset	Beset	Beset
Bet	Bet / Betted	Bet / Betted
Betake	Betook	Betaken
Bid	Bade	Bidden
Bind	Bound	Bound
Bite	Bit	Bitten
Bleed	Bled	Bled
Blend	Blended / Blent	Blended / Blent
Bless	Blessed / Blest	Blessed / Blest
Blow	Blew	Blown
Break	Broke	Broken
Breed	Bred	Bred
Bring	Brought	Brought
Broadcast	Broadcast	Broadcast
Build	Built	Built
Burn	Burnt / Burned	Burnt / Burned
Burst	Burst	Burst
Buy	Bought	Bought
Cast	Cast	Cast
Catch	Caught	Caught
Chide	Chided / Chid	Chided / Chid
Choose	Chose	Chosen
Cleave	Clove / Cleft	Cloven / Cleft
Cling	Clung	Clung
Come	Came	Come
Cost	Cost	Cost
Creep	Crept	Crept
Cut	Cut	Cut
Deal	Dealt	Dealt
Dig	Dug	Dug
Do	Did	Done
Draw	Drew	Drawn
Dream	Dreamed / Dreamt	Dreamed / Dreamt
Drink	Drank	Drunk
Drive	Drove	Driven
Dwell	Dwelled	Dwelt
Eat	Ate	Eaten
Fall	Fell	Fallen
Feed	Fed	Fed
Feel	Felt	Felt
Fight	Fought	Fought
Find	Found	Found

Verb	Past	Past Participle
Flee	Fled	Fled
Fling	Flung	Flung
Fly	Flew	Flown
Forbear	Forbore	Forborne
Forbid	Forbade / Forbad	Forbidden
Forecast	Forecast / Forecasted	Forecast / Forecasted
Forego	Forewent	Foregone
Foresee	Foresaw	Foreseen
Foretell	Foretold	Foretold
Forget	Forgot	Forgotten
Forgive	Forgave	Forgiven
Forgo	Forwent	Forgone
Forsake	Forsook	Forsaken
Forswear	Forswore	Forsworn
Freeze	Froze	Frozen
Gainsay	Gainsaid	Gainsaid
Get	Got	Got / Gotten
Gird	Girded / Girt	Girded / Girt
Give	Gave	Given
Go	Went	Gone
Grave	Graved	Graven
Grind	Ground	Ground
Grow	Grew	Grown
Hamstring	Hamstrung	Hamstrung
Hang	Hung / Hanged	Hung / Hanged
Have	Had	Had
Hear	Heard	Heard
Heave	Heaved / Hove	Heaved / Hove
Hew	Hewed	Hewed / Hewn
Hide	Hid	Hidden
Hit	Hit	Hit
Hold	Held	Held
Hurt	Hurt	Hurt
Inlay	Inlaid	Inlaid
Keep	Kept	Kept
Kneel	Knelt	Knelt
Knit	Knitted / Knit	Knitted / Knit
Know	Knew	Known
Lay	Laid	Laid
Lead	Led	Led
Lean	Leant / Leaned	Leant / Leaned
Leap	Leapt / Leaped	Leapt / Leaped
Learn	Learnt / Learned	Learnt / Learned
Leave	Left	Left
Lend	Lent	Lent
Let	Let	Let
Lie	Lay	Lain
Light	Lighted / Lit	Lighted / Lit
Lose	Lost	Lost
Make	Made	Made
Mean	Meant	Meant
Meet	Met	Met
Melt	Melted	Melted / Molten
Misdeal	Misdealt	Misdealt
Mislay	Mislaid	Mislaid
Mislead	Misled	Misled
Misspell	Misspelt	Misspelt
Misspend	Misspent	Misspent
Mistake	Mistook	Mistaken

Verb	Past	Past Participle
Misunderstand	Misunderstood	Misunderstood
Mow	Mowed	Mown / Mowed
Outbear	Outbore	Outborne
Outbid	Outbid	Outbid / Outbidden
Outdo	Outdid	Outdone
Outgrow	Outgrew	Outgrown
Outrun	Outran	Outrun
Outride	Outrode	Outridden
Outshine	Outshone	Outshone
Overbear	Overbore	Overborne
Overblow	Overblew	Overblown
Overcome	Overcame	Overcome
Overdo	Overdid	Overdone
Overdraw	Overdrew	Overdrawn
Overgrow	Overgrew	Overgrown
Overhang	Overhung	Overhung
Overhear	Overheard	Overheard
Overlay	Overlaid	Overlaid
Overleap	Overleapt / Overleaped	Overleapt / Overleaped
Override	Overrode	Overriden
Overrun	Overran	Overrun
Oversee	Oversaw	Overseen
Overshoot	Overshot	Overshot
Oversleep	Overslept	Overslept
Overtake	Overtook	Overtaken
Overthrow	Overthrew	Overthrown
Partake	Partook	Partaken
Pay	Paid	Paid
Pen	Pent	Pent
Prove	Proved	Proved / Proven
Put	Put	Put
Quit	Quit	Quit
Read	Read / Red	Read / Red
Rebuild	Rebuilt	Rebuilt
Recast	Recast	Recast
Redo	Redid	Redone
Relay	Relaid	Relaid
Remake	Remade	Remade
Rend	Rent	Rent
Repay	Repaid	Repaid
Rerun	Reran	Rerun
Reset	Reset	Reset
Rewrite	Rewrote	Rewritten
Rid	Rid / Ridded	Rid / Ridded
Ride	Rode	Ridden
Ring	Rang	Rung
Rise	Rose	Risen
Rive	Rived	Riven
Run	Ran	Run
Saw	Sawed	Sawn
Say	Said	Said
See	Saw	Seen
Seek	Sought	Sought
Sell	Sold	Sold
Send	Sent	Sent
Set	Set	Set
Sew	Sewed	Sewn / Sewed
Shake	Shook	Shaken
Shave	Shaved	Shaved / Shaven

Verb	Past	Past Participle
Shear	Sheared	Shorn , Sheared
Shed	Shed	Shed
Shine	Shone	Shone
Shoe	Shod	Shod
Shoot	Shot	Shot
Show	Showed	Shown / Showed
Shrink	Shrank / Shrunk	Shrunk / Shrunken
Shrive	Shrove / Shrived	Shriven / Shrived
Shut	Shut	Shut
Sing	Sang	Sung
Sink	Sank	Sunk / Sunken
Sit	Sat	Sat
Slay	Slew	Slain
Sleep	Slept	Slept
Slide	Slid	Slid
Sling	Slung	Slung
Slink	Slunk	Slunk
Slit	Slit	Slit
Smell	Smelt	Smelt
Smite	Smote	Smitten
Sow	Sowed	Sown
Speak	Spoke	Spoken
Speed	Sped / Speeded	Sped / Speeded
Spell	Spelt / Spelled	Spelt / Spelled
Spend	Spent	Spent
Spill	Spilt / Spilled	Spilt / Spilled
Spin	Spun / Span	Spun
Spit	Spat	Spat
Split	Split	Split
Spoil	Spoilt / Spoiled	Spoilt / Spoiled
Spread	Spread	Spread
Spring	Sprang	Sprung
Stand	Stood	Stood
Stave	Staved / Stove	Staved / Stove
Steal	Stole	Stolen
Stick	Stuck	Stuck
Sting	Stung	Stung
Stink	Stank / Stunk	Stunk
Strew	Strewed	Strewn / Strewed
Stride	Strode	Stridden
Strike	Struck	Struck
String	Strung	Strung
Strive	Strove	Striven
Swear	Swore	Sworn
Sweep	Swept	Swept
Swell	Swelled	Swollen / Swelled
Swim	Swam	Swum
Swing	Swung	Swung
Take	Took	Taken
Teach	Taught	Taught
Tear	Tore	Torn
Tell	Told	Told
Think	Thought	Thought
Thrive	Throve / Thrived	Thriven / Thrived
Throw	Threw	Thrown
Thrust	Thrust	Thrust
Tread	Trod	Trodden
Unbend	Unbent	Unbent
Unbind	Unbound	Unbound

Verb	Past	Past Participle
Underbid	Underbade	Underbidden
Undergo	Underwent	Undergone
Understand	Understood	Understood
Undertake	Undertook	Undertaken
Undo	Undid	Undone
Uphold	Upheld	Upheld
Upset	Upset	Upset
Wake	Woke	Woken
Waylay	Waylaid	Waylaid
Wear	Wore	Worn
Weave	Wove	Woven
Weep	Wept	Wept
Win	Won	Won
Wind	Winded / Wound	Winded / Wound
Withdraw	Withdrew	Withdrawn
Withhold	Withheld	Withheld
Withstand	Withstood	Withstood
Work	Worked / Wrought	Worked / Wrought
Wring	Wrung	Wrung
Write	Wrote	Written

24 INSTRUCTIONS ON ESSAYS

- **Introduction**

Begin describing the **phenomenon** , **the trend** or **the debate** that is focused on the **essay questions**. You should mention **both** the **opposite trends**. At the **end** of the introduction you can **expose your opinion**.

Useful expressions:

In contemporary times, it seems that...
From my perspective...
It is a fact that in contemporary times...
It is an indisputable fact that...
It is often claimed / said / asserted / stated...
Like almost everyone else in their life, I have experienced...
Nowadays, we are all realizing that...
Recently, we have all become concerned that...
There can be no doubt that...
There is little doubt that...
There is no doubt that nowadays...
There is no doubt that one of the most...
Today we are often confronted with the problem of...

- **Main body**

In the first part of the main body, we describe what we believe that is **people's first opinion**.
We **exemplify what many supporters of this view believe** or **what we believe** about this subject.
We mention **supporters' arguments (reasons)** of this view.
We close the first paragraph **elaborating** <u>why these people support this view</u>, or <u>why we support this view</u>, if asked.

Useful expressions:

...is believed to be...
I am a fervent supporter of...
It goes without saying that...
There are a host of reasons why...
There are several reasons as to why...
To elaborate...
To exemplify...
To illustrate my point of view...

In the second part of the main body, we describe **other people's opposite opinion** or **our opposite opinion**, if asked. We mention **supporters' arguments of this view**, or **our arguments relate to our view**, if asked.

Useful expressions:

A second point concerns...
Finally...
Last but not least...
Nonetheless, many are at odds with this idea...
Notwithstanding these facts...
On the other hand...

- **Final paragraph**

We recapitulate the **two different opinions**, adding our **personal opinion** about **what is necessary to be done**.

Useful expressions:

On the whole,
To recapitulate,
To sum up,

◊   **NOTE**:

■   These tips are only about how to write a good **essay** they are **not** about how to do the other kinds of writing tasks such as **a letter** , **a report** , **an article** , **a proposal** , a **competition entry** , **a review**.

■   Write about **one and a half** to **two** pages (**250-300** words).

◊   **Useful phrases found in essays**

At face value
At odds / Be odd with sb over sth
Be all about
Bewildering
Bewildering number
Beyond one's means
Blaze a trail
Contradictory
Detrimental impacts
Dicey
Dicey decisions
Equally poorly
Extraneous
Fervently advocate
Foil a plot
For what it is worth
From my perspective
Get blood out of stone
Go to any length
Gross misconception
Gross negligence
Have a field day
Have a good command of sth
Highly debated
Hold sb to account
In hordes
In order of priority
In tandem with
In that way
In the event of
In the sequel
Inherently dangerous
Melt into the background
Mend one's ways

More than ever
My firm conviction is that
Notwithstanding these facts
On any account
On the dire and adverse
On the whole
One's fair share
Out of senses
Overwhelm
Overwhelmingly
Propitious to sb / for sth
Repressed desire
Shift for oneself
Spell disaster
Stick to one's guns
Strike fear into
Subscribe to the idea that
This idea is flawed
To a whole new level
To elaborate
To exemplify
To recapitulate
To sum up
Tried and true
Turn over a new leaf
Unflagging energy
Weighty
Weighty issue
Window of opportunity
Wishful thinking
Without a shadow of doubt
Wreak havoc on sth
Wreak sth on sb

Essay sample

Groups and organizations form a vital part of people's life. Why do people join in groups? What role do groups in people's life? Support your opinion with specific reasons.

From the beginning of the history of the mankind, people preferred living in groups and small societies rather than living on their own. During human's evolution various forms of association appeared in the civilized communities, defining people's lifestyle. But why people are joined in groups and organizations?

It is indisputable fact that nowadays the difficulties and the challenges are more provocative , comparing to those of the previous decades. This condition leads people to join in groups in order to cope with the difficulties, that only a few would be able to surpass , following an isolated way of life.

To exemplify, there are professional organizations such as the commercial chambers which help the businessmen to boost their products in the foreign markets, organizing trade fairs, conferences, and so on.
The exchange of cultural activities is another reason why people join in groups. In almost every country there are clubs relate to theatre, music, and cinema. We should not miss to mention the sports clubs which tend to be more and more popular, and which contribute to transmit the competitiveness, in conjunction with emulation among the joint members.
Another reason why people join in clubs is the necessity, that most of us have, to share our concerns and worries with others, who are able to offer us their advices.

Taking in to consideration the above it is understandable why most of the people's unions play an active role in their life. They can also affect their character. From my perspective the most serious role that most of these societies can play in people's life is the role of the personal instructor. People who join in groups learn how to follow the laws and the regulations of the team, becoming by this way, more discipline and obedient. Everyone is taught to respect the peculiarities of the others and, if need be, to give his / her assistance to them.

It would be a remarkable omission if I didn't mention the international associations such as the "Red Cross" , "Doctors without Frontier" which have global presence, as they offer their services for the good of the humanity. Groups may also help almost everyone to surpass their superstitions relate to the lifestyle of other people, offering education and social guidance on this topic.

To recapitulate, It is necessary for almost all of us, to join in groups and organizations with active social and cultural orientation, as the difficulties and the challenges of life tend to create impassable obstacles that no-one is able to surpass without any guidance and support.

25 OTHER WRITING FORMS

◊ **HOW TO WRITE REPORTS**

A report is usually a **formal** report to **a boss, colleagues** or **members of a committee**. It **gives informa-tion on the progress** made on a project or for a meeting is held or decisions taken **regarding to the future of business**.

■ **Introduction**

In the introduction we **mention the purpose** for which we wrote the report and its contents.

Useful expressions:

As requested , this is a report regarding the subject of...
The information below summarizes the events which took place...
The purpose / aim / intention of this report is to present the progress of...

■ **Main body of the report**

In the main body we **present every aspect** of the topic of the report. **We develop each topic in separate paragraphs** with the **appropriate heading** for **each paragraph**.

Useful expressions: General comments for each paragraph

Although ... , **I should point out that** ...
It is a fact that ...
It is generally felt that...
On the whole, I found that ...

Useful expressions: To express facts and proportions

A large / small proportion of people surveyed replied / reported that...
Of the (number) people / students / workers who were questioned / interviewed...
The majority / minority of viewers believed that...

■ **Conclusion**

In the final paragraph we **mention briefly** the points that raised on the issue.

Useful expressions:

All things considered , I believe that ...
Fortunately , a number of difficulties have been encountered...
Taking all these points into consideration , I would recommend...
To conclude / To sum up , the current state of affairs is that...
Unfortunately , progress has not been as fast as expected...

Report sample

You belong to an international film club and you have been asked to write the club's annual report for this year. The report is written for members and it has to include information about the main events held over the last twelve months , to present plans for activities in the coming year and to summarize the current financial position of the club , in respect of money received and payments made.

Now use this advice to write your **report** in **280-320 words**.

Introduction

This report summarizes the activities of our film club for this year. It is a compendium of our plans and actions that took place this year, as well as a presentation of the financial results.

Main events

During this period many social and cultural activities have been organized by club's committee. It is worth mentioning the tribute to Italian cinema that was one of our best cultural activities for this year. The whole presentation has been characterized as an excellent effort , as it has shown us many unknown aspects of Italian movies. The annual diner for our sponsors was another celebration that had been orchestrated by the newcomers of the club, showing by this way their interest for it.

New members

As it was mentioned above the new members have already made their presence felt in the club. It is noteworthy that during this time more newcomers have been added, more than any other previous year, and this happened because of the unique presentation of our activities.

Advertising

Another serious initiative that the committee performed this period of time is the advertising campaign, that made a remarkable impression to everyone who planned to join us. Our web site as well as the presentation from the social media contributed to shape a new image for our club, adding by this way new members.

Future plans

In the near future new series of activities will be prepared by the members of our club. In particular:
a) In cooperation with the cinema institution of our local university we will organize a tribute to the European cinema at the turn of the 20th century, by the end of the next month.
b) An educational trip to Rome's cinema museum will take place at the end of the spring.
c) The inaugurations of the new cultural hall in Leeds will be orchestrated by our musicians, which is a great honor for our society.

Finances

All these actions that have mentioned above require financial resources. Thanks to our sponsors that come not only from our town but also from abroad, all the necessary financial resources have been ensured. The state contribution, although it is not enough, is remarkable.

◊   **HOW TO WRITE LETTERS**

LETTERS OF COMPLAINT

■   **Introduction**

We mention the **reason** for writing. We make clear the **purpose** of our letter.

Useful expressions:

I am writing to tell you how disappointed / annoyed I feel about ...
I am writing to complain about...
I am writing to draw your attention to the subject of...
I am writing to you in connection with...
I am writing to you to express my extreme dissatisfaction with...
I was amazed / distressed / horrified to find that ...

■   **Main body of the letter**

Details of problems , **justifying your complaint**.

Useful expressions:

Although
Besides that
Despite the fact that...
Firstly...
Furthermore...
In addition...
In spite of the fact that...
Moreover...

■   **Conclusion**

What you expect to change.

Useful expressions:

I am afraid that I will have to take effective measures if this (situation / noise , etc) continues ...
I hope this matter will receive your prompt attention...
I hope we can sort this matter out amicably...
I trust this will not happen again...
Your product is not up to my expectations...

Yours sincerely,

Your name

Letter of complaint sample

You bought some CDs to help you improve your English. You were not happy with the CDs and you have decided to write to the Publisher, CD World. Write a letter to CD World explaining why you bought the CDs, why you are dissatisfied and saying what you would like the company to do.

Write you answer in **180-220 words**

I am writing to express my extreme dissatisfaction with the set of 6 CDs concerning English lessons which I purchased from your company, two weeks ago.

First of all I would like to explain that I bought these CDs because I was persuaded by your misleading a-advertisement that I could learn to speak English within one month, whether for business purposes or just for pleasure. The knowledge of English has become a necessity for me. Unfortunately I am not able to afford money for tutorial lessons, nor have the time to attend them. For that reason I thought that your CDs would be the perfect solution for me, but unfortunately I was wrong.

Upon receipt of my 6 CDs, I started working. I followed your advice scrupulously, and after a week of practicing I realized , to my disappointment , that business conversations were not included in the CDs.
In addition the so-called innovative teaching method, supposedly that it should have been included in the cds, according to your ad, consisted only of "listen and repeat" units.
I still wonder about how you promised to the people that they will be able to speak English in such a short period of time, studying this poor teaching method. I have also been charged with 20 Euros per CD, unlike what was mentioned in your ad.

Your product is not up to my expectations and does not meet my requirements. I also believe that your advertisement was absolutely dishonest. If I don't receive compensation, by your side, I will be forced to take legal action.

Yours sincerely,

Alan Smith

LETTERS OF APOLOGY

- **Introduction**

In the introduction you should **summarize the reasons** why you write this letter.

Useful expressions:

I must / would like to apologize for...
I' am writing to apologize for... , please accept my sincere apologies for...

- **Main body**

You can develop the subject in **two** or **three** paragraphs giving **detailed explanations**.
In the **next** paragraphs you can **express your regret** as well as your **willingness to rectify the wrong you have caused** , **asking forgiveness**.

Useful expressions:

As far as I am concerned...
As regards...
I insist on (+ing) to make up for your loss...   (Express our regret)
Needless to say...
Please allow me to offer as compensation for... (Express our regret)
We know we have no right to expect you to forgive us, but we sincerely apologize.
With regard to...

- **Conclusion**

Summarize your **remarks**.

Useful expressions:

Counting with your kind generosity to accept my sincere apology...
Hoping that my sincere apology will be kindly accepted...
Hoping that you will have the generosity to accept my sincere apology...
We hope you are willing to give us another chance to...

Yours sincerely,

Your name

Letter of apology sample

Disturbing the neighbors

Dear Mr. and Mrs. Smith,

We would like to apologize for causing you such disturbance. Since we moved into our apartment you had to endure our bad behavior. Our frequent parties have not only been disturbing but also lasted until the early hours. Our guests had left bottles and trash in the parking lot , in front of the building.
To make matters worse, the trashes sometimes dropped from our balcony to your balcony. Since you live directly under our apartment, our inconsiderate behavior had affected you more, comparing to the rest of the neighbors.

You and the other neighbors , have complained to us about the parties. The apartments' manager had left warning notices out of our door as well. As you know, the police have come several times and reprimanded us about the noise. We had organized parties like this at our previous apartment , and we had received severe criticisms from the neighbors , which made us to feel really sad.

What happened last night was terrible. It was clear that someone , during the party , dropped a lit cigarette out off our balcony. It fell on the surface of the mulch , around the bushes , in front of your apartment.
It was horrifying to see how quickly the mulch ignited and the bushes began to burn. Fortunately we were able to put out the fire without having to call the fire department.
We were relieved that no one was injured , and the only damage in your property was only two semi-burnt bushes.

We know that we have no right to expect you to forgive us , but we sincerely apologize. We promise to limit our parties to one per four months. They will take place only on Friday evenings and they will last until midnight. We will also supervise the behavior of our guests , and we will clean up every trash which will be caused by them.

Counting with your kind generosity to accept our sincere apology , we are going to each apartment, in this wing, and we will apologize face-to-face. In addition, Lisa and I will go to the manager's office to inform him that we are willing to pay the costs associated with the bushes' restoration.

We hope that you are willing to give us another chance not only to be your neighbors , but also to be your good neighbors.

Yours sincerely,

Tom and Lisa Anderson

LETTERS OF OPINION

- **Introduction**

Make your **topic** and **opinion clear**.

Useful expressions:

I am writing to express my opinion about...
I am writing in response to...
I would like to comment on...

- **Main body**

First paragraph: Give **reasons** for your **disagreement**.

Useful expressions:

As I see it...
First of all I would like to say that I totally (dis)agree with...
I don't think that option 1 is the most suitable one for the following reasons...
I don't think you should...for the following reasons...

Second paragraph: Provide **solutions** to the **problem**.

Useful expressions:

I think it is true / false that...
I think that option 2 is the most suitable one for the following reasons...
I think you should...for the following reasons...
I would also like to add some ideas to your comments:
Option 2, on the other hand is more sensible...

- **Conclusion**

Restate your opinion **hoping that this problem will be solved**.

Useful expressions:

For the reasons / grounds (given) above I think...
I hope my ideas...will help...to...
I look forward to hearing (your final decision) in the near future...
To sum up...

Yours sincerely,

Your name

A Letter to an editor

I am writing in response to the article , of the last Wednesday's publication , of your newspaper regarding the proposal of increasing the care services of the newborn babies across the country. With this way young mothers will be encouraged to go back to their work after the birth of their babies.

First of all I would like to say that I totally agree with the statement that, providing better care services will allow women to return to their works as soon as possible. Improvements in child care programs will contribute to this , and I think this is a wonderful idea. In my opinion women should be able to have children without having to worry to lose their jobs, simply because they do their natural right.
Secondly, I would like to mention that the fear , that some companies have , that this legal provision will encourage women to have too many children , and therefore it can cause them serious economic problems is irrational. Women in nowadays are career-oriented and they have the right to choose to have one or more children. The companies should not worry about them when they are out of their duties , for a period of time. This does not mean that they lose their professionalism. On the contrary, studies have proven that the majority of these women are able to cope with the demands of their duties, when they return to their work.

I would like also to add some personal ideas to your comments: An improved care service provides an ideal opportunity for introducing a national programme related to pre-school activities of the young children. I believe that we have to take into consideration this matter seriously as it gives the ability to young mothers to develop their own actions , along with the upbringing of their children. I fully expect to see a change in such an important aspect of social providence in our country.

To sum up, women do not need to risk their careers when they decide to have a baby. It is at the governments responsibility to ensure that their children will be secure , from their early years , as well as to create an appropriate national educational program so as to inform the companies about the women's right to become mothers, and their respect that they ought to show on them.

I am looking forward to reading other readers views on this subject.

Yours sincerely,

Mary Smith

LETTERS OF APPLICATION

■ **Introduction**

In the introduction we **summarize the reasons** why we write this letter.

Useful expressions:

I am writing in order to ask you...
I am writing to apply for the post / position of...
I would like to be considered for admission to the course in...

■ **Main body**

In the main body within **four paragraphs** we expose:

Our **education** and also our **skills**.
Our **personal assets** (e.g. **patient to work** , **organized** , **hard worker** , etc.)
Our **previous experience**
Our **suitability** for work (**communicative person** , **pleasant with the customers** , **cooperative with colleagues** , **willing to work overtime** , **etc**)

Useful expression for experience / qualifications:

At present I am employed / working as...
My interest is to test my skills on...

■ **Conclusion**

In the final paragraph we finish our application, **emphasizing to useful remarks**. We **sign** the letter.

Useful expression for experience / qualifications:

I would appreciate a reply as soon as possible.
I would be available for an interview at any time...
If you hire me for...
Please contact me should you have further questions.
Please find enclosed my CV/references from...

Yours sincerely,

Your name

Letter of application sample

You are studying Business and English at your college. You want to spend two months during your vacation working in a company in an English-speaking country to get work experience and to practice your English. Write a letter to the personal manager of Arcon, an international company with branches in many countries; explaining **who you are** what **would you like to do**, and why **the company should employ you temporarily**. Offer to send further information about yourself if the company is interested to employ you.

Dear Mr. Johnson

I am writing in order to ask information concerning the post of sales' assistant manager. I am a student of the Economics College, University of Athens, section Outsourcing and Management. It would be a great honor for me if you accepted me as an apprentice at your company. I am willing to offer you my skills during the summer period.

As I have already mentioned I am studying at the university, actually I am a third year student, and I am expert in financial assessmnet and outsourcing. During my studies I had cooperated with smaller local companies in Athens and elsewhere. My basic role had to do with the assignment of sustainability studies with the use of the appropriate software.

Although I used to work on vital projects, nevertheless I should confess that till now I had the opportunity to attend the development of small projects, because I had never had the chance to be a member a internatial company with expanded field of work as well as with the most sophisticated methods of quality control.

My interest is to test my skills on international standards, which your company applies for many decades. I intend to do post-graduated studies in digital logistics and management and for that reason I would like to work at your company during the summer period in order to acquire specified knowledge as well as to improve my financial terminology in English.

If you hire me for two months , I will be able to offer you my duties, as well as my experience with low cost. I am willing to work overtime without extra payment. I have also developed a new software which is adapted to the model of the management of your company, which I am willing to provide you with no charge.

Yours Sincerely

Yannis Diamantis

COMPETITION ENTRY

Competition entry sample

You have seen this announcement in the English Language Learning Magazine:

English Language Teacher Of the Year Award.

Write and tell us **why your language teacher should win**.
Tell us about **his** or **her background**.
Say **why you think** he or she is an outstanding teacher.
Say **how** he or she **has helped** you to learn English.

The writer of the winning entry will receive a £250 prize and the winning teacher will be presented with a trophy.

Write your **competition entry** in **220-260** words.

I firmly believe that my teacher, Missis Ann Osborne, must be the winner of the competition. Although she is only thirty four years old she combines the essential knowledge with her dynamic personality.

She is a Saint Andrew's University graduate. She also holds a post graduate degree. Until her mid twenties she lived in Scotland with her parents. During this period she developed a sophisticated method of interactive learning. Despite the fact that during her studies she had to confront with a serious family situation, she he managed to graduate with the higher score in her class.

It is not only her impressive school performance that makes her to distinguish among the other teachers but also her personality. As I have already mentioned she is a dynamic lady. In almost every lesson she transmits her knowledge in a friendly way without exaggerations. There are many students in our class coming from foreign countries who have to confront, apart from understanding the pronunciation, with the local idioms and the phrasal verbs. Missis Osborne from the beginning of the school year had prepared an English course suitable for students from abroad. According to it they have the ability to get accustomed with the pronunciation as well as with the idioms, without wasting their time.

When I joined in this class, three years ago, I had to face problems relate to writing and listening tests. She became aware about it and she told me that she was willing to offer me extra material on these specific topics. I should confess that this kind of tests helped me to enter into the essence of the English Language with a rather unique way. Without her help I wouldn't be able to surpass all the obstacles in such a short time. Her communication style as well as the excellent knowledge of the English language are the keys of her success.

Yours Sincerely

Ornella Rossi

◊   **HOW TO WRITE ARTICLES**

What is the difference between essay and article?

Very little in practice, except that an essay usually develops some **form of argument** and therefore begins with an **introduction** , has a number of intermediary paragraphs in which the argument is developed and then arrives at a conclusion which is mentioned in the final paragraph.

An article **does not necessary develop an argument** or even **display a point of view**. It is a simple as well as a succinct way of imparting information. It targets at readers **who seek to be informed** rather than be entertained , for that reason it has **shorter paragraphs** than an essay. In other words , **it is "punchier"** Although it is likely to contain links and references from other articles , it **does not necessary reach to any conclusion**.

■   **Introduction**

In the introduction **advises the reader** about the topic that will be presented in the article.

Useful expressions:

In the past , people used to... , but now...
It is often stated / claimed / said that...
Recently , we have all become concerned that...

■   **Main body**

1st Paragraph We mention the **positive points** or the **negative points** of our topic , giving a **description** of each point.
2nd Paragraph We mention the **positive points** or the **negative points** of our topic , giving **extra information** to the reader.
3rd Paragraph Make the **positive suggestion and mention the result** or we present the **impacts** of the **negative points**.
4th Paragraph Make the **second positive suggestion and mention the result** or we present **other impacts** of the **negative points and mention the result**.

■   **Conclusion**

In the conclusion we make a **summary of what it was said** in the article. We express our opinion using **neutral expressions**.

Useful expressions:

In conclusion , the facts suggest that ...
What can be done is...

Article sample

An international current affairs magazine has invited readers to contribute articles entitled "Globalization – good news or bad?" for its next issue. You decide to write an article explaining your personal views on this topic.

Write your **article** in **280 - 320** words

It is often stated that globalization tends to be the plague of the mankind. More and more articles have been written by experts who have expressed various opinions. All things considered , might the globalization be a real threatening situation, which could effect people's life radically?

According to some sociologists the negative impact on the global community will be more feasible in a couple of decades from the present time. This will happen due to cultural deterioration which will be substantial in the developing countries. They also claim that the way of life of the poor nations will be mutated by the cultural and spiritual invasion from the developed ones. As a result the identity of the local population will have been gradually vanished. Languages and dialects , which now are in use , will pass to the history.

The impact on the education of the contacted nations is another drawback that the globalization is likely to bring about. According to some experts the school's schedule should be adapted to new global conditions. With this way the future generations will have less education links with their country's history and tradition. A national distortion from the inside , as it is called by some scientists.

Apart from the cultural and spiritual side effects the globalization can be the cause of rapid changes that can influence the developed countries. Eminent economists from almost every developed country have claimed that the new era will cause dramatically changes to almost all employees who once were confident about their jobs.

The relocation of the manufactures from the rich and expensive countries to the poorest ones will cause the increase of the unemployment in the industrial countries , as more and more firms are going to choose other locations with lower salaries for their facilities.

What can be done is a question that might be answered only by those who are responsible for it, and there are not others except for the global financial elite that rules the planet. They ought to take into consideration not only their financial benefits but also the rights of the simple people in order the humanity to avoid transforming into a productive unit without cultural identity and tradition.

◊ **HOW TO WRITE PROPOSALS**

A proposal is a **formal document** in which you can "**propose**" or you can **give ideas for a project**. It is a typical informational report that highlights **projects** and **initiatives for future actions**, and is **submitted for approval** from the boss or from a committee.

■ **Introduction**

In the introduction we mention the **purpose** of this proposal.

■ **Main body of the proposal**

In the main body we **present every aspect** of the topic of the proposal. **We develop each topic in separate paragraphs** with the **appropriate heading** for **each paragraph**.

■ **Conclusion**

In the conclusion, we mention our **recommendations** in brief using official language.

Proposal sample

Proposal on how to attract more members to the English-cultural society.

Introduction

The aim of this proposal is to give recommendations about the new events that will be organized in order to attract more people to our society. It also suggests various ways with which we can make our current activities more appealing.

The current situation

There is a number of cultural activities that we can offer in our society such as the book club. This institution is taken place on Saturday afternoons giving the ability to our members to discuss about classic books. The cinema club , is also a remarkable association , in which black and white films are projected once a month. Both events have proved to be popular among older people , mainly in the middle-aged women. Unfortunately very few young people have shown their interest in participating to these activities. As a result the society has failed to attract new members and in fact, according to our statistics, we have start losing members little by little.

How to attract new members

I suggest that we should create events aiming to attract young people in their mid-twenties. For example we can organize pop concerts , inviting the local bands of our town which play pop songs , as well as to contact with other cultural societies , where our members will be able to expose their common views , giving them the ability to talk even with well-known British artists , sharing their views.
We should also try to attract more male members to our society , and an easy way to achieve this is through sports events. I would recommend that we should form a new football club or a tennis club.
Regarding our current events , the book club and the cinema club , I think we should keep them active adding a new list with more modern books and films.

Conclusion

There should be no delay in creating new enjoyable activities so as to attract new members, as the suggested pop concerts and sports events. We should also maintain the book club as well as the cinema club, which have proved to be a success. For that reason the old members of our society must submit their views without wasting time , so as to with this common effort to make a new beginning with positive effects for all of us.

◊ **HOW TO WRITE REVIEWS**

■ **Introduction**

You can start the review mentioning **the title** , **the type of the book / play / film** , **the setting (where - when)** , **the theme** as well as **the main characters**.

Useful expressions:

Each chapter / scene is devoted to / involves...
I found the photography / acting / ending...
It conveys a sense of...
It portrays the story of...
The book / film / program deals with... / **tells the story of**... / **focuses on**... / **includes**...
The story / plot is based on...
The...is...situated in the...
As you enter into the place you...

■ **Main body**

In two or more paragraphs you can develop the **main points of the plot** (without revealing the ending) as well as you can **comment on various features** (e.g. acting , setting , plot , characters , etc). **Don't forget to justify your points** (explanation , reason - example).

Useful expressions:

It is remarkable that...
The beginning of the film is...
The story / drama / comedy takes place on...
What a pitty that...

■ **Conclusion**

It can include an **overall assessment** of the work and a **recommendation** , usually **with justification**.

Useful expressions:

All in all , It is well worth seeing / reading , Since...
Despite the...for that reason I highly recommend...
It is a classic of its kind... , **It is sure to be a hit**... , **It is sure to be best seller**...
On the whole , I wouldn't recommend it...
You should definitely see / read...

Review sample

Your local newspaper is asking its readers to write a review of a restaurant where you have eaten recently and would recommend to others.

Write your **review** in **280-320** words

The Open House Polo Restaurant

The "Open House Polo" is a restaurant situated in the heart of a small village between two national forests and close to the horse´s capital city, Chantilly. It is the favorite hangout for people from the polo, the horse races, and from the world of golf.

As you enter into the place you are impressed by the magnificent setting , a delightful space with antique chiseled stones , and the luxuries of modernity. Sitting in any table you have a wonderful view of the kitchen where you can see the chefs working. For those who have not booked a table and are in waiting , there is a cozy lounge with leather armchairs and pictures of polo players displayed on the walls.

The menu offers a wide variety of mouth-watering starters. I had ordered white asparagus accompanied with mousseline sauce and poached eggs , while my friend chose the zucchini carpaccio served with tomatoes and a mozzarella strudel. They were exquisite. The main course consisted of a risotto with scallop, cooked in cream , as well as a cassolette of coley with mussels , which really thrilled us. All of them are followed by a delicious apple pie served with a scoop of vanilla ice cream for dessert.

All the products were fresh and the dishes had the warmth of home-made food. The chefs had taken great care in selecting top quality ingredients. The restaurant also covers all tastes , providing a large selection of the best wines of the local region which , although are pricy , offer a unique delight to the consumer.

What a pity that the service does not accompany with the high quality of the cooking. You can't find neither one smiling waiter.Thankfully the owner and hostess of the restaurant , a middle-aged charming woman , are always close to the tables , and willing to exchange some kindly words with almost every client.

Despite the high price of the food and the not so attentive service , I had a pleasant dining experience with tastes of the most exquisite flavors. For this reason I recommend that it is a great choice, for everyone who want to taste top quality food , to visit the "Open House Polo restaurant".

■ **Instructions on how to write a film review**

Let's start from the basics. Whatever you do , **don't reveal end of the film**! If there is something , in the film reviews that readers hate , is spoilers. **When you are writing about the plot** it is better to describe it **in brief**. The reference of the **title** and the **main actors´names** are essential , and they should be mentioned. Something very important is to **give your opinion**.
Saying something about the **director**, the **special effects** and the **soundtrack** is something that it would give your text a plus. Use the **official language** , avoid using any word more than twice.

Film review sample

The Perfect Storm

The Perfect Storm is a Warner Bros disaster film which released in 2000. Based on a book by Sebastian Junger. It portrays the story of a fishing ship called the Andrea Gail, which has the misfortune of being trapped in most terrible storm that has ever happened in the North Atlantic.

This drama takes place in October 1991 in Gloucester, Massachusetts. After several unsuccessful fishing seasons , Captain Bobby Tyne , magnificently played by George Clooney , convinces his crew to head out in the cold Atlantic Ocean in search for fish , ignoring the warnings of the imminent arrival of a hurricane. Tyne has taken his decision to lead his crew to a dangerous place , the Flemish Cap , where they have to face inclement weather conditions. All of a sudden they get trapped in gigantic swirling waves.

The beginning of the film is disappointingly and boring. Quietness holds us back for one hour or so. However, things are getting better as the disaster approaches their door: Here comes the storm of the century , with its breath-taking special effects , which almost makes you feel seasick. The digital images are so awe-inspiring and realistic that they carry us into the disaster , swamping us with fear , and which rivet our attention on the screen. You may be surprised, riveted to your armchair, at the view of the nightmarish sea.

Even though the different personalities of the actors have led to on-board conflicts , the crew has shown a great courage and a strong team spirit , struggling with the storm against their fate. The dialogues as well as the choice of the music are successful , and in accordance with the subject , giving an extra suspense. "The Perfect Storm" is simply an outstanding movie with spotlessly special effects. I recommend it to all kinds of people especially to those who are fond of adventure movies, which could be an excellent choice for them.